# HOMEBREW

# 100

**How to brew 100 beers... and make them <u>your own</u>**

**Edited by Daniel Neilson**

BEER HAWK

Beer Hawk Ltd
Unit 16 Ash Way
Thorp Arch Ind. Est.
Wetherby
West Yorkshire
LS23 7FA

**HOMEBREW 100**

Text copyright Beer Hawk Ltd 2017
Images Rob Vanderplank
Design / illustration Adam McNaught-Davis

First Beer Hawk Ltd edition 2017

ISBN: 978-1-9998655-0-4

A catalogue record for this book is available from the British Library
Printed and bound in United Kingdom

Photos by Rob Vanderplank

# CONTENTS

## INTRODUCTION

Find recipes by beer style         12
Foreword                           14
Ownbrew                            16
Homebrew process                   20

## Chapters

## 1 INGREDIENTS

Malt + adjuncts                    24
Hops                               32
Yeast                              36
Fruit + spice                      40
Water                              42

## 2 EQUIPMENT

Homebrew set up                    46
Equipment                          48

## 3 BREWING

Glossary                           56
Cleaning                           58
Extract brewing                    60
All-grain                          62
Preparation                        63
Heating water                      64

Mashing in                         65
Sparging                           66
The boil                           67
Cooling + transfer                 68
Pitching yeast                     69
Fermentation + dry hopping         70
Conditioning                       71
Racking + priming                  72
Kegging                            74
Barrel ageing                      75
Sour beers                         76

## 4 RECIPES

Using the recipes                  80
British & Irish styles             82
German styles                     114
Belgian styles                    142
American styles                   158

## THE BACK

Get started                       190
Index                             192
Acknowledgements                  196

Ingredients 24

Equipment 44

Recipes 78

NOW BREWING

THE PLINIAN LEGACY

Brewing 54

# Find recipes by style

| RECIPE BY REGION | PAGE | EASE |
|---|---|---|
| **BRITISH & IRISH STYLES** | | |
| Ordinary bitter | 84 | ● |
| Best bitter | 85 | ● |
| ESB | 86 | ● ● |
| Pale ale | 87 | ● |
| English IPA | 88 | ● ● |
| Golden ale | 89 | ● |
| Amber ale | 90 | ● ● |
| Northern brown | 91 | ● |
| Southenr brown | 92 | ● |
| Mild | 93 | ● |
| Imperial mild | 94 | ● ● |
| Old ale | 95 | ● |
| Barley wine | 96 | ● ● ● |
| Porter | 97 | ● |
| Baltic poter | 98 | ● ● ● |
| Smoked porter | 99 | ● ● |
| Dry Irish stout | 100 | ● ● |
| Foreign extra stout | 101 | ● ● |
| Milk stout | 102 | ● ● |
| Oatmeal stout | 103 | ● ● |
| Coffee stout | 104 | ● ● |
| Breakfast | 105 | ● ● |
| Imperial stout | 106 | ● ● ● |
| Irish red | 107 | ● |
| Irish draft | 108 | ● |
| Scottish 60/ | 109 | ● |
| Scottish 70/ | 110 | ● |
| Scottish 80/ | 111 | ● |
| Wee heavy | 112 | ● ● |
| Heather ale | 113 | ● ● |
| **GERMAN STYLES** | | |
| Bohemian Pilsner | 116 | ● ● ● |
| German Pilsner | 117 | ● ● ● |
| Munich Helles | 118 | ● ● ● |
| Maibock | 119 | ● ● ● |

| RECIPE BY REGION | PAGE | EASE |
|---|---|---|
| Doppelbock | 120 | ● ● ● |
| Dunkels Bock | 121 | ● ● |
| Bock | 122 | ● ● |
| Dortmunder Export | 123 | ● ● |
| Kellerbier | 124 | ● ● ● |
| Schwarzbier | 125 | ● ● |
| Eisbock | 126 | ● ● ● |
| Vienna lager | 127 | ● ● |
| Marzen | 128 | ● ● |
| Roggenbier | 129 | ● ● ● |
| Raspberry wheat | 130 | ● ● ● |
| Hefewiezen | 131 | ● |
| Helles Weizen | 132 | ● |
| Weizenbock | 133 | ● ● |
| Dunkelweizen | 134 | ● ● |
| Dunkel | 135 | ● ● |
| Rauchbier | 136 | ● ● |
| Kolsch | 137 | ● |
| Altbier | 138 | ● |
| Sticke | 139 | ● ● |
| Berliner Weisse | 140 | ● ● ● |
| Gose | 141 | ● ● ● |
| StickeAlt | 146 | ● ● |
| Berliner Weisse | 147 | ● ● ● |
| Gose | 148 | ● ● ● |
| **BELGIAN STYLES** | | |
| Belgian blond | 144 | ● |
| Dubbel | 145 | ● |
| Tripel | 146 | ● ● |
| Golden strong | 147 | ● ● |
| Petite saison | 148 | ● |
| Saison | 149 | ● ● |
| Lambic | 150 | ● ● ● |
| Gueuze | 151 | ● ● ● |
| Fruit lambic | 152 | ● ● ● |
| Flanders red | 153 | ● ● ● |

| RECIPE BY REGION | PAGE | EASE |
|---|---|---|
| Old bruin | 154 | ● ● ● |
| Witbier | 155 | ● ● |
| Patersbier | 156 | ● |
| Bière de garde | 157 | ● |
| **AMERICAN STYLES** | | |
| American lager | 160 | ● ● ● |
| Pre-prohibition lager | 161 | ● ● ● |
| American pale | 162 | ● |
| Cream ale | 163 | ● |
| Amber ale | 164 | ● |
| Brown ale | 165 | ● ● |
| California common | 166 | ● ● ● |
| American porter | 167 | ● |
| American stout | 168 | ● |
| American IPA | 169 | ● ● |
| Session IPA | 170 | ● ● |
| West Coast IPA | 171 | ● ● |
| Rye IPA | 172 | ● ● ● |
| Black IPA | 173 | ● ● |
| Imperial Black IPA | 174 | ● ● ● |
| Red IPA | 175 | ● ● |
| White IPA | 176 | ● ● |
| Double IPA | 177 | ● ● |
| Grapefruit IPA | 178 | ● ● |
| Mosaic IPA | 179 | ● ● |
| American rye | 180 | ● ● |
| American red | 181 | ● |
| American wheat | 182 | ● |
| Pumpkin ale | 183 | ● ● |
| **SPECIALITY** | | |
| Italian grape ale | 184 | ● ● ● |
| Koyt | 185 | ● ● |
| Sahti | 186 | ● |
| Grodziskie | 187 | ● ● |
| Kvass | 188 | ● ● |
| Australian sparlkling lager | 189 | ● ● |

# Find recipes by type

| RECIPE BY TYPE | PAGE | EASE |
|---|---|---|
| **PALE ALES** | | |
| Ordinary bitter | 84 | ● |
| Best bitter | 85 | ● |
| ESB | 86 | ●● |
| Pale ale | 87 | ● |
| Golden ale | 89 | ● |
| Amber ale | 90 | ●● |
| Irish red | 107 | ● |
| Irish draft | 108 | ● |
| Scottish 60/ | 109 | ● |
| Scottish 70/ | 110 | ● |
| Scottish 80/ | 111 | ● |
| Heather ale | 113 | ●● |
| Belgian blond | 144 | ● |
| American pale | 162 | ● |
| Cream ale | 163 | ● |
| Amber ale | 164 | ● |
| California common | 166 | ●●● |
| American red | 181 | ● |
| **LAGER HYBRIDS** | | |
| Bohemian Pilsner | 116 | ●●● |
| German Pilsner | 117 | ●●● |
| Munich Helles | 118 | ●●● |
| Maibock | 119 | ●●● |
| Doppelbock | 120 | ●●● |
| Dunkels Bock | 121 | ●● |
| Bock | 122 | ●● |
| Dortmunder Export | 123 | ●● |
| Kellerbier | 124 | ●●● |
| Schwarzbier | 125 | ●● |
| Eisbock | 126 | ●●● |
| Vienna lager | 127 | ●● |
| Marzen | 128 | ●● |
| Dunkel | 135 | ●● |
| Rauchbier | 136 | ●● |

| RECIPE BY TYPE | PAGE | EASE |
|---|---|---|
| **LAGER HYBRIDS** | | |
| Kolsch | 137 | ● |
| Altbier | 138 | ● |
| Sticke | 139 | ●● |
| American lager | 160 | ●●● |
| Pre-prohibition lager | 161 | ●●● |
| **IPAs** | | |
| English IPA | 88 | ●● |
| American IPA | 169 | ●● |
| Session IPA | 170 | ●● |
| West Coast IPA | 171 | ●● |
| Rye IPA | 172 | ●●● |
| Black IPA | 173 | ●● |
| Imperial Black IPA | 174 | ●●● |
| Red IPA | 175 | ●● |
| White IPA | 176 | ●● |
| Double IPA | 177 | ●● |
| Grapefruit IPA | 178 | ●● |
| Mosaic IPA | 179 | ●● |
| **DARK/STRONG BEERS** | | |
| Northern brown | 91 | ● |
| Southenr brown | 92 | ● |
| Mild | 93 | ● |
| Imperial mild | 94 | ●●● |
| Old ale | 95 | ● |
| Barley wine | 96 | ●●● |
| Porter | 97 | ● |
| Baltic poter | 98 | ●●● |
| Smoked porter | 99 | ●● |
| Dry Irish stout | 100 | ●● |
| Foreign extra stout | 101 | ●● |
| Milk stout | 102 | ●● |
| Oatmeal stout | 103 | ●● |
| Coffee stout | 104 | ●● |
| Breakfast | 105 | ●● |

| RECIPE BY TYPE | PAGE | EASE |
|---|---|---|
| Imperial stout | 106 | ●●● |
| Wee heavy | 112 | ●● |
| Dubbel | 145 | ● |
| Tripel | 146 | ●● |
| Golden strong | 147 | ●● |
| Brown ale | 165 | ●● |
| American porter | 167 | ● |
| American stout | 168 | ● |
| **WILD/SOUR BEERS** | | |
| Berliner Weisse | 140 | ●●● |
| Gose | 141 | ●●● |
| Petite saison | 148 | ● |
| Saison | 149 | ●● |
| Lambic | 150 | ●●● |
| Gueuze | 151 | ●●● |
| Fruit lambic | 152 | ●●● |
| Flanders red | 153 | ●●● |
| Old bruin | 154 | ●●● |
| **WHEAT/RYE BEERS** | | |
| Roggenbier | 129 | ●●● |
| Raspberry wheat | 130 | ●●● |
| Hefewiezen | 131 | ● |
| Helles Weizen | 132 | ● |
| Weizenbock | 133 | ●● |
| Dunkelweizen | 134 | ●● |
| Witbier | 155 | ●● |
| American rye | 180 | ●● |
| American wheat | 182 | ● |
| **SPECIALITY BEERS** | | |
| Pumpkin ale | 183 | ●● |
| Italian grape ale | 184 | ●●● |
| Koyt | 185 | ●● |
| Sahti | 186 | ● |
| Grodziskie | 187 | ●● |
| Kvass | 188 | ●● |
| Australian sparlkling lager | 189 | ●● |

# FOREWORD

I remember brewing at home: my Dad bought kits from Boots, and, knowing nothing about brewing or fermentation, we managed to screw it up every single time.

We managed to get almost every single detail wrong, though with hindsight I'm pretty sure our biggest mistake was adding yeast to boiling water because we didn't see why waiting for it to cool was so important.

Kits are a great way to learn the basics of fermentation and the importance of cleanliness. But if you're reading this, you've probably moved beyond kits and are now using hops and whole grains. You're looking to expand your repertoire.

Home brewing has changed just as dramatically as every other aspect of the craft beer revolution. I'm often asked to judge home brew competitions, and when I do so we usually use the same judging sheets I've used in competitions for professional brewers. And I'm still shocked when, time after time, filling in those sheets I'm

# By Pete Brown

generally giving higher marks to the home brews in front of me than when I last used them to evaluate commercial brews.

Maybe I shouldn't be surprised: the commercial brewer is taking a bottle, can, cask or keg off the production line, while the home brewer is obsessing over each batch, choosing the very best samples to send into the competition. But I've seen several of those home brew champions make the transition to commercial beers, and they're still better than most.

We have too many deeply average commercial breweries all brewing similar beers. When I find a brewer who really stands out, they all have one thing in common: they all home-brewed for years before going commercial. So use this book as a springboard. Pimp your recipes. And when you no longer need to refer to it — when you're writing or re-writing your own recipes in your head — I'd love to try your beers.

Cheers, Pete Brown

# MAKE IT YOUR OWN

**This is a homebrew book like never before.
One that offers you the tools to make the beer <u>your own</u>**

We set out to make a homebrew book like never before. It is one that is not only easy to follow and has a mammoth 100 recipes, but one that gives you the tools to experiment, to make the beer your own. We also believe this is the easiest-to-use book out there.

I've been known to say that homebrewing is no more complicated than making a boeuf bourguignon. Yes, it takes a good few hours to make the meat tender, and yes it requires a fair few frantic steps followed by long periods of, well, getting on with other stuff, but the outcome, when made properly, is an unctuous assemblage that warms the soul. That sounds an awful lot like brewing to me: a matter of fine ingredients, following an agreed procedure and turning out something recognisable and delicious. For instance, an English IPA, a dark lager or a witbier. And in this book, we've offered 100 of these recipes, tried and tested by our friends across the pond at Northern Brewer or here at Beer Hawk, one of the most experienced and respected homebrew supply shops in America.

## THE RECIPES
We wanted to build on these recipes, however. Not only does this book include an easy-to-use core recipe covering almost every style in the world, we've also added a 'make it your own' column that demonstrates how far you can push the recipe but still keep it within the parameters for a certain style. For example, if you want to make an American pale ale, we'll give you a recipe that we think is pretty great. However, if you want to push the hop aroma, we'll tell you where, when and how many hops to add to the brew, while keeping it drinkable and within the recognised American pale ale style. If you didn't quite have enough pale malt left, but an abundance of something else lurking in the shed, this book will

tell you the maximum amount of a certain malt that you can put in the beer without making it taste acrid. The 'Homebrew 100' is different from everything else out there because we're visually demonstrating how far you can push each recipe yourself and still have a really good beer at the end of it.

Alongside each recipe, we also offer an extract recipe where possible. Although all-grain brewing (doing the mash yourself) is where our heart is and where you'll get the very best results, extract brewing is great for beginners, or if you're tight for time and space. It's not an exact replica but it will be pretty close to the all-grain recipe we've offered. Also, down the side of each page, is our easy-to-use timeline that at a glance you'll see where your hop or adjunct additions are.

## THE METHOD

The first half of the book tells you everything you need to know about brewing at home with a simple reference guide. The first chapter is dedicated to ingredients: hops, malts, water, yeast, adjuncts, plus fruit and spices you can add to your beer. The second chapter is all

# Welcome letter

about equipment. We'll tell you the minimum you need, plus some great pieces of gear that will markedly improve the taste of your beer. The third chapter is the one that's going to get dirty, the one you'll be flicking through with hands sticky with hops. It's the brewing process. We've broken the entire brew day down into easy-to-follow instructions plus a timeline so you'll know exactly what to do next and in the most efficient way possible.

It's often said that because of the love and care homebrewers put into their beer the end results can often be the best they've ever drank. We agree. That imperious IPA or boisterous bitter that you've put your soul and time into will be the best beer you've ever tried, and, what's more, it will be your recipe, all your own work. All we're doing in this book is giving you a nudge in the right direction.

With that in mind, you'd get your wellies on, it's brew day!

When I started Beer Hawk with Chris France in 2012, we had one simple aim: to bring the world's best beers to your doorstep. It's been quite a journey since then. We've grown rapidly, building on a reputation for excellent service and a huge selection of beers, now numbering around 1,000. In 2017, our journey took a new turn, and we started stocking homebrewing equipment. We partnered with our friends at Northern Brewer in America and became exclusive stockists for some of the world's best homebrew gear.

Northern Brewer's tremendous reputation in the US is as a result of the superb kits and gear (much of it designed bespoke for them) but also the generosity with which it shares the wealth of knowledge it has built up. The company has spent years honing recipes and advice, and we have used that as the basis for many of the recipes in this book: tried and tested methods for creating excellent beers. Our team at Beer Hawk also include plenty of very experienced

homebrewers and, combined with Northern Brewer's help, we've developed quite a knowledge base.

When we stood in the warehouse staring at several shipping containers of homebrew equipment and ingredients, we quickly realised we'd needed a book. A book that not only helped those at the beginning of their journey to confidently get brewing, but also offered something that had never been done before. I gave Daniel one simple brief: create a book that would allow people to make the beers uniquely theirs. After much trial and error, I'm confident we've achieved this. Whether you're an absolute beginner or a semi-pro, we're offering you a toolbox to make beers that are yours and yours alone. We'd love to know how you get on. Pop a picture to @ thebeerhawk or even drop us a bottle! We hope you enjoy brewing as much as we do.

**Mark Roberts**
**Co-Founder, Beer Hawk**

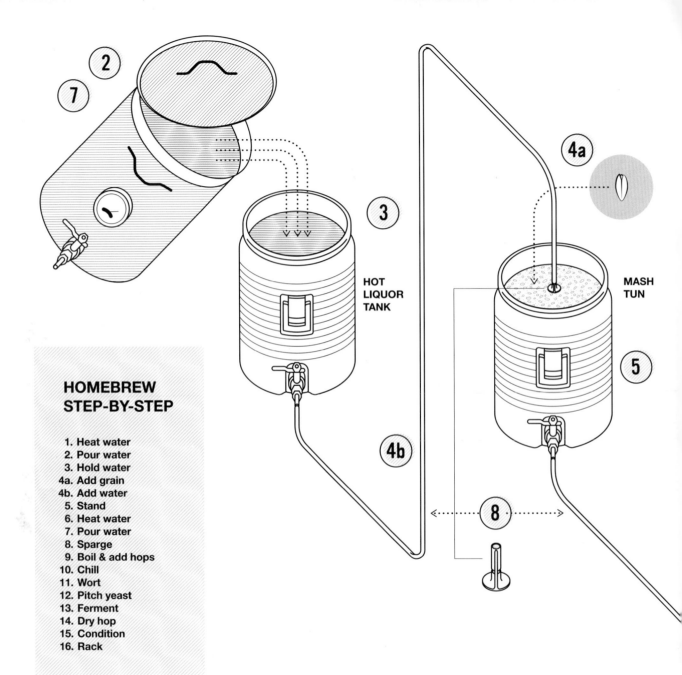

## HOMEBREW STEP-BY-STEP

1. Heat water
2. Pour water
3. Hold water
4a. Add grain
4b. Add water
5. Stand
6. Heat water
7. Pour water
8. Sparge
9. Boil & add hops
10. Chill
11. Wort
12. Pitch yeast
13. Ferment
14. Dry hop
15. Condition
16. Rack

HOT LIQUOR TANK

MASH TUN

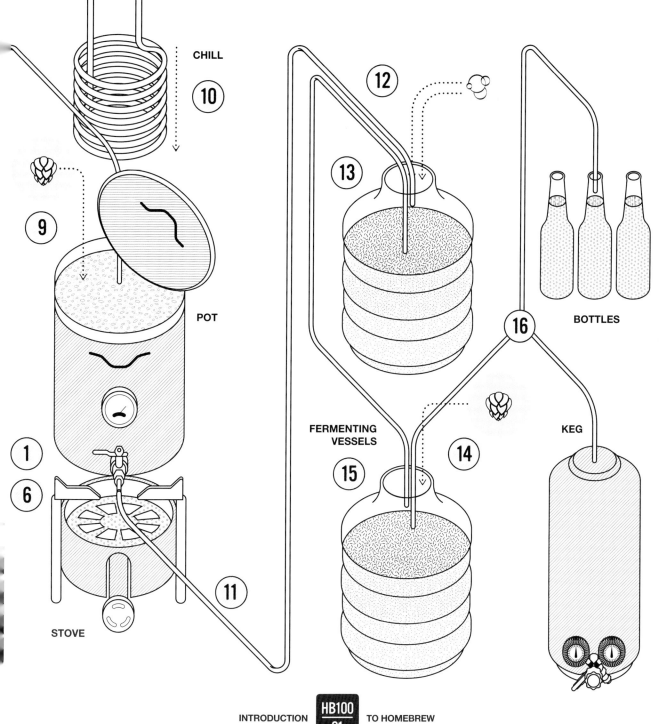

CHILL

10

9

POT

1

6

STOVE

11

12

13

FERMENTING VESSELS

15

14

16

BOTTLES

KEG

INGREDIENTS

# Meet the grains

**Munich:** Gives a smooth, deep maltiness. Used in Alts, Bock, Dunkel and amber ales.

**Pale:** Nutty maltiness, clean and used in many beers, especially English ales.

**Pilsner:** Bright, clean and full-bodied. Used in most lagers including Pilsner and Helles.

**Vienna:** Slightly toasty, darker and maltier than Pilsner. Used in Oktoberfest and Vienna lager.

**Chocolate:** Bittersweet chocolate and roasty. Used in porter, stout and brown ale.

**Roasted barley:** Bitter and roasty, commonly used in a dry Irish stout.

**Acidulated malt:** Used to give a sour flavour to beers such as a Berliner Weisse.

**Crystal:** Many types, but generally toasty with a toffee-like maltiness.

**Carafa III:** Smooth with slight roastiness. Used in Bock, Doppelbock and Alt.

**Black:** Roasty and very dark. Common in stouts, porters and Scottish ales.

# MALT

## Malt is the backbone of your beer. It provides colour, flavour, intensity and sugars

Beer is brewed by fermenting the sugars of malted barley and other cereal grains. Barley is the most common grain used to make malt for brewing because it can produce lots of fermentable sugars, but pretty much any grain can be used in beer from rice to rye. Adjuncts, covered on p28, offer even more flavours and characteristics.

Brewers use the process of malting to access the sugars in the grains. In brief, the grains are prompted to sprout by being soaked in water. The growth is then stopped, and the grain 'tumbled' to get rid of the rootlets. The grains are then roasted to different darknesses and, just like a piece of toast, these various shades create different flavours. A porter is black because it uses grain that has been kilned for longer than pale malts. Lighter malts have more potential to create sugars.

The malted grain then has to be crushed, the form that most homebrewers buy it in, although some will crush it themselves.

This crushed malt is then soaked in hot water in a process known as 'mashing'. Mashing activates the enzymes, which convert the grain's starch into sugars. These sugars are then rinsed from the grain, and the resulting liquid, known as 'wort', is boiled with hops and other ingredients. After boiling and cooling the hopped wort, yeast is added to kickstart fermentation and eventually produce beer.

There are a vast number of malts that brewers can use, and they fall into two broad categories: base malts that need to be mashed, and speciality malts that add extra flavour, colour and depth to a beer. Nearly all full-grain recipes are made from a majority of base malts and some speciality malts.

The blend of malts is called the 'grist'. Extract brewers will steep speciality malts to add flavour and colour and then use liquid malt extract or dry malt extract to brew.

### BASE MALTS

Base malts make up the majority of the grist in all-grain beer. This group includes pale malt, Pilsner malt, Vienna malt, Munich malt, and mild ale malt; there are also non-barley base malts such as wheat malt and rye malt. The variety is, frankly, astounding. Base malts can be described by their variety, for example, Maris Otter and Golden Promise. They can be named after the area where they were grown, such as America, England or Germany. American base malt, for example, is mild and relatively neutral; British malts tend to be maltier, bready, and biscuit-like. The European climate gives malts made from continental barley a clean, 'elegant' character. Finally, they can be categorised by the beer they are used to make, for example, Pilsner malt and Vienna malt. A Pilsner malt is lightly kilned and has a soft, delicate maltiness that defines pale lagers. Vienna malt, for instance, is 'high-kilned', darker and has a more toasty maltiness that you'd associate with a Vienna lager. Rye and wheat malts are also considered base malts because they can provide fermentable sugars. Rye is used in limited quantities, however, to give a spiciness to the beer (see other malts below).

## SPECIALITY MALTS

There are two sub-divisions for speciality malts: crystal/caramel malts and roasted or dark malts.

Crystal/caramel malts are steeped first when extract brewing, and they are used to add sweetness and colour to both extract and all-grain brews. They're usually named in relation to the Lovibond colour scale, for example Caramel 60L. As a general rule, the lighter-coloured crystal malts are more strictly 'sweet,' while darker crystal malts can add some roastiness or nuttiness in addition to sweetness. On the extreme light end, there are dextrin malts. These malts

also add dextrin, which contributes body and a thicker mouthfeel to the beer. To confuse things, many maltsters have their trademarked brand names for certain malts. For example, CaraFoam®, Briess Carapils®, Caramel Pils and Dextrin Malt are all different names for very similar malts. Anything labelled crystal, caramel, or Cara-something are crystal malts.

Roasted malts are any malts or grains that are roasted to a very high degree. The three most common roasted malts are black malt, chocolate malt and roasted barley. They offer roasty, bready, biscuity, coffee and dark chocolate notes for dark beers. Roasted malts can be steeped for extract brewing or mashed for all-grain, and add a lot of complexity and colour even in meagre quantities. Roasted malts are delicious, provided you don't go completely overboard: 10 per cent is about the most you would usually use. In this book, we have provided the maximum and minimum amounts in each recipe. Also see the table on p30.

## OTHER MALTS

There are also some malts which do not come from barley: oats, rye and wheat can be malted. These malts are primarily processed like, and can be treated as, their barley malt

cousins. Caramel wheat is similar to caramel barley malts and the same for non-barley wheat base malts, and so on. Other malts also include speciality malts which don't fall into the other categories of barley malts: things like biscuit malt or aromatic malt. These malts are used in low quantities to contribute unique flavours. Fortunately, the names given by their maltsters are usually obvious as to what sort of taste they provide. Biscuit malt, for example, contributes a very biscuity flavour (sometimes described as 'saltine cracker' taste), aromatic malt adds a very malty aroma and a complex malt flavour. There are some speciality malts which are less explicitly named. Some of the toasted malts like Victory, amber and brown malts and special roast, are less obvious. Brown malt and amber malt are similarly toasted malts with brown being darker and more toasty and bready. Amber malt is lighter in colour and has less of a pretzel-like flavour and more of a light bready character. Victory malt is another light one which lies in between biscuit malt and amber malt, with characteristics of both. The special roast is somewhat unique and will impart a slightly darker, reddish colour and has a relatively sharp, tangy, berry and deep almost alcohol-like flavour. All of these can be used in low quantities at 5 per cent of the fermentables.

## EXTRACT BREWING

The mashing process adds time (and equipment) to the brewing process so that some homebrewers will use malt extract. Liquid malt extract and dry malt extract are the concentrated results of mashing.

This malt extract is used as the base malt and will add the majority of the sugar to be fermented. However, many extract recipes require the steeping of some speciality grains (see p60) to provide more flavour and colour in the finished beer. To convert to extract recipes, see p66.

# Malt glossary

**ADJUNCT** Adjuncts are any ingredients such as fruits, sugars, spices, herbs and vegetables that are additional or required for the style of beer you are making.

**AMBER MALT** Amber malt is a more toasted version of pale malt. It is a traditional malt used in the making of brown porters and must be mashed.

**BASE MALT** Malt such as pale malt that serves as the 'backbone' of the beer, as well as the primary sugar source for fermentation.

**CARAMEL/CRYSTAL MALT** A malt that is made by raising the temperature of wet green malt to a level where the enzymes in the malt convert the starch to sugars, in effect mashing the grain 'in the husk'. Referred to interchangeably as 'crystal malt'. Usually used to add colour and sweetness to a beer.

**GRAIN BILL** A list of the types and quantities of malt, as well as other grains, used in a beer recipe.

**GRIST** Crushed malt grains used for mashing. Grist should be only gently crushed to expose the husk interior, not broken apart or ground into powder. Ground grains will result in tannins and astringency in beer.

**KERNEL** The inner, softer part of a cereal.

**LOVIBOND** Measurement with which malt and beer colour are compared against. The higher the Lovibond, the darker the colour. We use the EBC scale for the colour of the beer.

**MALT EXTRACT** A condensed/concentrated wort that is used by homebrewers. It is found in either a liquid or dry form. The malt extract is where most of the sugars are for fermentation. Using an extract negates the need for mashing grains, but speciality grains are often steeped.

**MALT** Usually, refers to malted barley but is also used to refer to any grain, such as

rye, wheat, or barley, etc., that has gone through the malting process.

**MALTING** The process which primarily consists of immersing or soaking grains in water until they start to germinate, then drying and kilning them in a way which creates the all-important enzymes that will be revived during the mash.

**MALTOSE** A crystalline sugar formed from starch by the action of amylase. It is dextrorotatory and the primary source of fermentable extract in brewing.

**ROASTED MALT** Malt used for colour, flavour and mouthfeel.

**WHEAT** The second most common grain used in beer brewing. Malted wheat makes up at least 50 per cent of the grist of traditional Weizen beers, and may also be added in lesser amounts to other styles (generally as an aid to head retention). Unmalted wheat makes up a substantial percentage of the grist in witbier and lambic.

# Meet
# the additions

**Torrified wheat:** Gives a smooth, bready flavour and is used widely in witbiers.

**Flaked rice:** Often used in very pale American lagers.

**Malted oats:** Adds a creamy, smooth texture and a grainy flavour to dark British beers.

**Maize:** Often used in American lagers to give a mild and a light body.

**Roasted rye:** Rye is added in limited quantities to give a spicy character to beers.

**Carapils:** A malted grain, but typically considered an adjunct for mouthfeel.

**Flaked oats:** Classically used in stouts and porters to add a creaminess to the beer.

# ADJUNCTS

## These additions will add all manner of flavours and characteristics to your beer

Adjuncts are unmalted, starchy things; even though adjuncts are typically considered a cereal grain, adjuncts can also be starchy pumpkins and potatoes. Starch adjuncts don't have sugars available like crystal malts, so they can't be steeped for extract brewing. Neither do they have enzymes like malted grains, so they need to be mashed with base malt to extract their sugars.

Under the adjunct umbrella are also sugars such as honey, maple syrup and candi sugar. These are added directly to the kettle during the boil or to the fermenter for flavour or alcohol.

### STARCH ADJUNCTS

So why would we add mashable adjuncts? Torrified wheat, for example, adds great head retention on your beer, while flaked oats are commonly used in oatmeal stouts and porters to give a silky mouthfeel to the beer. These are adjuncts that are used in pretty limited amounts.

### SUGAR ADJUNCTS

These adjuncts contain a lot of sugar already and are usually added to the kettle during the boil (they are also called kettle adjuncts). These are mainly sugars and syrups and added in minimal amounts. They are either used to give flavour characteristics to the beer or provide fermentable sugars that will make the beer stronger in alcohol.

Like most adjuncts, they need to be used in very limited quantities, usually less than 10 per cent, otherwise the beer may have an unpleasant alcoholic taste. Too much of these sugars and the yeast can struggle too. Some common are shown right.

1   *Corn sugar*. Commonly used in brewing, usually for priming bottles, but also to add more alcohol content.

2   *Honey*. Along with molasses, this is a typical adjunct that can impart the flavour of honey and boost fermentable sugars. It can be added to the fermenter to give honey notes.

3   *Maple syrup*. It has fermentable sugars but better to add it in secondary fermentation if you want a maple syrup flavour.

4   *Candi sugar*. This is used a lot in strong Belgian ales to increase the alcoholic strength.

5   *Lactose*. An unfermentable sugar and a key ingredient in milk stouts. It adds a smooth sweetness to the beer.

# Malts

| NAME | ABOUT | NEEDS MASHING | MAX % |
|---|---|---|---|
| **BASE MALTS** | | | |
| Belgian pale ale | Balanced, plain but makes a solid base for Belgian and Trappist ales. | Yes | 100 |
| Belgian pilsner | Clean, light flavour used in Belgian lagers and Trappist beers. | Yes | 100 |
| Dark Munich | Strong malt flavour, deep colour, used in Dunkel and Schwarzbier. | Yes | 50 |
| Dark wheat | Sweet and wheaty. Used in Dunkelweizen and Weizenbocks. | Yes | 60 |
| Maris Otter | Deep, nutty, malty, lovely. Use in all English styles. | Yes | 100 |
| Mild ale | Creates a more dextrinous wort than most other base malts. | Yes | 100 |
| Munich | Smooth, deep maltiness and used widely, especially in Alts and Bocks. | Yes | 50 |
| Pilsner | Bright, clean, full-bodied. Used in nearly all lagers. | Yes | 100 |
| Six-row | Neutral, slightly grainy for all styles of ales. | Yes | 100 |
| Two-row | Clean and smooth, good in most US style beers as a pale malt. | Yes | 100 |
| Vienna | Slightly toasty, a bit darker and maltier than Pilsner malt. | Yes | 50 |
| White wheat malt | Full, slightly sweet and used in American wheat beers. | Yes | 100 |
| **SPECIALITY MALTS** | | | |
| Acidulated malt | Used to balance PH and sometimes to add sour notes. | Yes | 10 |
| Amber malt | Biscuit and coffee notes for brown and red ales. | Yes | 10 |
| Aromatic malt | Rich maltiness commonly used in Belgian and British styles. | Yes | 10 |
| Belgian Special B | Adds a caramel flavour and colour. | No | 10 |
| Biscuit malt | Biscuity, 'saltine cracker' flavour. | No | 10 |
| Black malt | Roasty, black notes for stout, porter and Scottish ales. | No | 10 |
| Brown malt | Dark roasted flavour with a slight bitterness. | Yes | 10 |
| CaraAmber | Full flavour for Alt, stout, Bock and porter. | No | 20 |
| CaraAroma | Full flavour, improved aroma. | No | 15 |
| Carafa I | Smooth, slight roastiness. | No | 10 |
| Carafa II | Smooth, slight roastiness, darker than Carafa II. | No | 10 |
| Carafa III | Smooth, slight roastiness, darker than Carafa III. | No | 10 |
| Carahell | Full, round malt flavour, used in Oktoberfest, Maibock and Hefeweizen. | No | 15 |
| Caramunich | Sweet, slightly toasty and used in Belgian dubbels and dark ales. | No | 15 |
| Caramel malts | Usually go up in numbers relating to Lovibond scale of darkness. | No | 20 |
| Carapils | Gives impression of fullness and aids head retention. | No | 20 |
| CaraRed | Full body and used for Scottish ales, Bock and Altbier. | No | 10 |
| Chocolate | Add colour and aroma to dark beers. | No | 10 |

# Malts, adjuncts & sugars

| NAME | ABOUT | NEEDS MASHING | MAX % |
|---|---|---|---|
| SPECIALITY MALTS CONTINUED | | | |
| Chocolate rye malt | Roasty, spicy malt used for Dunkelweizen and Roggenbier. | No | 10 |
| Dark crystal | Sweet, grainy, malty and slightly roasty. Great for British styles. | No | 10 |
| Dextrin malt | Gives a subtle colour to beer but used for head retention and body. | Yes | 10 |
| Golden naked oats | Light caramel, creamy finish and used in oatmeal stouts. | No | 10 |
| Honey malt | Intense malt sweetness and honey. | No | 10 |
| Pale chocolate | Mild chocolate and coffee flavour. Good for mild ale, stout and porter. | No | 10 |
| Peated malt | Intense peat smoke character, used in some Scottish ales. | Yes | 20 |
| Medium crystal | Deep caramel and grainy. Used in British styles. | No | 20 |
| Melanoidin | Intense maltiness for dark lagers, red ales and Bocks. | Yes | 10 |
| Roasted barley | Bitter and roasty flavours for dry Irish stout. Not technically a malt. | No | 10 |
| Spelt malt | Gives a distinctive spelt aroma and flavour. | Yes | 10 |
| Smoked malt | Smooth smokiness and used in Rauchbier and smoked porters. | Yes | 70 |
| Victory | Bread-like, nutty and  toasty. Used in brown ales. | Yes | 20 |
| ADJUNCTS | | | |
| Barley hulls | Helps with mash run off. | - | - |
| Flaked barley | Grainy taste and increased head retention, creaminess, and body. | Yes | 20 |
| Flaked maize | Mild, neutral flavour in small amounts, moderate sweetness at higher loads. | Yes | 40 |
| Flaked oats | Use up to 30% of grist total for a distinct full-bodied flavor and creamy texture. | Yes | 15 |
| Flaked rye | Lends dry, crisp character and strong rye flavor. | Yes | 10 |
| Flaked wheat | Greatly increases head retention and body at as low as 8 per cent of the grist. | Yes | 40 |
| Rice hulls | Lightens the body and increases crispness of a beer. | Yes | 10 |
| Torrified wheat | Whole kernel version of flaked wheat — increase head retention and body. | Yes | 40 |
| SUGARS | | | |
| Corn sugar | Corn sugar (dextrose) for priming bottle-conditioned beer or boosting gravity. | | |
| Candi sugar | Comes as a syrup, soft sugar or crystals. | | |
| Honey | Adds a dry finish. Use in seconadry for honey flavour. | | |
| Lactose | A milk-based sugar that is not fully fermentable by beer yeast. | | |
| Maple syrup | Adds maple flavour and dryness. | | |
| Rice syrup solids | Adds gravity without impacting colour or flavour. | | |

## Pellets and cones

**Whole cone hops:**
Whole hops are often used in dry hopping as they are easier to remove from the beer and may give a slightly fresher aroma than pellet hops.

**Pellet hops:** Pellet hops are produced by grinding up the whole hop cones and pressing them into pellets. When used for bittering, pellet hops have a higher extraction efficiency by weight than whole hops. They are also less subject to oxidising than whole hops.

**Water:** See p42 for the importance of water for hops and malt.

# HOPS

## Hops. Mighty hops. This amazing flower is a major player in the taste of your beer

Hops, lovely hops. These little flowers are the cone-shaped head of the perennial *Humulus lupulus* plant. Hops are added to wort to impart a bitterness that balances the sweetness of malt and to provide a broad range of flavours and aromas. In addition to the bittering, flavouring and aromatic qualities that hops bring to beer, they also serve as a stability agent, prevent spoilage, contribute to head retention and act as a natural clarifier. In short, they're amazing.

It wasn't until the eleventh century that hop use was first documented in Germany, while English brewers had to wait until the sixteenth century before it's widespread use. Until then, hops were merely part of a blend of other plants such as heather, rosemary, anise, spruce and wormwood used to bitter the sweet beer.

Hops are grown in countless varieties all around the world from Kent to the Yakima Valley in north western America, and also in Argentina and Japan. Each type can give a wildly different flavour and aroma. That grapefruit and pine aroma in a big American IPA? That's the hops. That earthy, spicy note in an English golden ale? That's hops. Much like wine, hops are a product of their terroir; the climate, the soil, the altitude. Discovering hops is one of the great journeys of home brewing – nothing beats snipping open a new bag of hops and inhaling deeply on its complex aromas.

All hops contain alpha and beta acids, and it is these acids that contribute to the stability and bitterness of the beer. Knowing the alpha acid percentage in hops is useful when creating recipes. Hops contain a host of essential oils which can boil off if added early in the boiling process, but which lend characteristic flavour and aroma when added later in the boil or even after fermentation. Each hop varietal can contribute dramatically different qualities of bitterness, flavour and aroma to the beer. Therefore, hops usually fall into two categories: bittering hops that are added at the start of the one-hour boil and aroma hops that are added towards, or at, the end. Another common technique to extract all the marvellous aroma is dry hopping. This is when hops are added to the fermenter once the fermentation has finished to give a huge aroma.

Hop bitterness is measured in International Bitterness Units (IBUs). An American IPA could have an IBU count of up to 70 (or even more in some cases), whereas for a stout it could be as little as 15.

# Hops

| NAME | ORIGIN | ALPHA ACID | USE BIT | ARO | FLAVOUR | ALTERNATIVES |
|------|--------|------------|---------|-----|---------|--------------|
| Admiral | UK | 14-16 | ● | ● | Resinous, orange. | Target, Northdown, Challenger |
| Ahtanum | US | 7-9 | ● | ● | Adds citrus-zest character for moderate bittering and aroma. | Amarillo, Centennial, Simcoe |
| Amarillo | US | 6-9 | | ● | Floral, tropical, and citrus. Excellent aroma hop for American ales. | Cascade, Centennial, Summit |
| Apollo | US | 15-19 | ● | | Super high alpha hop has very strong bittering capabilities. | Zeus |
| Bramling Cross | UK | 5-8 | ● | ● | Spicy, blackcurrant notes. | Progress, Brewer's Gold |
| Brewer's Gold | Germany | 5-7 | ● | ● | Intense blackcurrant and spice aroma. | Bullion, Chinook, Galena |
| Cascade | US | 4.5-7 | | ● | Unmistakable grapefruit aroma and flavour. | Amarillo, Centennial, Summit |
| Centennial | US | 9-12 | ● | ● | A pleasant spicy citrus aroma and clean bitterness. | Amarillo, Cascade, Columbus |
| Challenger | UK | 5-9 | ● | ● | Dual purpose hop with moderate bittering and spicy aroma. | Perle, Admiral |
| Chinook | US | 11-15 | ● | ● | Intense, spicy and resiny aroma. | Brewers Gold, Columbus, Galena |
| Citra | US | 10-12 | ● | ● | Musky tropical fruit and strong citrus. | Galena, Eroica |
| Cluster | US | 5-8 | ● | ● | Underappreciated dual-use hop with pungent spicy aroma. | Galena |
| Columbus | US | 14-16 | ● | | Very pungent aroma, clean bittering properties. | Magnum, Chinook, Northern Brewer |
| East Kent Golding | UK | 4-6 | ● | ● | Smooth, spicy, floral. Quintessentially English. | Fuggle, Progress, First Gold |
| First Gold | UK | 6-9 | | ● | Versatile variety with spicy, Goldings-like aroma. | East Kent Goldings |
| Fuggles | UK | 3-5 | ● | ● | Wonderful earthy, pipe-tobacco and floral character. | Willamette, Styrian Golding, Tettnanger |
| Galaxy | Australia | 13-15 | | ● | Gentle citrus with passion fruit notes, with a high alpha acid. | Citra |
| Galena | US | 12-14 | ● | ● | Fruity, slightly citrusy and spicy. | Brewers Gold, Nugget, Cluster |
| Glacier | US | 5-6 | ● | ● | Earthy, slightly floral character and sweet citric edge. | Willamette, Fuggle, Tettnanger |
| Hallertau Mittelfrüh | Germany | 3-5 | | ● | Slightly fruity and spicy, flowery and haylike. | Liberty, Tettnanger, Mt. Hood |
| Hersbrucker | Germany | 2-4 | | ● | Moderate-intensity floral character are ideal for for aroma additions. | Mt Hood, Strisslespalt |
| Liberty | US | 3-5 | | ● | Spicy, sweet, resiny descendant of Hallertau. | Hallertau, Tettnanger, Mt. Hood |

# Hops

| NAME | ORIGIN | ALPHA ACID | USE BIT | USE ARO | FLAVOUR | ALTERNATIVES |
|------|--------|------------|---------|---------|---------|--------------|
| Magnum | Germany | 13-15 | ● | ● | Extremely clean bitterness with pleasant, mild aroma. | Horizon, Newport |
| Mosaic | US | 10+ | ● | ● | Everything from citrus, pine, earth, herbal, mint and bubblegum. | Simcoe |
| Motueka | NZ | 5-8 | ● | ● | Excellent variety for single hop bills with multiple applications. | Saaz, Sterling |
| Mt Hood | US | 4-7 | ● | ● | Mild, sweet and floral descendant of Hallertau. | Hallertauer, Liberty, Crystal |
| Neson Sauvin | NZ | 10-13 | ● | ● | Crushed gooseberry' is the term most commonly used. | Green Bullet |
| Northdown | UK | 6-9 | ● | ● | Moderate bittering and terrific spicy, resiny aroma. | Northern Brewer, Challenger |
| Northern Brewer | US | 8-10 | ● | ● | Dual purpose with unique woody, minty notes. | Nugget, Chinook, Columbus |
| Nugget | US | 9-11 | ● | ● | High-alpha hop giving clean bitterness and delicate herbal aroma. | Cluster, Galena, Brewers Gold |
| Perle | Germany | 6-9 | ● | ● | A smooth bitterness and spicy, slighly floral aroma. | Challenger, Northern Brewer |
| Pride of RIngwood | Australia | 6-8.5 | ● |  | Profoundly resinous, fruity, and pleasant herbal hop character. | Cluster, Galena |
| Progress | UK | 5-8 | ● | ● | Moderate bittering but strong, fruity and resiny aroma. | Fuggles, East Kent Goldings |
| Saaz | Czech R | 2-5 | ● | ● | Classic noble hop with delicate, refined aroma. | Sladek, Lublin, Sterling |
| Simcoe | US | 12-14 | ● | ● | Funky pine character, making it synonymous with American IPA. | Northern Brewer |
| Sorachi Ace | US | 10-16 |  | ● | High-alpha aroma hop with intense lemon character. | N/A |
| Strisselspalt | France | 2-4 | ● | ● | Hoppy, blackcurrant character. | Mt. Hood, Crystal |
| Styrian Goldings | Slovenia | 4.5-6 |  | ● | Spicy aroma with sweet, earthy edge. | Fuggle, Willamette |
| Summit | US | 17-19 |  | ● | Super high-alpha with funky, earthy, tangerine character. | Amarillo, Cascade |
| Target | UK | 9-12 | ● | ● | Herbal, haylike aroma. | Nugget, Fuggle, WIllamette |
| Tettnang | Germany | 3.5-6 | ● | ● | Classic noble hop with distinctive spicy, fruity aroma and flavour. | Hallertau, Liberty, Fuggle |
| Tradition | Germany | 5-7 |  | ● | Refined sweet floral and herbal character. | Hallertauer |
| Vanguard | US | 4-5.7 |  | ● | Sweet, slightly spicy aroma and flavor for use as a kettle addition. | Saaz, Hallertau |
| Willamette | US | 4-7 |  | ● | Earthy, spicy character. | Styrian Golding, Target, Fuggle |

# Dry or liquid

**Liquid yeast:** The range of available strains is the greatest benefit of liquid yeast. Because liquid yeast is a live culture, it is usually more expensive and more perishable. There are also fewer cells per pack than dry yeast, so when making a beer with a gravity above 1.060 (or when making any lager), the yeast should ideally be 'grown' by making a yeast starter (see p39) before brewing day. Many also come in a 'smack pack' that needs to be activated at least three hours before pitching.

**Dry yeast:** Dry yeast is sterile, strain-pure, and highly capable of producing great beer. The shelf life is often a year or more, and it is much more tolerant of warm storage or shipping conditions than liquid yeast. Dry yeast is also packaged with nutrient reserves and is ready to pitch directly without a yeast starter. For high gravity fermentations, more than one pack of dry yeast should be used.

# YEAST

## As the saying goes:
## brewers make wort, yeast makes beer

In 1516, the Reinheitsgebot, or Beer Purity Law, in what is now Germany listed the only ingredients allowed for brewing beer to be malt, hops and water. Yeast was then entirely unknown; it seemed like magic. And in fact, now we know more about how it works, it still retains plenty of that magic.

So just what is yeast? Well, yeast is a type of fungus. An organism that reproduces asexually, and unusual in that it can live with or without oxygen. In a low oxygen environment yeast cells consume sugars and in return produce carbon dioxide and alcohol as waste products. This process is fermentation. Once the yeast has munched all the sugars that it feeds on, the beer is complete, it has alcohol in it, and we are happy.

There are hundreds of species of yeast, but for brewing, we tend to use just two: *Saccharomyces cerevisiae*, an ale yeast, and *Saccharomyces pastorianus*, a lager yeast. Within these species, however, are dozens of different strains, each happy in different environments, and each offering a different flavour profile. Brewers also use *Brettanomyces*, either 100 per cent to ferment a beer, or after an ale yeast has mostly done its work, to impart a complex, earthy, spicy profile. Read more about brewing with *Brettanomyces* overleaf.

Brewing yeast tends to be classified as either 'top-fermenting' or 'bottom-fermenting'. As the names indicate, the yeast strains tend to be most active towards the top and bottom of the wort respectively, although the cells are dispersed throughout the wort. Top fermenting yeasts produce an ale style beer, bottom fermenting a lager style beer. Ale strains prefer warmer temperatures while lager strains ferment best at cooler temperatures. For a homebrewer, ale yeasts are easier because they require a steady 18-20°C while brewing a lager will often mean using a fridge.

Yeast also produces by-products that we as brewers need to be aware of, and often mitigate where possible. Esters are chemical compounds that give off fruity flavours and aromas. Esters may be welcome in a Belgian ale, but not in a lager. Controlling the temperature according to the recipe will limit (or accentuate) these flavours. The buttery diacetyl aroma is another common flaw in most styles caused by yeast. In short, we want our yeast to be as happy as possible, and that means keeping the temperature steady and within the parameters.

## CHOOSING A YEAST

It is said that British brewers talk mainly about malt, US brewers chat mostly about hops and the Belgians speak of yeast. There may be some truth in this, but more brewers around the world are experimenting with yeast. Certainly, there's more of a focus on it than there has ever been. It makes such a difference to beer, and like a sprinkle of salt on a steak, it should lift the aromas and flavours that hops and malt contribute. For instance, if you want to make an IPA full of tropical fruit, you can find a fruity yeast.

There are dozens of yeast strains available to the homebrewer. Fortunately, yeast suppliers name their yeasts with unerring logic. Wyeast, for example, has different yeasts called Bavarian Lager, Bohemian Lager, Munich Lager, Czech Pils and so on. All recipes will also suggest a yeast to use that is best suited to that beer style. Throughout this book we will suggest a dry yeast and a liquid yeast. Therefore, much of the work in choosing a yeast has already been done for you, but there are some things to bear in mind when experimenting with yeast, especially flocculation and attenuation.

## ATTENUATION & FLOCCULATION

Eh? Attenuation and flocculation. At least one of those words sounds made up, but they are readily thrown around by knowledgeable homebrewers. In fact, they are both pretty simple concepts.

Attenuation is the degree to which yeast ferments the sugar in wort. High attenuation and the yeast is eating up loads of sugars, low attenuation and it's not doing so well. If you have 50 per cent attenuation, it means that 50 per cent of the sugars have been converted into alcohol and $CO_2$ by yeast. If you have 100 per cent attenuation, all of the sugars have been consumed by yeast (although you'll never reach 100 per cent). Different yeasts have different attenuation rates.

Flocculation refers to how quickly the yeast falls out of the wort. If it falls out quickly, the beer will also clear quickly. However, highly flocculating yeasts often have low attenuation rates: it may clear up quickly, but it hasn't finished fermenting.

So where does this leave homebrewers? Well, firstly, don't worry. As we said earlier, if you're making a particular beer style, you've a relatively limited range of choice (in a good way). Where there are a few to choose from, such as with an English ale yeast, bear in mind attenuation and flocculation. If you're aiming for something pretty strong, pick a yeast with high attenuation rates. If you're wanting a lowish-alcohol, crystal clear golden ale, then read up about the flocculation characteristics of the yeast. The manufacturer's website will have all that information about the yeast. Choosing yeast can, and has been, the subject of a book in itself. Safe to say, don't stress and let us suggest it for you.

## BREWING WITH BRETT

*Brettanomyces* is a yeast that is used when making 'wild' beers. Sometimes brewers will only use Brett for 100 per cent of the fermentation, but more commonly, they'll use an ale yeast first and then Brett to 'finish it off'. Brett imparts flavours such as pineapple, hay, apple and barnyard. It is often described as funky. It is an acquired taste, but once you have it, you'll continue to search out these beers. Sour beers also often use Brett in conjunction with lactic acid. We cover sour beers on p76. Also, note that fermenting with Brett can take many months.

# Making a yeast starter

### WHY MAKE A YEAST STARTER?

1  **Increase cell count**. Having a high pitching rate makes better beer.
2  **Increase cell viability**. Healthy yeast cells ferment quickly, produce minimal fermentation by-products, attenuate sufficiently (ferment to a proper final gravity), can ferment high-gravity worts, and have more tolerance for high concentrations of alcohol.
3  **Reach full attenuation**. An insufficient amount of cells may ferment sluggishly or incompletely, especially in a high-gravity or lager wort.
4  **Shorten growth**. Reducing the duration of the lag and growth phases minimises the opportunity for wort contamination and the formation of fermentation by-products.
5  **Improve beer flavour and aroma**. Underpitching creates stress and too much work for too few cells. Stressed cells are more likely to create off-flavours or aromas in the finished beer. Unpredictability is not something a brewer needs.

### WHAT SIZE YEAST STARTER?

A 1000ml starter is appropriate for a 20-litre (five-gallon) batch of ale of up to about 1.080 starting gravity, or a lager of up to about 1.060 starting gravity. A 2000ml starter is appropriate for a 20-litre (five-gallon) batch of ale of gravity over 1.080 or a lager up to 1.080.

### USING A STIR PLATE

Putting your yeast starter on a stir plate (see p51) will greatly increase the rate of growth and the size of the yeast culture. A 0.5-litre starter on a stir plate will produce the same cell count as a two-litre non-stirred culture. A starter on a stir plate will usually be ready to pitch in about 12 hours instead of 24.

### INSTRUCTIONS

The following instructions are for making a one-pint starter in a 1000 mL flask using a Wyeast Activator 'smack' pack.

1  Break the inner pouch to activate the yeast; ideally, the yeast would be allowed to incubate for three hours, but it can be pitched immediately.
2  In a pan, bring 650 ml of water to a boil. Once the water reaches a boil, remove from heat and stir with 120ml of dry malt extract. Return to heat and gently boil the wort for 15 minutes.
3  Sanitise the flask, foam stopper, yeast pack, and a pair of scissors.
4  Carefully pour the wort into the flask, then attach the foam stopper. Using a hot pad or potholder, move the container to a cold-water bath. Add ice or cold water to speed cooling.
5  Once the wort has cooled to 29°C or lower, remove the stopper and pitch the yeast. Re-attach the foam stopper and shake or swirl the flask to aerate the wort and help the yeast.

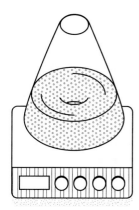

6  Allow the yeast starter to ferment for at least 12 hours. Usually, a fermenting yeast starter will not exhibit the same indicators of fermentation as your main batch such as krausen and a bubbling airlock). Instead, look for a cloudy appearance, 'yeasty' or 'beery' aroma (instead of sweet and 'worty'), and a layer of white sediment on the very bottom of the flask.
7  Pitch the starter into the main batch. Swirl the flask to pick up the sediment at the bottom, and pour it into the fermenter. Alternatively, you may wish to decant the spent wort from the flask and add only the thick yeast slurry at the bottom. To decant the spent wort – chill the flask for several hours to cause the yeast cells to settle, then pour the wort off of the top. Before pitching, add 100-200 ml of boiled and cooled water or wort to the flask and swirl vigorously to dislodge the slurry.

To make a 2000ml batch use 1300ml of water and 230ml of dry malt extract and follow the same instructions.

**Ginger:** Use sparingly in beer. Grate it and add it to the boil. Good with pumpkin.

**Chilli:** Used in Mexican beers, but also increasingly common in dark beers. Add to fermenter.

**Cherries:** Used in a Belgian kriek to add a sweetness. Add a few days into fermentation.

**Cardamom:** Often used in Belgian beers. Add a few days into fermentation.

**Coriander seeds:** Commonly used with orange peel in a witbier. Add to end of boil.

**Pumpkin:** A popular adjunct that is added to the mash. Good with ginger.

**Star anise:** Used in Christmas beers. Add to end of boil or a few days into fermentation.

**Orange peel:** Classic in a witbier with coriander. Add to end of boil or early fermentation.

# Aroma & flavour

**Raspberries:** Great brewing fruit. Add a few days into fermentation.

**Lemon peel:** Great addition to summer ales. Add at end of boil or in fermenter.

**Lime peel:** This can work well in light summer ales when added to boil or fermentation.

# FRUIT & SPICE

## Sugar and spice and all things nice all make great beer too. And you can pretty much put anything in it

You can have a lot of fun with fruit and spices in beer. It's not a new method, of course, brewers throughout the ages have added whatever they find in their local environment to flavour beer. Before the widespread use of hops, yarrow and heather were common in the British Isles for example. Belgians have long used cherry and raspberry to add a sweetness and balance to their sour lambic beers.

For the homebrewer, the availability of spices and fruits from around the world means we have an infinite variety of flavours to play with. But it's not a matter of just lobbing in a few cherries and getting a lovely, blushed beer out the other end. Different additions act in very different ways, and it's all dependent when you add them too: in the kettle or in the fermenter?

### FRUIT
There are a couple ways in which fruit is used in beer. One is to put the fruit at the centre stage, such as in a Belgian kriek where the cherries dictate the beer. A second method is to lift the flavours already provided by the hops, hence the popularity of adding grapefruit to big American IPAs to boost the aroma already present. A third is to add a natural tartness to the beer. However, when using fruit, the effect is often very subtle. It is often best to use lightly-hopped pale or wheat beers if you are adding fruit.

If adding fresh fruit, freeze and thaw it to room temperature first. Puree rather than fruit juice is probably the best bet for adding loads of flavour, and citrus zest is also a common addition. It's nearly always best to add your fruit during secondary fermentation.

The addition will cause another and usually rapid fermentation, so leave plenty of room at the top and also ensure that the airlock isn't blocked. If you're bottling a beer with fruit that hasn't fully fermented beware of bottle bombs. The final word is that beer with fruit added works best when it has aged considerably. Open the first after a month, but leave some for at least six months and make notes. It's not easy when homebrewing to get the profile of a fruit beer right first time.

### SPICES
If fruit is unpredictable, wait till you try spices. All spices are like this. Whereas you probably need plenty of fruit for an assertive profile, go easy on spices. Herbs are a similar story if you're putting in mint or nettle for example. Spices and herbs are added to the boil.

# WATER

## Most of your beer is water. It's important, but often overlooked. Here's how to make it the best you can

Water makes up 90-95 per cent of beer, but it's often overlooked on brew day. Understanding how water affects beer can take your recipe from good to great, but taking it for granted can render an otherwise great recipe underwhelming. In general, if your water tastes good or better still doesn't taste at all, you're probably in good shape. But if you have a water softener in your house or find yourself filtering your drinking water you might want to start treating your water more like an ingredient than an afterthought. Remember: Good in = good out. If you want to explore water more, the first step is to find out what kind of water profile you have at home. This information should be on your supplier's website. Take a note of the numbers (in part per million) for calcium, magnesium, sulphate,

chloride and sodium, as well as pH, total hardness, and alkalinity as CaCo3 (calcium carbonate). There are several excellent brewing water calculators available online. Start by inputting your own water's data and then adjust these to the ideal ranges as needed.

### CALCIUM
Calcium and magnesium, the minerals that attribute to hardness, are essential for yeast health and promote clarity and shelf life. If your water tastes minerally or leaves scale in your kettle, the easiest way to prep your water for brew day is to dilute it 1:1 with distilled, deionised or reverse osmosis water, readily bought from your local supermarket. The optimal brewing water range for calcium is 50-150 ppm. If your calcium concentrations are lower than the

ideal range, just add few grams of gypsum (calcium sulphate) or calcium chloride. It is available from homebrew suppliers.

### CHLORINE
For extract brewers, chlorine and chloramine are probably the most detrimental to beer flavour. Filtering with a carbon filter or treating your water with a Campden tablet will eliminate the potential for chlorophenols that impart a medicinal taste.

### ALKALINITY & PH
Alkalinity and pH are often confusing terms for all-grain brewers. Alkalinity (expressed as either 'Total Alkalinity as CaCO3', 'Bicarbonate' or 'HCO3') represents the concentration of anions like bicarbonate in your water and can be problematic at levels over 250 ppm. Alkalinity acts as a pH buffer.

The higher the concentration, the more resistant to change your mash pH will be. Ideal mash pH should be between 5.1-5.5. If higher, mash enzymes are still very active but tannin extraction from husk material is more likely especially around a pH of 6. A pH lower than 5.1 will hinder enzymatic activity, therefore reducing efficiency and could potentially affect flavour.

Brewers are more likely to find themselves battling high mash pH as a result of high alkalinity more than other factors. The speciality malts in your recipe will help lower your mash pH but not drastically. This acidity can contribute to counteract higher mash pH, but if you're still not in that 5.1-5.5 range, you may need additional acid. You can find acid in multiple forms including acidulated malt, lactic and phosphoric acid. Acidulated malt is also useful to have on hand. One per cent of your total grist by weight should lower your mash pH by one-tenth of a point.

Brewing water pH can vary widely depending on the source. An ideal range is 6.5-8.5, but the pH of your water is far less important than the pH of your mash. Mashing in first, allow it to settle for five minutes. Then take a pH reading and adjust appropriately.

So, keep your calcium levels between 50-150 ppm, your alkalinity between 0-250 ppm, your mash pH between 5.1-5.5 and adjust your ratio of chloride to sulphate to the characteristics of the style you intend to brew.

# SET-UPS

## From a stove top to a 20-litre all-grain brew. Here's how to get started

There are almost as many different homebrew set-ups as there are homebrewers. And like all good hobbies, it can be started with very little investment, but as you become more experienced, you can begin to improve your gear and get better and better results. Throughout this book, we have used our favourite set up, but much of it can be substituted. Think of it as a modular system where you can upgrade elements when you want to work on bigger batches, go all-grain or make the brew day a little shorter.

The first aspect to consider is the size of the brew. In homebrewing terms, the two most common brew sizes are 3.8 litres (one gallon) and 23 litres (five gallons). All the recipes in this book are for 23 litres but can be easily scaled down. One gallon brews (usually extract) can be made on the stove top with a large stock pot and a plastic fermenting bucket. As you jump up to five gallons, it's unlikely your stove will have enough energy to bring it all to a rolling boil (and your kitchen ceiling will thank you). You'd need to invest in an electric kettle (a converted tea urn basically) or, our preference, a burner and a large pot.

The next consideration is whether you are extract brewing or all-grain brewing. Many homebrewers start with extract but quickly upgrade to all-grain to get more flavour out of their beer. The key addition for all-grain brewing is a mash tun which is usually a converted coolbox.

The final consideration is storing it. You can keep it in a pressurised plastic barrel, bottles or a small keg system. Once you answer those questions, you can be making great beer with very little investment, and add to your gear as you go along.

## Stove top

The most basic kit you'll need for a four-litre extract homebrew on a stove top is a very large stock pot as your brew kettle and a food-grade plastic fermenting bucket or demi-john. Other essential items you may need to buy are an airlock, cleaning and sanitising chemicals and plastic tubing. Equipment you will probably have lying around are a long spoon, colander, digital scales and a thermometer. You also need to consider where you're going to keep it. A homebrew pressure barrel is less hassle than bottling.

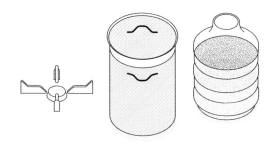

## 23-litre extract brewing

The next logical move is to up the size of the brew to 23 litres (five gallons). Two key pieces require spending: a brew kettle and larger fermenting vessel. The kettle is the biggest investment. It can be either an electric kettle (a converted tea urn) or large pot with a propane burner (our preference as it's more reliable). You'll also need a larger fermenting vessel (a bigger bucket!). At this level, you should also be looking at a hydrometer to measure alcohol, airlocks, syphons and a wort chiller to cool the wort as quickly as possible.

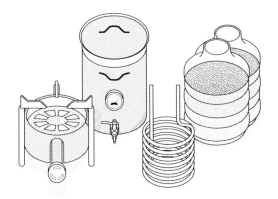

## All-grain brewing

All-grain brewing means you'll be mashing your malted grain rather than using liquid or dry malt extract. It adds another step (and a couple of hours) to your brew day, but the results are noticeably better. Regarding equipment, then the essential addition is a mash tun, usually some form of converted insulated coolbox with a false bottom to separate the grain from the wort. There also needs to be a mechanism to sprinkle the water over the grain bed when sparging. A wort chiller is also necessary for quality of the beer. A hot liquor tank is also handy, but not essential.

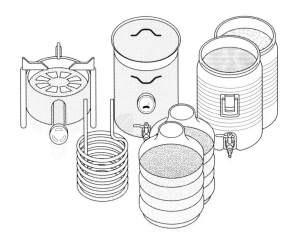

# BREW GEAR

## Go basic, go big, go pro, go geek. Here's some of our favourite gear, admittedly not all essential

When looking at what gear you need, break down the brew day into component parts, writing down what you have and what you need as you go through the process. Some items (kettle, digital scales, spoon, hydrometer) you'll need more than once. It's often useful to draw a quick sketch (perhaps based on the process in this book) to make sure you have everything you need. There's nothing more disheartening than organising a brew day and realising you have the wrong attachment to the mash tun (yes we are speaking from experience).

Many homebrewers are incredibly resourceful, making mash tuns out of cool boxes, kettles out of tea urns, using demi-johns from boot sales and much else besides. The second-hand market for equipment such as Corny kegs to store your beer is also active. And that's all part of the fun of homebrewing. You can, of course, start with the best of everything, but it's wise to work up slowly. Firstly, to make sure you're going to keep the brewing up (and most of us do – it becomes an obsession), but also to settle into your gear and add where you think the next leap in brew quality will come from.

Several items, however, seem at first like luxuries but we'd argue are essential almost from the get-go. An immersion wort chiller will certainly aid the quality of your beer, but also speed up the brewing process. Similarly, a hydrometer is an important device and not too expensive. And don't forget about where you'll be putting your beer once it's finished either. But maybe the most important item? A notebook or spreadsheet to record your progress.

## Other stuff

Some other items you may consider.

- Airlock and bung
- Bottles
- Bottle caps
- Bottle drying tree
- Bottle filler
- Digital scales
- pH meter
- Malt mill
- Muslin grain and hop bags
- Water pumps
  (if you're going really pro)
- Syphon

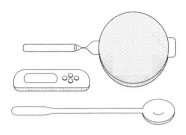

### Thermometer, spoon, colander

A few essential basics. The thermometer is by far the most important item, and we'd always use an electric one for a quick reading. You'll be using it all the time. A long spoon that can almost reach the bottom of your kettle is also useful (if you don't want to burn your fingers). A large, stainless steel colander is also handy.

### Cleaning equipment

By now you'll have heard that brewing is 90 per cent cleaning. It's an exaggeration, but only slightly. Cleaning and sanitising products are non-negotiable, see Cleaning p58 for more details. A small bottle cleaner, long-arm brush and spray gun for sanitisers are handy. Dedicated bottle washers, drying trays and racks are also available.

### Kettle (steel pot or electric kettle)

The kettle is where you heat the water for your mash and also where you boil your wort with the hops. You can either use an electric brewing kettle or a large pot with a burner. We've found the latter more reliable and faster, but more expensive and needs to be used outside. Ideally, they'll have a built in thermometer and a tap at the bottom.

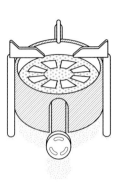

## Burner

We're fans of propane burners. They are reliable; they heat water very quickly, you can use the pot with an ice bath. They are, however, pretty fierce. The Edelmetall Brü Burner pictured, for example, churns out a whopping 72,000 BTUs. You'll need to invest in a propane cylinder and the gas, and we do recommend it is used outside.

## Hot liqour tank

A hot liquor tank (HLT) isn't an essential piece of kit, but it is convenient. A home brewing HLT is very similar to a mash tun and is often an insulated cool box with a tap towards the bottom. The only difference is that there's no false bottom to separate the wort from grains. Use it to fill with strike water and sparge water.

## Mash tun and sparge sprayer

A mash tun is essential for all-grain brewing. It is usually an insulated cool box that has a tap at the bottom and either a false bottom to separate the wort or a gauze around the tap that works just as well. Some mash tuns also have spinning arms at the top to sparge. We just attach a gizmo that sprays the water reasonably well over the bed.

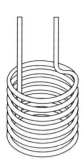

## Immersion wort chiller

A wort chiller, we'd argue, should be filed under essential. It markedly improves your beer and lessens the chance of infection. For the price, a copper or stainless steel coiled immersion wort chiller is the best value for money. Simply hook one end up to a tap, immerse in the wort (to sterilise), and leave to run for half an hour or so.

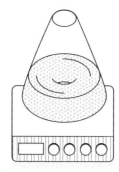

## Stir plate

Unlike the wort chiller, the stir plate is filed under wow-that's-cool-I-want-one. The stir plate is used with a conical flask to make a yeast starter (see p39). The Maelstrom one pictured has a rare earth magnet that is rapidly spun by the electronic device, creating a whirlpool and the perfect environment to propagate yeast.

## Fermenting vessel

An essential item, but if you're are secondary fermenting/conditioning you'll need two. A food grade, sealable plastic bucket with an airlock and bung drilled through the top works well, as does a demi-john or larger carboy. We use a Big Mouth Bubbler available in glass or plastic. It is easy to clean and keep an eye on fermentation.

## Hydrometer and test jar

A hydrometer is used to measure the alcohol content and see how the fermentation is going. Use it to measure the sugar content in the wort before pitching the yeast, any time the beer is moved (for example into a secondary fermenter), to monitor fermentation and at the end to ensure it has finished fermenting. A specific beer one is required.

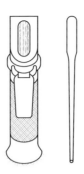

## Refractometer

A refractometer will instantly read the gravity of your wort, in either Brix or SG. Just apply a couple of drops onto the prism with the pipette, close the cover and look through the eyepiece while aiming your refractometer at a light source. It helps to know when to stop sparging (usually 2-3 Brix), or to take readings during the boil.

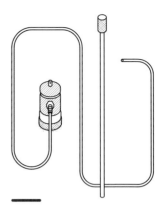

## Oxygenation kit

Healthy, happy yeast is essential to avoiding off-flavours in the finished beer while making sure your wort has enough dissolved oxygen for the yeast to grow is a sure-fire step towards clean and consistent quality beer. This aeration wand tipped with a stainless steel 0.5-micron air stone will do just that. Not essential, but makes a difference.

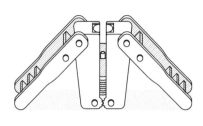

## Bottle capper

Needed if you are bottling. Bottling works with any regular pry-off bottles (not screw-off bottles). Just balance the bottle caps on the top of the bottle and pull down on the two levers. It seals the cap tightly over the bottle. Another option is to collect the 'Grolsch-style' bottles with the flip off cap. They can be bought new.

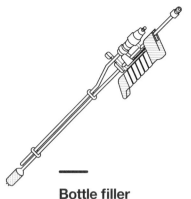

## Bottle filler

This rather attractive bottle filler is for use with kegged beer that has been force carbonated. With the press of a button the Last Straw purges your bottle with $CO_2$, then by pushing the tip of the straw to the bottom of your bottle, it is filled with carbonated beer from your keg. It's an easy way to fill a few bottles for a party or competition.

## Keg and regulator

If you are kegging your beer (and after a few bottle filling sessions we're pretty sure you'll seriously be considering it), you'll need a full keg system. This includes a Cornelius (Corny) keg or a new Draft Brewer keg, $CO_2$ tank, gas tubing and a $CO_2$ regulator – the pictured CO2PO one has pressure marked by beer styles.

# GLOSSARY

## Your ready reference to the main homebrew terms

| TERM | EXPLANATION |
| --- | --- |
| Adjunct | Ingredients that are additional to the grist that help define a style. |
| Airlock | A piece of equipment or lid designed to let CO2 out without letting air back in to your fermentation vessel. |
| Ale | Beer fermented with top-fermenting yeast. It can also sometimes refer to beers with more body or darker in color. |
| Alkali | Alkalis are what you would use to raise the pH of your mash water if it is too acidic. |
| Alkalinity | Alkalinity is the measurement of an alkali solution's ability neutralise an acid. |
| Alpha acid | Alpha acids are responsible for the bitterness we taste in beer. Heat extracts these compounds and isomerizes them into iso-alpha acids. |
| Amino acids | Amino acids are compounds that join to gether to form proteins. |
| Amylases | Amylases are enzymes responsible for breaking large starches into smaller sugars so that the yeasts used in brewing can easily digest them. |
| Bacteria | Bacteria are microscopic organisms typcially undesireable it beer. Some bacteria are cultivated for their ability to create sour flavours in sour beers. |
| Base malt | Malt such as pale malt that serves as the 'backbone; of the beer, as well as the main sugar source for fermentation. |
| Batch | Quantity of beer produced at one time. |
| BJCP | Beer Judging Certification Program. Also defines beer styles in US |
| Blow-off | A type of airlock arrangement with a tube exiting from the fermenter into a bucket of water allowing the release of carbon dioxide. |
| Carbon dioxide | A heavy, colorless, gas (CO2). Two grams fermented wort extract will produce about 1 gram of alcohol and 1 gram of CO2. |
| Coldbreak | Materials that precipitate out of the wort when it is chilled in the fermenter, consisting primarily of proteins and tannins |
| Cone | Any of several cone-like flower or fruit clusters, as in the hop. |
| Copper | A British term for the kettle. |
| Crown caps | Common metal caps used to seal beverage bottles by being crimped or squeezed on. |
| Decoction | Mash method involving the boiling of parts of the mash and returning it to heat the overall mash temperature. |
| Dry hopping | Adding hops to finished beer which provides hop aroma and flavour but no bitterness. |
| Ester | Product of a reaction between an acid and alcohol, often giving off aromas sometimes unwanted. |
| Grain bill | A list of the types and quantities of malt and other grains used in a beer recipe. |

| TERM | EXPLANATION |
|------|-------------|
| Grist | Crushed malt grains used for mashing. Grist should be only gently crushed to expose the husk interior, not broken apart or ground into powder. |
| Gypsum | Sulfate of lime combined with water forms gypsum. Used to increase levels of calcium in water. |
| Hardness | The hardness of water is equal to the concentration of dissolved calcium and magnesium ions. Usually expressed as ppm of ($CaCO_3$). |
| Hopback | Hopback is a sealed chamber that is inserted in between the brewing kettle and counter-flow wort chiller. Hops are added to the chamber. |
| Hydrometer | Hydrometer is a floating instrument for determining specific gravities. A calculation allows you to find the ABV of beer. |
| IBU | International Bitterness Unit. A measure of the bitterness in beer. |
| Infusion | Infusion is the process of extracting flavours from plant material by allowing the material to remain suspended within water. |
| Infusion mash | Simplest procedure for conducting a mash in which crushed grain is mixed with hot water to arrive at a pre-determined rest. |
| Initial mashing | The temperature at which malt and water are brought together at Temp commencement of mashing. |
| Isinglass | A semi-transparent, whitish and form of gelatine, prepared from the air-bladders of certain fish, to clear beer. |
| Krausen | Krausen, pronounced, kroy-zen, is the foamy and bubbly head that forms on top of beer during primary fermentation. |
| Lactic acid | Small amounts of pure lactic acid are commonly used as a brewing water additive to reduce pH. Desirable in lambic, Berliner Weisse and oud bruin. |
| Lauter tub | Vertical and usually cylindrical, straining tank having a false bottom for separating the wort from the spent grains. |
| Lupulin | The fine, yellow, resinous powder on the strobile of hops. |
| Malt extract | A condensed/concentrated wort that is used by homebrewers. It is found in either a liquid or dry form. |
| Malt | Usually refers to malted barley but is also used to refer to any grain, rye, wheat, or barely, etc, that has gone through the malting process. |
| Maltose | A crystalline sugar formed from starch by the action of amylase. It is dextrorotatory and the main source of fermentable extract in brewing. |
| Must | Raw wine. The mixture of fruit juice, sugar, water and yeast which eventually ferments into wine. |
| Original gravity | The density of the wort before fermentation occurs. Measure after fermentation to get ABV. |
| pH | pH values in water range from 0 to 14, below 7 being the acid range and above 7 the basic range. |
| Phenols | Off-flavour in most beer styles (except weizens and some Belgian styles) which can manifest themselves as a medicinal/clovey/band-aid type flavor or aroma |
| Pitch | Adding yeast to the cooled wort. |
| Priming | Addition of a fermentable sugar to a finished beer to carbonate in the bottle. Also called bottle conditioning. Corn sugar is a common priming sugar. |
| Rack | Also referred to as 'transfer'. To move beer from one vessel to another, usually through siphoning. |
| Sparging | Rinsing excess sugars from the grain after mashing. |
| Starter | A vigorous yeast culture prepared in advance to ensure a strong initial ferment. Also describes reserving and nurturing a sample of yeast for future use. |
| Steeping grains | The process of soaking grains (usually specialty grains) in water to extract color/flavor/aroma/body. |
| Torrified | Puffed. Many grains are available in torrified form, alas, all must be mashed. |
| Trub | The whitish, scummy layer that forms on the bottom of fermenting wort containing precipitated proteins, dead or dying yeast cells and other molecules. |
| Wort | Unfermented beer. Made after mashing and sparging process. Liquid or dry malt extract is a concentrated wort. Pronounced 'wert'. |
| Yeast | A group of unicellular organisms of the family Saccharomycetaceae which ferment sugars to alcohol and carbon dioxide by virtue of its enzymes. |
| Wild yeast | Uninvited yeast other than our cultured yeasts. |

# CLEANING

## The most important part of brewing? Afraid so. Here's how to make it faff-free

Yeast is king. It's what is making your beer. We love it, and we want it to be happy. We don't want to upset it in any way. We don't want anything to compete with it, and nothing can stop it. Yeast is our master, and we shall obey it. If we don't follow its orders, it'll either give up fermenting or let something take over, like bacteria. We don't want that. So we clean, vigorously, and sanitise, often.

You must clean well everything that your beer may come in contact with, and just before use, you must sanitise this equipment as well (except the brew kettle). A surface cannot be sanitised until it is clean. If something does not look or smell clean, it probably isn't.

### CLEANING

Cleaning chemicals are very potent, often alkaline chemicals which remove organic deposits. These cleaners need to be thoroughly rinsed after use (unless noted otherwise). Powdered Brewery Wash (PBW) is our favourite.

### SANITISING

All equipment needs to be fully immersed in a sanitising solution for a certain amount of time to reduce the number of microorganisms. Star San, our preferred sanitiser, for example, needs one minute. All unboiled water is a potential source of contamination in fermentations. Rinsing can cause infection, so it is important to use cleaning chemicals designated 'No Rinse' or 'Final Rinse' – examples include Star San and One Step. These are very effective against bacteria, but harmless to beer and people when used as directed. Brewers often fill a trigger spray bottle with sanitiser for quick cleaning.

## Using Star San

1. Find a clean container large enough to hold all the items you are going to be sanitising. Larger items, like fermenters and carboys, can have the sanitising solution prepared inside them.

2. Mix a solution of Star San by adding two tablespoons in 23 litres (5 gallons) of warm water. Stir to mix. Halve quantities for less.

3. Ensure that all surfaces get at least a couple of minutes of contact time. Remove the items from the sanitising solution when needed. If any items or your hands touch an unsanitary surface, they should be re-sanitised.

4. Star San solution loses its ability to sanitise. It only lasts a couple of days.

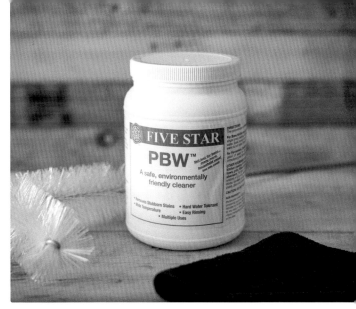

# EXTRACT

## Most people start with an extract brew: it's quick, easy and the results are great

Extract brewing is where many people begin on this great beer journey. The process is pretty straightforward: steep grains in warm water, bring to boil, add malt extract (dried or liquid), add hops, cool, pitch yeast, ferment, drink. The brew day is around five hours, not too much equipment is needed (especially if doing a small batch), and the beer is likely to be very drinkable. You can make most beer styles as an extract brew, and the quality can be exceptionally high (they've even been known to win competitions).

Most extract recipes (and those in this book) involve steeping speciality grains in hot water, much like a tea bag, for around half an hour. These malts add extra colour and flavour to the finished beer. The water should be around 65°C.

After removing the steeping grains, bring the liquid to a boil. Many recipes require you to add the malt extract (liquid or dry) once the liquid reaches a boil. For best results, remove the kettle from your heat source first, then slowly add the malt extract and stir until dissolved. Then return the kettle to the heat source and bring it back to a boil. If you add the extract while boiling, it may simply scorch to the bottom of your kettle and create burnt flavour in the beer. Watch the heat level carefully, as the foam can very quickly boil over and make a hideous mess.

Once it is boiling, add the hops according to the recipe and follow the process in this book as normal: chill the beer as quickly as possible, pitch the yeast and wait for it to ferment into beer.

## Converting recipes

Converting an all-grain recipe to extract brewing isn't an exact science because the process of extract and all-grain is so different. The primary goal is to keep the gravity and bitterness level the same. There are calculators online, but in this book we have stuck to a relatively easy rule of thumb. Steep the same amount of grains that aren't the base malt at the beginning. If using liquid malt extract, use 3/4 of the amount of base malt (x 0.75). For example, if the recipe calls for 4kg of pale malt, use 3kg of liquid extract. If using dry malt, multiply the amount by 0.6. So 4kg of pale malt is 2.4kg of dry malt extract. For hops, as a rough guide, add 20 per cent more. BeerSmith has a useful calculator.

# ALL-GRAIN BREW

## To make the best beer you can, it has to be all-grain. Here's how

All-grain brewing is the best way to make beer, no doubt about it. You'll nearly always achieve a greater depth of flavour than with extract brewing. The process is more intricate (and longer), but everything is 100 per cent in your control, and you'll get the satisfaction that the beer you crack open with your mates will be all your own work. It's never long before those who started on extract kits invest in a mash tun and take the next step. There's nothing like full-grain homebrewing. We love it, and we know you will too.

So what are the main differences? The key aspect is that you will be extracting the sugars from the grain yourself. This is known as mashing. Simply put, it is soaking the grains in hot water to extract all those sugars. That usually takes an hour. Hot water is then run through the grain bed (known as the sparge) and out of the tap on your mash tun back into your kettle. The liquid that runs through is wort, a sugary liquid you'll add hops to during the boil. The fermentation process will then eat up all those sugars and create alcohol.

A mash tun is the key investment here. It is often an insulated cool box that has a tap and a false bottom to separate the wort from the grain. Some kind of mechanism to 'sprinkle' the water evenly across the grain bed during sparging is also required. We use a little plastic device that fits into a tube, but some mash tuns come with spinning sprinkler arms. A hot liquor tank is also useful so you can be heating water while another process is happening.

It's a full day for sure, but there is the odd half hour of downtime to read a book or paint the shed.

OK, wellies on, scales out, tap on, it's time to get brewing.

 **Timeline**

Throughout this section, we've created a timeline so you know what you can be doing at any given point. Each homebrewer will do things slightly differently, and it's a matter of finding what works for you, but this is the process we usually follow. The timings are only there as a guide too. For your first brew day put aside eight hours or so. It's also worth going through the kit and ingredient list the day before so you are all set in the morning.

# PREPARATION

**EQUIPMENT LIST**

Hot liquor tank
(optional)
Mash tun
Kettle
Burner (or
electric kettle)
Tubing
Fermenting vessel
Two large jugs
Bowls for weighed
out hops and malt
Hydrometer and
test jar

**INGREDIENTS**

Malts
Hops
Yeast
Water
Any adjuncts
Any fruit and spices

Success, so the saying goes, is 90 per cent preparation and 10 per cent perspiration, and so it is with beer. Having your brew day planned out will not only save you time but also eliminate the chances of anything ruining your beer.

**1/ Clean all items**. Clean everything your beer will come into contact with for the mash (sanitise other equipment just before you need it). This includes your hot liquor tank, mash tun, kettle, pots and jugs, spoons, thermometer and tubing. We've covered cleaning and sanitising on p58.

**2/ Lay out all items**. Having all equipment and ingredients quickly to hand will make the brew day quicker. See the list left.

**3/ Weigh out ingredients**. Weigh out all your malts (they can be thrown in together once weighed) and your hops for each addition in the boil or dry hop.

**4/ Prepare yeast**. If using a 'smack pack', activate the pack by breaking the inner pouch with a firm smack and incubate at room temp for a least three hours. Bring dry yeast to room temperature.

| | | | | |
|---|---|---|---|---|
| 0h | | | | 1h |
| Read recipe | Layout ingredients | Equipment check | Take yeast out of fridge, or active 'smack pack' | Fill kettle |

# HEATING WATER

The water you'll be heating now is for the mash – the porridge-like mixture of water and malts from which you'll get your wort. The water can be heated in an electric kettle or with a propane burner (our method). The latter is quicker but needs to be used outside.

**1/ Calculate the amount of water**. A general rule of thumb is 2.5 litres for every kilogram of malt. Add another litre to this to ensure you have enough if the consistency of your mash is too thick.

**2/ Heat water to strike temperature**. You need to heat your water to the strike temperature. The strike temperature is higher than the mash temperature because it will lose around 10-12°C as it hits the malt. Presuming the mash temperature is 67°C, heat the water to 79°C. The temperature of the mash must not go above 75°C.

**3/ Transfer water to HLT**. Once the water has hit the strike temperature, transfer the full amount to the hot liquor tank (or directly into the mash tun). Heat more water for the sparge.

---

**A HOT LIQUOR TANK?**

There are several methods for heating water depending on your set up. Our chosen method is to use a hot liquor tank (HLT). This separate insulated vessel holds water at a steady temperature to use. It's not essential, but it allows you to heat water for the sparge while you are mashing plus it is often easier to move around.

1h — Set strike temp — Weigh out grains — Clean HLT and mash tun — Check temp with thermometer (aim for 79°C) — 2h

# MASHING IN

### STEP INFUSION MASHING

A multiple-step infusion mash is different from a singe-step infusion mash because it includes a protein rest of 20-30 minutes at different temperatures. This is particularly used in lager and Belgian brewing. A protein rest reduces haze, improves body and head retention and creates a nutrient-rich wort for yeast.

Mashing in is the process that extracts all the fermentable sugars from the malt.

**1/ Transfer water to mash tun**. Using a jug, transfer your water, heated to strike temperature, to the mash tun.

**2/ Add grist**. Slowly pour in your malts (no need to keep different malts separated)

stirring all the time with a long spoon. There can't be any clumps of malt, instead it should be a smooth porridge-like mixture.

**3/ Take temperature**. The temperature should stabilise at 67°C. Be aware that there can be cool spots in the mash so test it in a couple of areas. If it's not hot enough heat some water in a regular kettle and

stir in well. If it's too hot add a little cold water. It must not go over 75°C.

**4/ Rest for an hour**. During this saccharification rest, malt enzymes convert the grain's starch into fermentable sugars.

**5/ Heat sparge water**. While the mash is resting, heat 2.5 litres for every kilogram of dry malt to 76°C.

Gradually pour in grains, stirring constantly

Heat sparge water to 76°C

3h

Transfer water to HLT

Make a porridge-like mixture, and stir occasioanlly

Ensure mash temp is 67°C

# MASH OUT + SPARGING

**1/ Mash out.** Add two litres of hot water to the mash, stirring constantly, raising the temperature to 76°C and leave for 10 minutes. This helps sparging.

**2/ Recirculate.** The initial run-off from the mash tun is cloudy and filled with draff — small solid grain particles. The run-off should be clarified by recirculating through the grain in the mash tun. Open the valve slightly and collect the runoff in a jug with at least a litre capacity. Fill one vessel and pour it gently down the side of the mash tun, while filling the other one, until the wort appears clear of draff (after 5-15 minutes).

**3/ Sparge.** Open the valve on the sparge water tank and gently disperse the 76°C sparge water over the top of the grain bed. We use an attachment that sprays the water. Some mash tuns come with spray attachments in the lid. Don't allow the grain bed to dry out until the end.

**4/ Stop sparging.** Stop once you have collected the right amount of wort (27L in our recipes) back in your kettle.

## STUCK MASH?

A stuck mash occurs when the runnings slow or stop because the filter bed of husks has clogged. This may be caused by crushing the grain too fine, putting too much sparge water on the grain bed, losing too much heat, and/or using glutinous adjuncts like wheat, oats or unmalted barley. Try stirirring gently, and recirculate again. Failing that, remove mash and start again

Open valve on HLT and mash tun to sparge

Ensure hops weighed out

3h

4h

Add 2 litres of water at 76°, rest for 10 mins

Draw off wort, recirculate until clear

Stop when 27 litres has been collected

Heat kettle to boil

# THE BOIL

## FININGS

Fining agents clarify the beer. They make many of the bits floating around in the beer to clump together and drop out. Common homebrew fining agents are Protofloc and Irish moss added 10 minutes before the end of boil. Isinglass, made from a fish's swim bladder, is often added by brewers after fermentation has finished.

The boil is when you add the hops, and it usually lasts an hour. Spices and sugars are often treated like hops and added to the kettle at specific times.

**1/ Heat wort**. You'll have collected your wort back into your kettle. Begin to heat it to a low, steady boil.

**2/ Add first hops**. Hop additions are made

according to a hop schedule which is the order and time the hops go in. It is a countdown, usually from 60 minutes to 0 minutes or 'flame out'. Bittering hops are added as soon as the wort comes to the boil.

**3/ Follow hop schedule**. The next additions are towards the end of the boil and contribute to flavouring and aroma in the beer.

**4/ Sanitise chiller**. An immersion chiller needs to santised. Some homebrewers add it for the last 10 minutes of the boil — but be careful.

**4/ Flame out**. When 60 minutes of boil time has finished, turn out the flame, or switch off the electricity, and add the final hops if needed. It now needs to be cooled as quickly as possible.

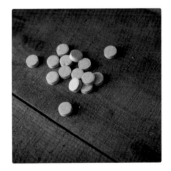

Immerse chiller in boiling wort 10 mins before end

5h

At boil, add bittering hops

Towards end of boil add aroma hops and Protofloc if using

Hook up chiller

# COOLING + TRANSFER

**1/ Prepare chiller**. If using an immersion chiller, hook it up to the tap and turn it on.

**2/ Start cooling**. Carefully lower the coil into the kettle and turn on the tap. The cool water will travel around the coil and conduct the heat out. The first run of water out of the chiller can be very hot (use the water to clean your fermenter). Gently stir the wort in a circular motion opposite to the flow of water through the chiller. Start with the tap on full, before slowing the flow down as the wort chills.

**3/ Take temperature**. With a sanitised thermometer measure the temperature of the water (everything has to be sanitised that touches the beer from now on). It needs to reach the optimum level of the yeast that you are using – it will say on the yeast packet, (for an ale usually between 18-24°C).

**4/ Transfer wort**. You will need to transfer it to a sanitised fermentation vessel. Do this slowly and steadily. Leave behind any thick sludge in the bottom of your kettle. While you are transferring the wort, take a sample for hydrometer in the glass test jar.

## WHICH CHILLER?

There are several ways to cool your wort. An ice bath is the simplest way to cool wort, but also takes the longest and can't be used with an electric kettle. Immersion coil chillers are our preferred method and are efficient for the price. Plate and counterflow chillers are quicker, but more expensive and you usually need a pump

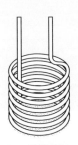

Take temperature

Transfer cooled wort to fermenter

5h

6h

Turn on tap

Gently stir wort in opposite direction

# PITCHING YEAST

## WHAT IS A YEAST PITCHING RATE?

This is the amount of yeast added to the cooled wort. It is measured in millions of yeast cells per millilitre of wort. Simply, the higher the original gravity, the more yeast you need, and the colder you ferment, the more yeast you need. The cleaner you want your beer, the more yeast you would use and vice versa. See Making a Starter on p39.

The brewing term for adding yeast to wort is pitching. You will have activated the yeast smack pack, made a starter (see p39) or got the yeast out of the fridge to room temperature.

**1/ Measure original gravity**. Before pitching the yeast take a sample in the glass test jar and measure the original gravity. Record the figure.

**2/ Sanitise everything**. Sanitise a pair of scissors and the area of the pack of yeast you'll be cutting, as well as the airlock and bung. Place some sanitiser in the airlock.

**3/ Pitch yeast**. Open your packet, if you have liquid yeast, go ahead and pour it directly into the wort; if you have dry yeast, sprinkle it on the surface of the wort.

**4/ Seal lid**. Seal the lid of your fermentation vessel, fill the airlock with some of your sanitising solution (not pure), or vodka.

**5/ Move your wort**. Move your vessel into a dark, quiet spot. Choose somewhere with a steady temperature and little exposure to light. Pick an area that is easily accessible too.

Week

0w

Measure original gravity with hydrometer

Pitch yeast

Seal fermenter, filling airlock with diluted sanitising solution

# FERMENTING + DRY HOPPING

Fermentation, the process that converts our wort to beer, begins on brew day and ends a week or two later.

**1/ Watch for fermentation**. Within a day or two of brew day, fermentation starts. As the yeast converts malt sugars into $CO_2$ and alcohol, you will see bubbles come through the airlock. The specific gravity will steadily drop, and a cap of thick foam called krauesen forms above the beer. If not, see right.

**2/ Fermentation ends**. Roughly a week from brew day, fermentation stops. Bubbles coming through the airlock become very slow or stop entirely; the specific gravity is stable, and the cap of foam starts to subside.

**3/ Measure gravity**. The specific gravity will drop during fermentation. Only check when you transfer your beer, either to another container or, finally, during bottling/kegging to ensure it has finished. You're checking to see if you have hit your final gravity target in the recipe. You may miss your target, but if it's near you are good. If it's way off it could be stuck (see right).

## STUCK FERMENTATION?

If not much seems to be happening after a couple of days first check the gravity; it could be that your fermenter isn't sealed and the yeast is fine. If nothing is changing, maybe fermenter is too cold Check temperature and perhaps wrap it in something warm like an old sleeping bag. Maybe add more yeast and nutrients.

Dry hop beer when fermentation slows

Transfer to secondary fermenter

1w     2w     3w

When moving beer, check gravity

# CONDITIONING/SECONDARY FERMENTATION

**BREWING A LAGER?**

Lager is a different beast: it requires a lower fermentation temperature and takes significantly longer. Pitching sufficient quantities of yeast under the correct conditions should allow you to wrap up the primary fermentation in 10-21 days, depending on the style. The beer can then be transferred to the secondary to finish up for another 7-14 days.

In brewing term, secondary fermentation, or conditioning, is moving the beer into a new, clean fermenter. During our fermentation process, we see a layer of krausen form on top of our beer. That krausen dissipates over time and any remaining grain particles, hop particles and dead yeast cells will accumulate instead at the bottom of your fermenter in a mass known as 'trub'. Sitting on this trub for a short while can impart flavours we want to see in a beer, but letting our brew sit atop this trub for too long can create characteristics we don't want.

To avoid unwanted flavours setting in, we suggest 'racking' (syphoning) – (see overleaf) the brew out of the first fermenter, being careful to leave the trub behind and into a new, sanitised fermenter. Doing so allows the beer to settle out and condition in flavour. This is also when we would add some adjuncts or more hops for dry hopping a week before we're planning to bottle the beer. It can usually sit here for two weeks – we specify in the recipe. Check the gravity with a hydrometer when transferring the beer.

4w — If an ale, bottle or keg - see overleaf

5w

6w — Bottle/keg lager / Bottled ale ready

# RACKING + PRIMING

Racking is the process of carefully moving beer off of the trub – the hop pieces, dead yeast and malt brewing materials at the bottom of the fermenter – into a secondary fermenter (see p71), or directly into bottles or a keg (see p74). It's worth stating again that sanitation is the most important task of the entire brewing process. Priming beer is adding sugar that will ferment and carbonate your beer in the bottle.

**1/ Sanitise everything.**
For bottling this means bucket, bottles, caps, tubing and attachments. For a Cornelius keg, this includes the keg and all attachments .

**2/ Priming**. Mixing in the priming sugar will allow the yeast to carbonate your beer in the bottle.

There are several methods. Racking to a bottling bucket lets you fully mix your priming solution and beer before bottling. This is the quickest way, and if using it see 'Syphoning' right. An alternative if you don't have a bottling bucket or similar, is to add sugar to the individual bottles. The amount of priming sugar to be used depends on the style of beer.

---

**WHICH BOTTLES?**

Any bottles that are 'pry-off' style can be capped. Capping our bottles assures we protect our brew from any errant bacteria and it is vital that our caps, just like any of our other equipment, are sanitised and in good condition. The caps are cheap, and a bottle capper is simple to use (plenty of small commercial breweries still bottle and cap manually).

Prime bottles with Fizz Drops or add solution to bottling bucket

0h            1h

Sanitise everything           Begin syphoning

Large PET bottles are now less common, but also provide a quick option for bottling. The downsides are that if scratched they are hard to sanitise, and if they are transparent, it may lead to an off flavour due to the light hitting it. One of the best options is the 'Grolsch-style' flip off caps. They can be bought from most homebrew shops, but it's also worth keeping an eye out for these bottles at supermarkets.

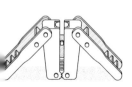

More sugar = more carbonation. There's a good online calculator here: northernbrewer.com/priming-sugar-calculator. If you are priming your beer directly in a bottle, by far the easiest solution is to use Fizz Drops. They drop directly into the bottle. The downside is that you can't control the amount of sugar for different styles.

**3/ Syphoning**. It is worth getting a syphon that has a tip on the end that does its best at leaving some of the trub at the bottom. It is usually called a racking cane. Your syphon should be deep enough to syphon yet not so deep as to disturb the trub. Start with your syphon about seven centimetres deep into your beer and slowly deeper as your liquid is displaced

into the bottling bucket or bottles. Be very careful not to draw in any sediment. Siphon smart!

**4/ Bottling**. The best way to bottle is to use a bottle filler attached by a short length of tubing to your bottling bucket's spigot. Funnel in priming sugar or add Fizz Drops first. Leave a little space of headroom at the top of your bottle.

Fill bottles to just below the top

Cap bottles

2h

# KEGGING

Kegging is the fastest and easiest way to serve beer. Each kegging system is slightly different but will contain four items: tap lines, a carbon dioxide tank, a regulator to control carbonation and a keg.

The most common type of keg for homebrewers is a Cornelius (Corny) keg that were used widely for soft drinks. There's now plenty about and you'll find some on eBay. New kegs with the same system are also available. We use Draft Brewer's keg system. It is the same as a regular Corny keg set up, but the regulator is designed specifically for beer, even showing the styles on the pressure gauge. There is some outlay on kegging but, as you'll soon realise, bottling is a bit of a faff!

The keg system comes with comprehensive instructions, but simply, the carbon dioxide tank is connected to a gas regulator, which in turn is connected via gas tubing to the 'in' connection of the keg. The CO2 carbonates the beer and also pushes the beer out of the 'out' side which is connected to a tap. It's ideal for storing beer, and no oxygen is present.

## WHICH BEER TO AGE?

Dark and strong beers (over 5%) fare best when ageing (in wood or fermenter). Partly because it can stand the time, but also, the dominant flavour from oak is vanilla – delicious in a stout. In fact,

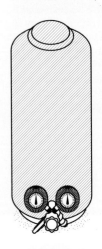

Gently fill the keg with beer and seal keg

0h

1h

Sanitise kegs and tubing by pushing sanitation fluid through the keg with CO2

Begin adding CO2 according to instructions and beer style

# BARREL AGEING

any beers that have a good punch of chocolate and coffee notes work well with ageing in barrels or with oak chips. Imperial stouts and porters are perfect for it. Strong lighter coloured beers work too. Barley wines of course, but maybe big IPAs and double IPAs, can be aged. Lambics too are traditionally aged for up to three years and often blended with younger beers.

Ageing beer in barrels is increasingly popular among commercial craft brewers looking at adding a complexity, a certain amount of whim, and just to have some fun. It's not a new thing, of course, beer was traditionally kept in wooden barrels, but this is a new era of experimentation. Barrels that once contained tequila, sherry, bourbon and burgundy are snapped up by brewers to put their beers in. The market for used barrels is vibrant and demand high. Homebrewers can readily buy them, but at a price. A good alternative is to add oak chips or spirals to the secondary fermenter. The lightest touch is probably from American oak chips which is a good starting place. But you can easily get hold of chips that have been soaked in bourbon or sherry. Of course, you can soak the chips in anything you fancy.

Using oak chips, and especially ageing in barrels, is a matter of trial, error and accurate recording. It's one of the most unpredictable aspects in brewing, but that's why it is such good fun. Buy some chips, make something dark and try it.

0y ————————————————————— 2y

Clean barrel or add oak chips    Return regularly to try beer    Bottle or keg as normal

# SOUR BEERS

## The popularity of sour beers shows no sign of abating, and it is well within the scope of a homebrewer

Sour beers have been part of the fabric of Belgian beer culture for centuries. Only recently gaining popularity in the States and then the international beer market. So-called 'sour' or 'wild' beers include some styles that are one way or another sour, tart, funky, barnyard-like or acidic thanks to the introduction of wild yeasts and bacteria during fermentation.

### LACTOBACILLUS

Called 'lacto' in beery circles, lactobacillus is a bacteria which eats the sugars in wort and, instead of converting them to alcohol, converts them to lactic acid. The result is a clean yet sour taste and is what gives Goses and Berliner Weisses their distinctive flavours.

### PEDIOCOCCUS

AKA 'pedio', this is another bacteria which converts sugars to lactic acid. The result is more of a sour character than lactobacillus and can give off more funky flavours. It works well alongside Brett (see p38) in Flanders reds or lambics.

### WILD YEASTS

Or bacteria or microfauna, these little critters are found everywhere! Whichever ones are found in a particular environment define a terroir AND a beer's flavour.

### SPONTANEOUS FERMENTATION

While many brewers today control which yeasts or bacteria come in contact with their beer, historically sour beers were created by exposing them to whichever wild yeasts or bacteria were in the air, floorboards or rafters of the brewery. Cantillon in Brussels is the most famous brewery to practice this method.

## Kettle sours

Kettle souring is a technique that allows brewers to rapidly sour unfermented wort in just a matter of days, often taking only a mere 24 hours. It could not be more simple – after creating wort and conducting a brief boil for sanitation, the wort is cooled to 24ºC – 35ºC and a cultured strain (or blend of strains) of pure lactobacillus is introduced. Once introduced, the lactobacillus will go to work and begin consuming sugars in the wort transforming them into lactic acid, providing the tart flavour. Given some time, usually one to three days, the souring will be complete. For a subtle sourness, target a pH in the mid to upper 3s or if you want that awesome lip-puckering sourness, shoot for a pH in the lower 3s.

# RECIPES

**9**

# The magic of 'make it your own'

The reason for this book is to offer you the tools to 'make it your own'. We give you a core recipe that we're confident will taste amazing, but the 'make it your own' column allows you to see how much of a particular ingredient you can use to be either still within a style, or without it tasting rubbish.

The 'variance score' is an at-a-glance indication of how far you can push an individual element. We also show the maximum recommended usage of a malt or hop, plus the main ways it will impact your beer. We've also suggested hop substitutes and a liquid yeast. Enjoy!

# HOW TO

## Your guide to our ground-breaking recipe cards

**1**

### ABOUT THIS BREW

| | |
|---|---|
| Volume | 23 litres |
| Boil volume | 27 litres |
| Alcohol | 5.6% (5.5% – 9%) |
| Bitterness / IBU | 25 IBU (50 – 90 IBU) |
| Colour | 50 EBC (40 – 80 EBC) |
| Original Gravity | 1.062 (1.050– 1.085) |
| Final Gravity | 1.016 (1.010 – 1.018) |

**2**

**EXTRACT RECIPE:**
Steep 250g caramel 80, 170g of Carafa III and 170 of chocolate malt in 27 litres of water for half an hour. Remove and then add 3.3kg of light dried malt extract or 4.1kg of Maris Otter pale liquid malt extract, bring to the boil and add hops as normal to the boil.

# BLACK IPA

**7**

An ebony-hued tipple topped with a beige head and surrounded by an aromatic citrus-and-pine force field, backed by a smooth roastiness redolent of cocoa and French roast coffee. Full-bodied, hop-bitter, and boozy, this beer is compelling enough to both fuel and quash the argument of its stylistic integrity, and it goes great with a blue-cheese stuffed sirloin burger or steak.

**5**

**ADJUNCTS:** 500g of corn sugar is added at the end of the boil to increase alcoholic strength.

**9**

**3**

| CORE RECIPE | | | | MAKE IT YOUR OWN | | | | | |
|---|---|---|---|---|---|---|---|---|---|
| MALT | Ideal qty | % | Overall qty kg | Qty min | Variance score | Qty max | max % | Impacts | |
| **Pale malt** | 5.5kg | 90 | 6.09 | 5kg | | 6.5kg | 80 | ABV + colour | |
| **Caramel 80L** | 250g | 4 | | 250g | | 500g | 10 | Colour + flavour | |
| **Carafa III** | 170g | 3 | | 100g | | 300g | 10 | Colour | |
| **Chocolate malt** | 170g | 3 | | 100g | | 300g | 10 | Colour + aroma | |

 **Mash in** at 64°C for 60min ▬▬ **Mash out** at 76°C for 10min

**4**

| HOP | Qty g | AA | Time | g min | Variance score | g max | Impacts | Alternatives |
|---|---|---|---|---|---|---|---|---|
| ⓪ Summit | 25 | 17.5 | 60 | 15 | | 30 | Aroma + bitterness | Amarillo / Cascade |
| ⓪ Chinook | 30 | 13 | 15 | 15 | | 35 | Aroma + bitterness | Brewers Gold / Columbus |
| ⓪ Centennial | 30 | 10.5 | 10 | 15 | | 35 | Aroma | Amarillo / Cascade |
| ⓪ Cascade | 30 | 5.8 | 5 | 20 | | 40 | Aroma | Amarillo / Centennial |
| ⓪ Centennial | 30 | 10.5 | 0 | 20 | | 40 | Aroma | Amarillo / Cascade |
| ⓪ Cascade | 30 | 5.8 | Dry hop | 30 | | 40 | Aroma | Amarillo / Centennial |
| Corn sugar | 500g | | | 0 | | | | |

**5**

| YEAST | Temp °C | | Condition / Wks | | | Alternative yeasts | Temp °C | |
|---|---|---|---|---|---|---|---|---|
| | Min | Max | 1st | 2nd | Bot | | MIN | MAX |
| **MJ's M44 West Coast IPA** | 18 | 23 | 1-2 | 1-2 | 2 | Wyeast #1272 American Ale Yeast II | 15 | 22 |

**6**

Mash 67°C

Mash out 74°C

0

60
70
60

**8**

Boil

15

10

5

0

Dry hop in secondary 1 week before packaging

## 1 About this brew

Here you'll find the valuable information about the beer. In brackets are the accepted parameters for this style according to the BJCP guidelines.

## 2 Extract recipe

We've converted the all-grain recipes according to a calculation (see p60). It's impossible to get an exact clone, but this will get you started.

## 3 Core recipe table

The core recipe will give you a great tasting beer within the style guidelines. It shows the malt bill and the percentage each element one makes up.

## 4 Hop table

The hop table shows the type of hop, the quantity, the alpha acids and the time they are to be added. The final column shows any substitutions.

## 5 Notes, adjunct info and table

Any information outside the regular recipe, including adjunct additions, souring or ageing information, and traditional mash options.

## 6 Yeast table

Here we recommend a Mangrove Jack's (MJ's) dry yeast strain, as well as a Wyeast liquid option, plus ideal temperatures. Also the conditioning times.

## 7 Beer example

Where possible we've shown a commercial example of the beer style, or near to it. Note: the recipe is not a clone.

## 8 The tremendous timeline tool

Maybe 'tremendous' is over-stating it a little, but our handy timeline gives you a quick look at the brew day and the times for key hop and adjunct additions. The time counts up for the mash and always includes a 10-minute mash out that we find useful for mashing.

The hop timeline counts down, as is the accepted convention. A hop addition at '15' indicates 15 minutes from the end of the one-hour boil. '0', also known as 'flame out' is when you turn the heat off. The hops are usually left in for 20 minutes at this point before cooling. Dry hopping information is also given. Adjunct additions, when added to the boil, are also listed.

# BRITISH & IRISH

## ABOUT THIS BREW

| | |
|---|---|
| Volume | 23 litres |
| Boil volume | 27 litres |
| Alcohol | 3.8% (3.2 – 3.8%) |
| Bitterness / IBU | 28 IBU (25 – 35 IBU) |
| Colour | 22 EBC (16 – 28 EBC) |
| Original Gravity | 1.039 (1.032 – 1.040) |
| Final Gravity | 1.010 (1.007 – 1.011) |

### EXTRACT RECIPE:

Steep 350g of crystal 120L in 27 litres of water at 65°C for half an hour. Remove and then add 2.2kg of golden light dried malt extract or 2.7kg of Maris Otter pale liquid malt extract bring to the boil and add hops as normal in boil.

# ORDINARY BITTER

With its roots in the Burton-on-Trent pale ales of the late 1800's, the ordinary bitter is a low-gravity version of the quintessential English bitter. Usually served on cask, this ale is noted for its bready, biscuity malts and a moderate sweetness which is tempered by a moderately-high bitterness and creamy carbonation.

### CORE RECIPE | MAKE IT YOUR OWN

| MALT | Ideal qty | % | Overall qty kg | Qty min | Variance score | | Qty max | max % | Impacts |
|---|---|---|---|---|---|---|---|---|---|
| Pale malt (Maris Otter) | 3.5 | 91 | 3.85 | 3 | | | 3.8 | 8 | ABV |
| Crystal 120L | 350g | 9 | | 100g | | | 500g | 5 | Colour |

⊂⊃ **Mash in** at 67°C for 60min ▬▬ **Mash out** at 76°C for 10min

| HOP | Qty g | AA | Time | g min | Variance score | | g max | Impacts | Alternatives |
|---|---|---|---|---|---|---|---|---|---|
| ❶ East Kent Goldings | 28 | 5.5 | 60 | 23 | | | 35 | Aroma | Fuggles |
| | | | | | | | | | Progress |
| | | | | | | | | | Challenger |
| ❷ East Kent Goldings | 28 | 5.5 | 15 | 50 | | | 70 | Aroma + bitterness | Fuggles |
| | | | | | | | | | Progress |
| | | | | | | | | | First Gold |
| ❸ East Kent Goldings | 14 | 5.5 | 1 | 50 | | | 70 | Aroma | Fuggles |
| | | | | | | | | | Progress |
| | | | | | | | | | First Gold |

| YEAST | Temp °C | | Condition / Wks | | | Alternative yeasts | Temp °C | |
|---|---|---|---|---|---|---|---|---|
| | Min | Max | 1st | 2nd | Bot | | MIN | MAX |
| MJ's M36 Liberty Bell | 18 | 24 | 1 | N/A | 2 | Wyeast #1098 British Ale | 18 | 24 |

## ABOUT THIS BREW

| | |
|---|---|
| Volume | 23 litres |
| Boil volume | 27 litres |
| Alcohol | 4.2% (3.8 – 4.6%) |
| Bitterness / IBU | 40 IBU (25 – 40 IBU) |
| Colour | 16 EBC (8 – 32 EBC) |
| Original Gravity | 1.044 (1.040 – 1.048) |
| Final Gravity | 1.011 (1.008 – 1.012) |

### EXTRACT RECIPE:

Steep 250g of dark crystal in 27 litres of water for half an hour. Remove and then add 2.4kg of golden light dried malt extract or 3kg of Maris Otter pale liquid malt extract bring to the boil and add hops as normal in boil.

# BEST BITTER

While the name suggests that this version of bitter is the very best, it instead is the name used to describe a maltier, somewhat higher gravity type of English bitter. This style displays the characteristic English hops on top of a sturdy malt profile while still being exceptionally drinkable and balanced.

| CORE RECIPE | | | | MAKE IT YOUR OWN | | | | |
|---|---|---|---|---|---|---|---|---|
| **MALT** | Ideal qty | % | Overall qty kg | Qty min | Variance score | Qty max | max % | Impacts |
| Pale malt (Maris Otter) | 4 | 94 | 4.25 | 3.7kg | | 4.3% | 95 | ABV + colour |
| Dark crystal | 250g | 6 | | 250g | | 350g | 10 | Colour + flavour |

◁▭▷ **Mash in** at 64°C for 60min ▬▬ **Mash out** at 76°C for 10min

| **HOP** | Qty g | AA | Time | g min | Variance score | g max | Impacts | Alternatives |
|---|---|---|---|---|---|---|---|---|
| ❶ East Kent Goldings | 45 | 5.5 | 60 | 25 | | 45 | Aroma | Fuggles |
| | | | | | | | | Progress |
| | | | | | | | | Challenger |
| ❷ Fuggles | 25 | 4.8 | 15 | 10 | | 30 | Aroma + bitterness | East Kent Goldings |
| | | | | | | | | Progress |
| | | | | | | | | First Gold |
| ❸ Fuggles | 25 | 4.8 | 5 | 10 | | 30 | Aroma | East Kent Goldings |
| | | | | | | | | Progress |
| | | | | | | | | First Gold |

| **YEAST** | Temp °C Min | Max | Condition / Wks 1st | 2nd | Bot | Alternative yeasts | Temp °C MIN | MAX |
|---|---|---|---|---|---|---|---|---|
| MJ's M36 Liberty Bell | 18 | 23 | 1-2 | 2-4 | 2 | Wyeast #1275 Thames Valley Ale Yeast | 17 | 22 |

## ABOUT THIS BREW

| Volume | 23 litres |
|---|---|
| Boil volume | 27 litres |
| Alcohol | 5% (4.6% – 6.2%) |
| Bitterness / IBU | 42 IBU (30 – 50 IBU) |
| Colour | 16.7 EBC (16 – 36 EBC) |
| Original Gravity | 1.056 (1.048 – 1.060) |
| Final Gravity | 1.014 (1.010 – 1.016) |

### EXTRACT RECIPE:

Steep 250g of crystal 60L, 100g of torrified wheat and 100g chocolate malt in 27 litres of water at 65°C for half an hour. Remove and then add 3kg of golden light dried malt extract or 3.75kg of Maris Otter pale liquid malt extract and bring to the boil. Add hops as normal to the boil.

# ESB BITTER

Think of the Extra Special Bitter as a bitter squared: it has more malt, more hops, a higher gravity, more bitterness and more of, well, everything. An ESB is a showcase for high-quality hops and brewing skill, meant to be enjoyed with consideration rather than merely quaffed.

//////////////////////////////

**ADJUNCTS:** The addition of torrified wheat can add to the head retention and flavour.

## CORE RECIPE / MAKE IT YOUR OWN

| MALT | Ideal qty | % | Overall qty kg | Qty min | Variance score | | | | Qty max | Max % | Impacts |
|---|---|---|---|---|---|---|---|---|---|---|---|
| Pale malt (Maris Otter) | 5kg | 92 | | 4.7 | | | | | 6 | 95 | ABV |
| Crystal 60L | 250g | 4 | 5.45 | 250g | | | | | 500g | 10 | Colour |
| Torrified wheat | 100g | 2 | | 0 | | | | | 500g | 10 | Head retention/flavour |
| Chocolate malt | 100g | 2 | | 0 | | | | | 200g | 5 | Colour |

Mash in at 67°C for 60min ▬▬ Mash out at 76°C for 10min

| HOP | Qty g | AA | Time | g min | Variance score | | | | g max | Impacts | Alternatives |
|---|---|---|---|---|---|---|---|---|---|---|---|
| ❶ Challenger | 50 | 7 | 60 | 35 | | | | | 60 | Bitterness | East Kent Goldings |
| | | | | | | | | | | | Willamette |
| | | | | | | | | | | | Northdown |
| ❷ East Kent Goldings | 20 | 5.5 | 15 | 10 | | | | | 35 | Aroma/bitterness | Fuggles |
| | | | | | | | | | | | Progress |
| | | | | | | | | | | | First Gold |
| ❸ Fuggles | 13 | 4.8 | 0 | 0 | | | | | 20 | Aroma | East Kent Goldings |
| | | | | | | | | | | | Progress |
| | | | | | | | | | | | First Gold |

| YEAST | Temp °C | | Condition / Wks | | | Alternative yeasts | Temp °C | |
|---|---|---|---|---|---|---|---|---|
| | Min | Max | 1st | 2nd | Bot | | MIN | MAX |
| MJ's M15 Empire Ale | 18 | 22 | 1-2 | 2 | 2 | Wyeast #1968 ESB Ale Yeast | 18 | 22 |

## ABOUT THIS BREW

| Volume | 23 litres |
|---|---|
| Boil volume | 27 litres |
| Alcohol | 4.8% (4.6% – 6.2%) |
| Bitterness / IBU | 38 IBU (30 – 65 IBU) |
| Colour | 16.3 EBC (16 – 35 EBC) |
| Original Gravity | 1.049 (1.048 – 1.060) |
| Final Gravity | 1.012 (1.010 – 1.016) |

### EXTRACT RECIPE:

Steep 300g of medium crystal in 27 litres of water at 65°C for half an hour. Remove and then add 2.7kg of golden light dried malt extract or 3.35kg of Maris Otter pale liquid malt extract and bring to the boil. Add hops as normal to the boil.

# PALE ALE

The English Pale Ale is renowned for its drinkability, enhanced bitterness and balancing malts. Yeast strains used in this style lend a bit of fruitiness while English-variety hops display an earthy, herbal hop character. Medium-bodied, golden to amber-coloured and served clear, this quintessential English ale is one from which many others have derived.

| Mash | Mash out | |
|---|---|---|
| 67°C | 76°C | |

0 · 60 · 70 · 60

Boil

0

| CORE RECIPE | | | | | MAKE IT YOUR OWN | | | | |
|---|---|---|---|---|---|---|---|---|---|
| MALT | Ideal qty | % | Overall qty kg | Qty min | Variance score | Qty max | max % | Impacts | |
| Pale malt (Maris Otter) | 4.5 | 94 | 4.8 | 4.5 | | 5.5 | 95 | ABV + colour | |
| Medium crystal | 300g | 6 | | 300g | | 900g | 20 | Colour | |

**Mash in** at 67°C for 60min ━━ **Mash out** at 76°C for 10min

| HOP | Qty g | AA | Time | g min | Variance score | g max | Impacts | Alternatives |
|---|---|---|---|---|---|---|---|---|
| ① East Kent Goldings | 60 | 5.5 | 60 | 55 | | 80 | Bitterness | Fuggles |
| | | | | | | | | Challenger |
| | | | | | | | | Target |
| ② East Kent Goldings | 30 | 5.5 | 0 | 25 | | 60 | Aroma | Fuggles |
| | | | | | | | | Challenger |
| | | | | | | | | Target |
| ③ Styrian Goldings | 15 | 5.3 | 0 | 0 | | 20 | Aroma | Challenger |
| | | | | | | | | Williamette |
| | | | | | | | | East Kent Goldings |

| YEAST | Temp °C | | Condition / Wks | | | Alternative yeasts | Temp °C | |
|---|---|---|---|---|---|---|---|---|
| | Min | Max | 1st | 2nd | Bot | | MIN | MAX |
| MJ's Liberty Bell Ale | 18 | 23 | 1-2 | 2 | 2 | Wyeast #1098 British Ale Yeast | 18 | 22 |

## ABOUT THIS BREW

| | |
|---|---|
| Volume | 23 litres |
| Boil volume | 27 litres |
| Alcohol | 6% (5% – 7.5%) |
| Bitterness / IBU | 42 IBU (40 – 60 IBU) |
| Colour | 12 EBC (12 – 26 EBC) |
| Original Gravity | 1.062 (1.050 – 1.075) |
| Final Gravity | 1.016 (1.010 – 1.018) |

### EXTRACT RECIPE:

Simply use 3.6kg of golden light dried malt extract or 4kg of Maris Otter pale liquid malt extract and bring to the boil. Add hops as normal to the boil.

# ENGLISH IPA

With its origins dating to the late 1700s, the English IPA was no more than a pale ale that had been extra-hopped in order to survive the voyage to India. What we've got today is a dry and moderately-strong ale that is balanced towards the hops with a supportive maltiness.

/ / / / / / / / / / / / / / / / / / / / / /

**ADJUNCTS:** The addition of candi sugar can boost sweetness and alcohol. Add 500g at the beginning of the boil. 

## CORE RECIPE / MAKE IT YOUR OWN

| MALT | Ideal qty | % | Overall qty kg | Qty min | Variance score | | | | Qty max | Max % | Impacts |
|---|---|---|---|---|---|---|---|---|---|---|---|
| Pale malt (Maris Otter) | 6kg | 94 | 6.4 | 5 | | | | | 7kg | 100 | ABV |
| Crystal malt | 400g | 5 | | 0 | | | | | 1kg | 20 | Colour |

Mash in at 67°C for 60min ▬ Mash out at 76°C for 10min

| HOP | Qty g | AA | Time | g min | Variance score | | | | g max | Impacts | Alternatives |
|---|---|---|---|---|---|---|---|---|---|---|---|
| ❶ Fuggles | 70 | 4.8 | 60 | 30 | | | | | 70 | Bitterness | Stryian Golding |
| | | | | | | | | | | | Willamette |
| | | | | | | | | | | | Tettanger |
| ❷ East Kent Goldings | 50 | 5.5 | 15 | 10 | | | | | 55 | Aroma/bitterness | Fuggles |
| | | | | | | | | | | | Progress |
| | | | | | | | | | | | First Gold |
| ❸ Fuggles | 50 | 4.8 | 15 | 0 | | | | | 20 | Aroma | Stryian Golding |
| | | | | | | | | | | | Willamette |
| | | | | | | | | | | | Tettanger |

| Candi sugar | 500g | | 60 | |
|---|---|---|---|---|

| YEAST | Temp °C | | Condition / Wks | | | Alternative yeasts | Temp °C | |
|---|---|---|---|---|---|---|---|---|
| | Min | Max | 1st | 2nd | Bot | | MIN | MAX |
| MJ's M42 Strong Ale | 16 | 22 | 2 | 4 | 2+ | Wyeast #1098 British Ale | 18 | 22 |

## ABOUT THIS BREW

| | |
|---|---|
| Volume | 23 litres |
| Boil volume | 27 litres |
| Alcohol | 4.2% (3.8% – 5%) |
| Bitterness / IBU | 35 IBU (20 – 45 IBU) |
| Colour | 8 EBC (4 – 12 EBC) |
| Original Gravity | 1.044 (1.038 – 1.053) |
| Final Gravity | 1.011 (1.006 – 1.012) |

### EXTRACT RECIPE:

Add 2.4kg of light dried malt extract or 3kg of Maris Otter pale liquid malt extract and bring to the boil. Add hops as normal to the boil.

# GOLDEN ALE

The golden ale was first brewed as the English ale answer to the lager. As such, this style is exceptionally refreshing and thirst-quenching. It features delicate hops, often American, and a firm bitterness which is accompanied by a subtle biscuity maltiness. The golden ale is best served a bit colder than your standard bitter.

| CORE RECIPE | | | | | MAKE IT YOUR OWN | | | | |
|---|---|---|---|---|---|---|---|---|---|
| **MALT** | Ideal qty | % | Overall qty kg | Qty min | Variance score | Qty max | Max % | Impacts | |
| Pale malt (Maris Otter) | 4kg | 94 | 4.25 | 3.5 | | 4.8kg | 95 | ABV | |
| Torrified wheat | 250g | 6 | | 100g | | 900g | 20 | Colour + flavour | |

**Mash in** at 67°C for 60min **Mash out** at 76°C for 10min

| **HOP** | Qty g | AA | Time | g min | Variance score | g max | Impacts | Alternatives |
|---|---|---|---|---|---|---|---|---|
| ① Citra | 20 | 12 | 60 | 15 | | 30 | Bitterness | Galaxy |
| | | | | | | | | Taurus |
| ② East Kent Goldings | 10 | 12 | 15 | 10 | | 30 | Aroma | Galaxy |
| | | | | | | | | Taurus |
| ③ Styrian Goldings | 10 | 12 | 0 | 0 | | 20 | Aroma | Galaxy |
| | | | | | | | | Taurus |

| **YEAST** | Temp °C | | Condition / Wks | | | Alternative yeasts | Temp °C | |
|---|---|---|---|---|---|---|---|---|
| | Min | Max | 1st | 2nd | Bot | | MIN | MAX |
| MJ's Liberty Bell Ale | 18 | 23 | 1-2 | 2 | 2 | Wyeast #1098 British Ale Yeast | 18 | 22 |

## ABOUT THIS BREW

| | |
|---|---|
| Volume | 23 litres |
| Boil volume | 27 litres |
| Alcohol | 4% |
| Bitterness / IBU | 25 IBU |
| Colour | 28 EBC |
| Original Gravity | 1.041 |
| Final Gravity | 1.010 |

### EXTRACT RECIPE:

Steep 150g of crystal malt, 150g of chocolate malt and 150g of biscuit malt in 27 litres of water at 65°C for half an hour. Remove and then add 2.1kg of golden light dried malt extract or 2.6kg of Maris Otter pale liquid malt extract bring to the boil and add hops as normal to the boil.

# HONEY ALE

Not an actual style, but the honey beer has certainly risen in popularity over the last few years. At their best, they should be tasty, refreshing and not too cloying. This recipe has a caramel and roasty notes with a note of honey, while remaining dry and drinkable.

**ADJUNCTS:** 500g of honey is added at the end of the boil.

## CORE RECIPE

## MAKE IT YOUR OWN

| MALT | Ideal Qty kg | % | Overall qty kg | Qty min | Variance score | | | | Qty max | max % | Impacts |
|---|---|---|---|---|---|---|---|---|---|---|---|
| Pale malt | 3.6 | 88 | | 3.5 | | | | | 4.5 | 85 | ABV + Colour |
| Crystal malt | 150g | 4 | 4.05 | 100g | | | | | 300g | 5 | Colour |
| Chocolate malt | 150g | 4 | | 100g | | | | | 300g | 5 | ABV + Colour |
| Biscuit malt | 150g | 4 | | 100g | | | | | 300g | 5 | ABV + Colour |

**Mash in** at 64°C for 60min **Mash out** at 76°C for 10min

| HOP | Qty g | AA | Time | g min | Variance score | | | | g max | Impacts | Alternatives |
|---|---|---|---|---|---|---|---|---|---|---|---|
| ❶ Cluster | 30 | 7 | 60 | 20 | | | | | 50 | Aroma + bitterness | Galena |
| | | | | | | | | | | | Eroica |

| Honey | 500g | | 0 | | | | | | | | |
|---|---|---|---|---|---|---|---|---|---|---|---|

| YEAST | Temp °C | | Condition / Wks | | | Alternative yeasts | Temp °C | |
|---|---|---|---|---|---|---|---|---|
| | Min | Max | 1st | 2nd | Bot | | MIN | MAX |
| MJ's M36 Liberty Bell Ale | 18 | 23 | 1-2 | 2 | 2 | Wyeast #1098 British Ale | 18 | 24 |

## ABOUT THIS BREW

| | |
|---|---|
| Volume | 23 litres |
| Boil volume | 27 litres |
| Alcohol | 4.5% 4.2% – 5.4% |
| Bitterness / IBU | 22 IBU (20 – 30 IBU) |
| Colour | 39 EBC (22 – 40 EBC) |
| Original Gravity | 1.047 (1.040 – 1.052) |
| Final Gravity | 1.012 (1.008 – 1.014) |

### EXTRACT RECIPE:

Steep 250g of dark crystal, 250g of chocolate malt and 250g of CaraRed in 27 litres of water at 65°C for half an hour. Remove and then add 2.4kg of light dried malt extract or 3kg of Maris Otter pale liquid malt extract and bring to the boil. Add hops as normal to the boil.

# NORTHERN BROWN ALE

Maltier than a bitter and stronger than a mild, describing the British brown ale is a bit of a conundrum. Modern versions of this style display a caramelly maltiness that can, at times, come across as a bit sweet. While it is not known for being refreshing, it is perfect for supping.

| CORE RECIPE | | | | MAKE IT YOUR OWN | | | | | |
|---|---|---|---|---|---|---|---|---|---|
| MALT | Ideal Qty kg | % | Overall qty kg | Qty min | Variance score | Qty max | max % | Impacts | |
| Pale malt (Maris Otter) | 4 | 85 | | 3.8 | | 4.5 | 85 | ABV + Colour | |
| Dark Crystal | 250g | 5 | 4.75 | 100g | | 300g | 5 | Colour | |
| Chocolate malt | 250g | 5 | | 0 | | 250g | 5 | ABV + Colour | |
| CaraRed | 250g | 5 | | 0 | | 700g | 10 | ABV + Colour | |

◁▭▷ **Mash in** at 64°C for 60min ▭▭ **Mash out** at 76°C for 10min

| HOP | Qty g | AA | Time | g min | Variance score | g max | Impacts | Alternatives |
|---|---|---|---|---|---|---|---|---|
| ⓘ Fuggles | 40 | 4.8 | 60 | 40 | | 55 | Aroma + bitterness | Stryian Golding Willamette Tettanger |

| YEAST | Temp °C | | Condition / Wks | | | Alternative yeasts | Temp °C | |
|---|---|---|---|---|---|---|---|---|
| | Min | Max | 1st | 2nd | Bot | | MIN | MAX |
| MJ's M36 Liberty Bell | 18 | 23 | 1-2 | 1-2 | 2 | Wyeast #1098 British Ale Yeast | 17 | 22 |

Mash 67°C

Mash out 74°C

0

60

70

60

Boil

0

## ABOUT THIS BREW

| | |
|---|---|
| Volume | 23 litres |
| Boil volume | 27 litres |
| Alcohol | 4% (2.8 – 4.1%) |
| Bitterness / IBU | 17 IBU (12 – 20 IBU) |
| Colour | 42 EBU (20 – 60 EBC) |
| Original Gravity | 1.041 (1.033 – 1.042) |
| Final Gravity | 1.010 (1.010 – 1.014) |

### EXTRACT RECIPE:

Steep 200g of brown malt, 200g of crystal malt and 200g of black malt in 27 litres of water at 65°C for half an hour. Remove and then add 2.1kg of light dried malt extract or 2.6kg of Maris Otter pale liquid malt extract bring to the boil and add hops as normal to the boil.

# SOUTHERN BROWN

This increasingly rare, yet historically important beer style is also known as a London brown ale. Medium to dark brown in colour, and low in alcohol, it is most distinguished for its exceptionally sweet flavour profile. While some fruity notes can be present, it is otherwise clean allowing the rich, creamy maltiness to be uninterrupted.

| CORE RECIPE | | | | MAKE IT YOUR OWN | | | | |
|---|---|---|---|---|---|---|---|---|
| MALT | Ideal Qty kg | % | Overall qty kg | Qty min | Variance score | Qty max | max % | Impacts |
| Pale malt (Maris Otter) | 3.5 | 85 | | 2.7 | | .5 | 85 | ABV + Colour |
| Brown malt | 200g | 5 | 4.1 | 100g | | 300g | 10 | Colour + flavour |
| Crystal malt | 200g | 5 | | 100g | | 300g | 10 | Colour + flavour |
| Black malt | 200g | 5 | | 100g | | 300g | 5 | Colour |

**Mash in** at 64°C for 60min ▬▬ **Mash out** at 76°C for 10min

| HOP | Qty g | AA | Time | g min | Variance score | g max | Impacts | Alternatives |
|---|---|---|---|---|---|---|---|---|
| ❶ Bramling Cross | 20 | 6 | 60 | 15 | | 30 | Aroma + bitterness | East Kent Goldings |
| | | | | | | | | UK Progress |
| | | | | | | | | First Gold |
| ❷ East Kent Goldings | 20 | 5.5 | 5 | 10 | | 40 | Aroma | Fuggles |
| | | | | | | | | Progress |

| YEAST | Temp °C | | Condition / Wks | | | Alternative yeasts | Temp °C | |
|---|---|---|---|---|---|---|---|---|
| | Min | Max | 1st | 2nd | Bot | | MIN | MAX |
| MJ's M42 Strong Ale | 16 | 22 | 1 | N/A | 2 | Wyeast #1187 Ringwood Ale | 18 | 24 |

## ABOUT THIS BREW

| | |
|---|---|
| Volume | 23 litres |
| Boil volume | 27 litres |
| Alcohol | 3.4% (2.8% – 4.5%) |
| Bitterness / IBU | 22 IBU (10 – 25 IBU) |
| Colour | 27 EBC (26 – 48 EBC) |
| Original Gravity | 1.035 (1.030 – 1.038) |
| Final Gravity | 1.009 (1.008 – 1.013) |

### EXTRACT RECIPE:

Steep 400g of dark crystal and 100g of chocolate malt in 27 litres of water at 65°C for half an hour. Remove and then add 2.4kg of light dried malt extract or 3kg of Maris Otter pale liquid malt extract and bring to the boil. Add hops as normal to the boil.

# MILD

The ancestor of the modern British Mild can be traced back to the 1800s with the darker versions appearing in the 20th century. Milds are typically light to medium-bodied with low bitterness and full of nutty, roasty malt flavour with a nice balance between quaffability and character.

**NOTE:** Maris Otter pale malt can substitute mild malt, but you'll need to add more brown malt.

## CORE RECIPE / MAKE IT YOUR OWN

| MALT | Ideal qty | % | Overall qty kg | Qty min | Variance score | Qty max | max % | Impacts |
|---|---|---|---|---|---|---|---|---|
| Mild malt | 3kg | 86 | | 2.5kg | | 3.2kg | 100 | ABV + colour |
| Dark Crystal | 400g | 11 | 3.5 | 100g | | 500g | 20 | ABV + colour |
| Chocolate malt | 100g | 3 | | 100g | | 500g | 5 | Colour |

**Mash in** at 64°C for 60min **Mash out** at 76°C for 10min

| HOP | Qty g | AA | Time | g min | Variance score | g max | Impacts | Alternatives |
|---|---|---|---|---|---|---|---|---|
| ❶ East Kent Goldings | 30 | 5.5 | 60 | 15 | | 30 | Aroma + bitterness | Fuggles |
| | | | | | | | | Progress |
| | | | | | | | | First Gold |
| ❷ Bramling Cross | 10 | 6 | 5 | 0 | | 30 | Aroma | East Kent Goldings |
| | | | | | | | | UK Progress |

| YEAST | Temp °C Min | Max | Condition / Wks 1st | 2nd | Bot | Alternative yeasts | Temp °C MIN | MAX |
|---|---|---|---|---|---|---|---|---|
| MJ's M36 Liberty Bell | 18 | 23 | 2 | 1-2 | 2 | Wyeast #1968 London ESB Yeast | 17 | 22 |

Mash 67°C
Mash out 74°C — 60 70 60
Boil
❷ 5
0

## ABOUT THIS BREW

| | |
|---|---|
| Volume | 23 litres |
| Boil volume | 27 litres |
| Alcohol | 5.9% |
| Bitterness / IBU | 24 IBU |
| Colour | 35 EBC |
| Original Gravity | 1.061 |
| Final Gravity | 1.015 |

### EXTRACT RECIPE:

Steep 200g each of dark crystal, extra dark crystal, pale chocolate and Victory malt in 27 litres of water at 65°C for half an hour. Remove and then add 2.7kg of dried malt extract or 3.375kg of liquid malt extract bring to the boil and add hops as normal to the boil, plus the corn sugar at the end.

# IMPERIAL MILD

While not a traditional style, per se, think of an Imperial Mild as an amped-up version of the classic Mild. This reddish-brown session beer crams twice as much Mild-goodness into every pint: double the nutty, roasty maltiness with dark fruit notes and a hint of English hops with a luxurious body.

**ADJUNCTS:** Dextrose (corn sugar) is used at the end of the boil to boost the alcohol.

## CORE RECIPE / MAKE IT YOUR OWN

| MALT & SUGAR | Ideal qty | % | Overall qty kg | Qty min | Variance score | Qty max | max % | Impacts |
|---|---|---|---|---|---|---|---|---|
| Mild malt | 4.5kg | 78 | | 4kg | | 5kg | 90 | ABV + colour |
| Dark crystal | 200g | 3 | | 100g | | 300g | 20 | ABV + colour |
| Extra dark crystal | 200g | 3 | 5.8 | 100g | | 300g | 20 | ABV + colour |
| Pale chocolate | 200g | 4 | | 100g | | 300g | 10 | Colour |
| Victory malt | 200g | 3 | | 100g | | 300g | 15 | ABV + colour |

**Mash in** at 64°C for 60min   **Mash out** at 76°C for 10min

| HOP | Qty g | AA | Time | g min | Variance score | g max | Impacts | Alternatives |
|---|---|---|---|---|---|---|---|---|
| ① Fuggles | 30 | 4.8 | 60 | 15 | | 45 | Aroma + bitterness | Palisade |
| | | | | | | | | Willamette |
| | | | | | | | | Tettanger |
| ② Fuggles | 15 | 4.8 | 30 | 10 | | 20 | Aroma + bitterness | Stryian Golding |
| | | | | | | | | Wilamette |
| | | | | | | | | Tettanger |
| ③ Fuggles | 15 | 4.8 | 15 | 10 | | 20 | Aroma + bitterness | Stryian Golding |
| | | | | | | | | Willamette |
| | | | | | | | | Tettanger |

| Corn sugar | 500g | 0 |
|---|---|---|

| YEAST | Temp °C Min | Temp °C Max | Condition / Wks 1st | 2nd | Bot | Alternative yeasts | Temp °C MIN | Temp °C MAX |
|---|---|---|---|---|---|---|---|---|
| MJ's M42 Strong Ale | 16 | 22 | 1-2 | 1-2 | 2 | Wyeast #1187 Ringwood Ale | 18 | 24 |

## ABOUT THIS BREW

| | |
|---|---|
| Volume | 23 litres |
| Boil volume | 27 litres |
| Alcohol | 7.7% 6% – 9% |
| Bitterness / IBU | 55 IBU (30 – 60 IBU) |
| Colour | 39 EBC (20 – 43 EBC) |
| Original Gravity | 1.080 (1.060 – 1.090) |
| Final Gravity | 1.020 (1.015 – 1.022) |

### EXTRACT RECIPE:

Steep 300g each of dark crystal and 200g of chocolate malt in 27 litres of water at 65°C for half an hour. Remove and then add 3.6kg of dried malt extract or 4.5kg of liquid malt extract bring to the boil and add hops as normal to the boil, plus the corn sugar at end.

# OLD ALE

Warming, rich, dark in colour and full on the palate, the Old Ale finds itself situated between the ESB and English barley wine. Its hefty malty sweetness and flavours of dried fruit and complex malts take well to ageing. This style is often defined by its lactic qualities when aged.

/ / / / / / / / / / / / / / / / /

**ADJUNCTS:** Corn sugar is used to boost sweetness and ABV. ●

## CORE RECIPE / MAKE IT YOUR OWN

| MALT & SUGAR | Ideal qty | % | Overall qty kg | Qty min | Variance score | Qty max | max % | Impacts |
|---|---|---|---|---|---|---|---|---|
| Pale malt (Maris Otter) | 4.5 | 60 | | 5 | | 6.5 | 8 | ABV + colour |
| Munich malt | 2kg | 27 | 7.5 | 0.25 | | 1.5 | 5 | ABV |
| Dark crystal | 300g | 4 | | 5 | | 6.5 | 6 | ABV + colour |
| Chocolate malt | 200g | 3 | | 0.25 | | 1.5 | 5 | ABV |

▭ **Mash in** at 64°C for 60min ▬ **Mash out** at 76°C for 10min

| HOP | Qty g | AA | Time | g min | Variance score | g max | Impacts | Alternatives |
|---|---|---|---|---|---|---|---|---|
| ❶ East Kent Goldings | 100 | 5.5 | 60 | 15 | | 45 | Bitterness | Fuggles |
| | | | | | | | | Progress |
| | | | | | | | | First Gold |
| ❷ East Kent Goldings | 50 | 5.5 | 10 | 10 | | 20 | Aroma + bitterness | Fuggles |
| | | | | | | | | Progress |
| | | | | | | | | First Gold |
| ❸ Stryian Goldings | 20 | 5.5 | 0 | 10 | | 20 | Aroma | Fuggle |
| | | | | | | | | Willamette |

| Corn sugar | 500g | | 0 | | | |
|---|---|---|---|---|---|---|

| YEAST | Temp °C Min | Max | Condition / Wks 1st | 2nd | Bot | Alternative yeasts | Temp °C MIN | MAX |
|---|---|---|---|---|---|---|---|---|
| MJ's M15 Empire Ale | 18 | 22 | 1-2 | 1-2 | 2 | Wyeast #1028 English ale | 17 | 22 |

## ABOUT THIS BREW

| | |
|---|---|
| Volume | 23 litres |
| Boil volume | 27 litres |
| Alcohol | 8.5% (8 – 12%) |
| Bitterness / IBU | 44 IBU (35 – 70 IBU) |
| Colour | 23 EBC (16 – 43 EBC) |
| Original Gravity | 1.087 (1.080 – 1.120) |
| Final Gravity | 1.022 (1.018 – 1.030) |

## EXTRACT RECIPE:

Steep 300g each of dark crystal and 800g of Carapils in 27 litres of water at 65°C for half an hour. Remove and then add 4.5kg of dried malt extract or 5.7kg of liquid malt extract bring to the boil and add hops as normal to the boil.

# BARLEY WINE

Usually the strongest ale in a traditional brewery's lineup, the English-style barley wine has an intense, concentrated malt flavour with vinous, dried fruit and molasses notes laced with a charge of hop bitterness. A considerable alcohol content, chewy body and interesting complexity can take on port-like flavours when aged.

//////////////////////////////////

**ADJUNCTS:** Honey can be added to the boil to increase ABV. Add 500g for the last 10 mins.
**NOTES:** Because of the strength, a yeast starter and two stage fermentation is recommended.

## CORE RECIPE     MAKE IT YOUR OWN

| MALT & SUGAR | Ideal qty | % | Overall qty kg | Qty min | Variance score | Qty max | max % | Impacts |
|---|---|---|---|---|---|---|---|---|
| Pale malt (Maris Otter) | 7.5kg | 87 | | 7kg | | 10kg | 90 | ABV + colour |
| Dark crystal | 300g | 3 | 8.6 | 100g | | 300g | 20 | Colour + flavour |
| Carapils | 800g | 9 | | 100g | | 300g | 20 | Body + flavour |

🌡 **Mash in** at 64°C for 60min ▬ **Mash out** at 76°C for 10min

| HOP | Qty g | AA | Time | g min | Variance score | g max | Impacts | Alternatives |
|---|---|---|---|---|---|---|---|---|
| ❶ Northdown | 60 | 8 | 60 | 15 | | 45 | Aroma + bitterness | Admiral |
| | | | | | | | | Challenger |
| ❷ Willamette | 15 | 5 | 15 | 10 | | 20 | Aroma + bitterness | Stryian Golding |
| | | | | | | | | Target |
| | | | | | | | | Tettanger |
| ❸ Target | 15 | 11 | 0 | 10 | | 20 | Aroma + bitterness | Fuggles |
| | | | | | | | | Willamette |
| | | | | | | | | Admiral |

| YEAST | Temp °C Min | Temp °C Max | Condition / Wks 1st | Condition / Wks 2nd | Condition / Wks Bot | Alternative yeasts | Temp °C MIN | Temp °C MAX |
|---|---|---|---|---|---|---|---|---|
| MJ's M42 Strong Ale | 16 | 22 | 1-2 | 5m | + | Wyeast #1945 NeoBritannia | 18 | 24 |

## ABOUT THIS BREW

| | |
|---|---|
| Volume | 23 litres |
| Boil volume | 27 litres |
| Alcohol | 4.7% (4% – 5.4%) |
| Bitterness / IBU | 31 IBU (18 – 35 IBU) |
| Colour | 47 EBC (10 – 58 EBC) |
| Original Gravity | 1.048 (1.040 – 1.052) |
| Final Gravity | 1.012 (1.008 – 1.012) |

### EXTRACT RECIPE:

Steep 500g each of medium crystal and 300g of chocolate malt in 27 litres of water at 65°C for half an hour. Remove and then add 2.7kg of dried malt extract or 3.375kg of liquid malt extract bring to the boil and add hops as normal to the boil.

# PORTER

The classic porter dates back to 18th-century London and is the predecessor to all stouts. Noted for its restrained roasted character and bitterness, the porter is a moderately strong English brown-coloured beer. Leaning to the sweet side, the porter features a significant caramel or toffee character and malty complexity.

/ / / / / / / / / / / / / / / / / / / / / /

**NOTES:** See the next couple of pages for stronger versions.

## CORE RECIPE / MAKE IT YOUR OWN

| MALT & SUGAR | Ideal qty | % | Overall qty kg | Qty min | Variance score | Qty max | max % | Impacts |
|---|---|---|---|---|---|---|---|---|
| Pale malt (Maris Otter) | 4.5kg | 83 | | 3.5 | | 4.3 | 90 | ABV + colour |
| Medium crystal | 500g | 11 | 4.8 | 100g | | 500g | 20 | Colour + flavour |
| Chocolate malt | 300g | 6 | | 300g | | 400g | 10 | Colour + flavour |

**Mash in** at 64°C for 60min **Mash out** at 76°C for 10min

| HOP | Qty g | AA | Time | g min | Variance score | g max | Impacts | Alternatives |
|---|---|---|---|---|---|---|---|---|
| ❶ First Gold | 30 | 7.5 | 60 | 15 | | 35 | Bitternes | East Kent Goldings |
| | | | | | | | | Progress |
| | | | | | | | | Fuggle |
| ❷ First Gold | 20 | 7.5 | 10 | 0 | | 25 | Aroma + bitternes | East Kent Goldings |
| | | | | | | | | Progress |
| | | | | | | | | Fuggle |

| YEAST | Temp °C Min | Max | Condition / Wks 1st | 2nd | Bot | Alternative yeasts | Temp °C MIN | MAX |
|---|---|---|---|---|---|---|---|---|
| MJ's M15 Empire Ale | 18 | 22 | 1-2 | 1-2 | 2 | Wyeast #1187 Ringwood Ale | 17 | 22 |

Mash 67°C — 0
Mash out 74°C — 60 / 70 / 60
Boil — ❶
❷ — 10
0

## ABOUT THIS BREW

| Volume | 23 litres |
|---|---|
| Boil volume | 27 litres |
| Alcohol | 8,1% (5.5 – 9.5%) |
| Bitterness / IBU | 32 IBU (20 – 40 IBU) |
| Colour | 50 EBC (33 – 60 EBC) |
| Original Gravity | 1.083 (1.060 – 1.090) |
| Final Gravity | 1.021 (1.015 – 1.024) |

### EXTRACT RECIPE:

Steep 250g of Chocolate malt and 100g of Carafa III in 27 litres of water at 65°C for half an hour. Remove and then add 3kg of light dried malt extract or 3.75kg or Maris Otter pale liquid malt extract, along with 1.8kg of dry Munich extract or 2.25kg of lisquid Munich extract and bring to the boil and add hops as normal to the boil.

# BALTIC PORTER

Influenced by the imperial stout, the Baltic porter was brewed by brewers from Eastern Europe (not an English style, but fits in well here) and Scandinavia using continental ingredients and techniques. A Baltic porter is a big beer with notes of roasted malts and chocolate and an assertive hop bitterness. Brewed with lager yeast, this style has a clean finish.

## CORE RECIPE / MAKE IT YOUR OWN

| MALT | Ideal qty | % | Overall qty kg | Qty min | Variance score | Qty max | max % | Impacts |
|---|---|---|---|---|---|---|---|---|
| Bohemian Pilsner malt | 3kg | 36 | | 1.5kg | | 3.5kg | 80 | ABV + colour |
| Munich malt | 3kg | 36 | | 1.5kg | | 3.5kg | 80 | ABV + colour |
| Vienna malt | 2kg | 24 | 8.35 | 1.5kg | | 3.5kg | 50 | ABV + colour |
| Chocolate malt | 250g | 3 | | 5g | | 300g | 10 | Colour + flavour |
| Carafa III | 100g | 1 | | 0 | | 100g | 5 | Colour + flavour |

⊂⊃ **Mash in** at 67°C for 60min ▭ **Mash out** at 76°C for 10min

| HOP | Qty g | AA | Time | g min | Variance score | g max | Impacts | Alternatives |
|---|---|---|---|---|---|---|---|---|
| ❶ Perle | 40 | 8,3 | 60 | 25 | | 50 | Aroma | Saaz |
| | | | | | | | | Northern brewer |
| | | | | | | | | Challenger |
| ❷ Mt Hood | 15 | 6 | 15 | 0 | | 25 | Aroma + bitternes | Hallertauer |
| | | | | | | | | Liberty |
| | | | | | | | | Saaz |
| ❸ Mt Hood | 15 | 6 | 5 | 0 | | 30 | Aroma | Hallertauer |
| | | | | | | | | Liberty |
| | | | | | | | | Saaz |

| YEAST | Temp °C Min | Max | Condition / Wks 1st | 2nd | Bot | Alternative yeasts | Temp °C MIN | MAX |
|---|---|---|---|---|---|---|---|---|
| MJ's M84 Bohemian Lager | 10 | 15 | 1-2 | 6-8 | 2 | Wyeast #2112 California Lager | 14 | 20 |

## ABOUT THIS BREW

| | |
|---|---|
| Volume | 23 litres |
| Boil volume | 27 litres |
| Alcohol | 5.6% (4.8% – 6.5%) |
| Bitterness / IBU | 37 IBU (25 – 50 IBU) |
| Colour | 60 EBC (40 – 69 EBC) |
| Original Gravity | 1.058 (1.048 – 1.065) |
| Final Gravity | 1.015 (1.012 – 1.016) |

### EXTRACT RECIPE:

Steep 400g of black malt, 100g of smoked malt, 100g of medium crystal malt in 27 litres of water at 65°C for half an hour. Remove and then add 2.1kg of light dried malt extract or 2.6kg or Maris Otter pale liquid malt extract, along with 1.2kg of dry Munich extract or 1.5kg of liquid Munich extract and bring to the boil and add hops as normal to the boil.

# SMOKED PORTER

This is a midnight black strong porter with an assertive profile: roasty, bitter, and big with underlying herbal, briny smoke character. Caramel malts emphasise the full body and bring a bit of balancing sweetness.
This beer is a great wintertime nightcap.

//////////////////////

**ADJUNCTS:** Peat smoked malt adds a new dimension.

| CORE RECIPE | | | | MAKE IT YOUR OWN | | | | | |
|---|---|---|---|---|---|---|---|---|---|
| **MALT** | Ideal qty | % | Overall qty kg | Qty min | Variance score | Qty max | max % | Impacts | |
| Pale malt (Golden Promise) | 3.5kg | 59 | | 3kg | | 4kg | 80 | ABV + colour | |
| Munich malt | 1.8kg | 31 | 5.9 | 500g | | 1.8kg | 50 | ABV + colour | |
| Black malt | 400g | 7 | | 200g | | 450g | 10 | Colour | |
| Smoked malt | 100g | 2 | | 100g | | 200g | 20 | Colour + flavour | |
| Medium crystal | 100g | 1 | | 100g | | 200g | 10 | Colour + flavour | |

🮥 **Mash in** at 64°C for 60min 🮥 **Mash out** at 76°C for 10min

| **HOP** | Qty g | AA | Time | g min | Variance score | g max | Impacts | Alternatives |
|---|---|---|---|---|---|---|---|---|
| ❶ Cluster | 40 | 7 | 60 | 15 | | 45 | Aroma + bitterness | Galena |
| | | | | | | | | Eroica |
| | | | | | | | | Challenger |
| ❷ Willamette | 20 | 5 | 30 | 10 | | 40 | Aroma + bitterness | Styrian Golding |
| | | | | | | | | Target |
| | | | | | | | | Tettnanger |
| ❸ Willamette | 30 | 5 | 15 | 10 | | 50 | Aroma | Styrian Golding |
| | | | | | | | | Target |
| | | | | | | | | Tettnanger |

| **YEAST** | Temp °C Min | Temp °C Max | Condition / Wks 1st | Condition / Wks 2nd | Condition / Wks Bot | Alternative yeasts | Temp °C MIN | Temp °C MAX |
|---|---|---|---|---|---|---|---|---|
| MJ's M42 Strong | 16 | 22 | 1-2 | 2-4 | 2 | Wyeast #1056 American Ale | 15 | 22 |

Mash 67°C
Mash out 74°C

0
60
70
60

① 

Boil

② 30

③ 15

0

0

60
70
60

0

## ABOUT THIS BREW

| | |
|---|---|
| Volume | 23 litres |
| Boil volume | 27 litres |
| Alcohol | 4.2% (4 – 5%) |
| Bitterness / IBU | 39 IBU (30 – 45 IBU) |
| Colour | 70 EBC (48 – 80 EBC) |
| Original Gravity | 1.044 (1.036 – 1.050) |
| Final Gravity | 1.011 (1.07 – 1.011) |

### EXTRACT RECIPE:

Steep 400g of flaked barley and 400g of roasted barley in 27 litres of water at 65°C for half an hour. Remove and then add 2.1kg of light dried malt extract or 2.6kg of Maris Otter pale liquid malt extract, bring to the boil and add hops as normal to the boil.

# DRY IRISH STOUT

The Irish stout evolved from the popular London porters of the late 1800s. A noticeable roasted character with a rather high hop bitterness is often accompanied by creamy mouthfeel especially when served on draught. A moderate alcohol content leads to an overall drinkability for generally bold and dry style.

/ / / / / / / / / / / / / / / / / / / / / / / / / / / / / / / /

**ADJUNCTS:** Stouts are one of the most styles of beer with anything from dark cherries to vanilla being added.

| CORE RECIPE | | | | MAKE IT YOUR OWN | | | | | |
|---|---|---|---|---|---|---|---|---|---|
| MALT | Ideal qty | % | Overall qty kg | Qty min | Variance score | Qty max | max % | Impacts | |
| Pale malt (Maris Otter) | 3.5kg | 81 | | 3.4kg | | 3.6kg | 80 | ABV + flavour | |
| Flaked barley | 400g | 11 | 4.3kg | 200g | | 400g | 10 | Flavour + head retention | |
| Roasted barley | 400g | 9 | | 300g | | 400g | 10 | Flavour + colour | |

🡪 **Mash in** at 67°C for 60min ▬ **Mash out** at 76°C for 10min

| HOP | Qty g | AA | Time | g min | Variance score | g max | Impacts | Alternatives |
|---|---|---|---|---|---|---|---|---|
| ❶ East Kent Goldings | 60 | 5.5 | 60 | 48 | | 69 | Bitterness | Fuggles<br>Progress<br>First Gold |

| YEAST | Temp °C | | Condition / Wks | | | Alternative yeasts | Temp °C | |
|---|---|---|---|---|---|---|---|---|
| | Min | Max | 1st | 2nd | Bot | | MIN | MAX |
| MJ's M42 Strong Ale | 16 | 22 | 1-2 | 1-2 | 2 | Wyeast #1084 Irish Ale | 17 | 22 |

## ABOUT THIS BREW

| | |
|---|---|
| Volume | 23 litres |
| Boil volume | 27 litres |
| Alcohol | 6.5% (5.5% – 8%) |
| Bitterness / IBU | 60 IBU (30 – 70 IBU) |
| Colour | 70 EBC (60 – 80 EBC) |
| Original Gravity | 1.067 (1.056 – 1.075) |
| Final Gravity | 1.017 (1.010 – 1.018) |

### EXTRACT RECIPE:

Steep 500g of flaked barley and 500g of roasted barley in 27 litres of water at 65°C for half an hour. Remove and then add 3kg of light dried malt extract or 3.75kg of Maris Otter pale liquid malt extract, bring to the boil and add hops as normal to the boil.

# FOREIGN EXTRA STOUT

With a history dating back to the 18th century, the Foreign Extra Stout is a heavily hopped stout that is brewed for the export market. A noticeable bitterness accompanies a bold roasted or coffee character with a smooth, creamy mouthfeel. The overall impression is one of a dry, moderately strong stout.

**ADJUNCTS:** Corn sugar helps with alcohol strength and sweetness. It is added at the end of the boil. ●

**NOTES:** This version uses US bittering hops, but you can try it with East Kent Goldings for a more authentic flavour.

### CORE RECIPE / MAKE IT YOUR OWN

| MALT + SUGAR | Ideal qty | % | Overall qty kg | Qty min | Variance score | Qty min | max % | Impacts |
|---|---|---|---|---|---|---|---|---|
| Pale malt (Maris Otter) | 5kg | 78 | | 4.1kg | | 5.5kg | 80 | ABV + flavour |
| Flaked barley | 500g | 8 | 6.6kg | 100g | | 1kg | 10 | Flavour + head retention |
| Roasted barley | 500g | 8 | | 400g | | 600g | 10 | Flavour + colour |

⊂⊃ **Mash in** at 64°C for 60min ▬▬ **Mash out** at 76°C for 10min

| HOP | Qty g | AA | Time | g min | Variance score | g max | Impacts | Alternatives |
|---|---|---|---|---|---|---|---|---|
| ❶ Summit | 30 | 17.5 | 60 | 15 | | 45 | Aroma + bitterness | Amarillo |
| | | | | | | | | Cascade |
| | | | | | | | | East Kent Goldings |
| ❷ Fuggles | 20 | 4.8 | 30 | 10 | | 40 | Aroma + bitterness | Styrian Golding |
| | | | | | | | | Willamette |
| | | | | | | | | Tettnanger |

| Corn sugar | 400g | | 0 | |
|---|---|---|---|---|

| YEAST | Temp °C Min | Temp °C Max | Condition / Wks 1st | Condition / Wks 2nd | Condition / Wks Bot | Alternative yeasts | Temp °C MIN | Temp °C MAX |
|---|---|---|---|---|---|---|---|---|
| MJ's M42 Strong Ale | 16 | 22 | 1-2 | 3m | 4 | Wyeast #1084 Irish Ale | 17 | 22 |

# ABOUT THIS BREW

| Volume | 23 litres |
|---|---|
| Boil volume | 27 litres |
| Alcohol | 4.9% (4% – 6%) |
| Bitterness / IBU | 27 IBU (20 – 40 IBU) |
| Colour | 70 EBC (60 – 79 EBC) |
| Original Gravity | 1.051 (1.044 – 1.060) |
| Final Gravity | 1.013 (1.012 – 1.024) |

## EXTRACT RECIPE:

Steep 350g pale chocolate malt, 100g of dark crystal and 350g of Carafa II in 27 litres of water at 65°C for half an hour. Remove and then add 2.7kg of light dried malt extract or 3.375kg of Maris Otter pale liquid malt extract, bring to the boil and add hops as normal to the boil.

# MILK STOUT

Otherwise known as sweet stout, this early 20th century beer style gets its name due to the addition of lactose.This jet-black ale has a roasted-malt character that is offset by a residual sweetness which suggests coffee-and-cream. A moderate hop bitterness could be present but, overall, this is a rich, sweet style.

**ADJUNCTS:** Oats can improve the silky mouthfeel. Put in about 200g. Add 500g of lactose at the end of the boil. Turn it into a chocolate milk stout by adding 100g of cacao nibs to the secondary fermenter two weeks before bottling.

## CORE RECIPE / MAKE IT YOUR OWN

| MALT | Ideal qty | % | Overall qty kg | Qty min | Variance score | | | Qty max | max % | Impacts |
|---|---|---|---|---|---|---|---|---|---|---|
| Pale malt (Maris Otter) | 4.5 | 87 | | 4kg | | | | 5.4kg | 8 | ABV |
| Pale chocolate | 350g | 6 | 5.3 | 250g | | | | 500g | 10 | Colour + flavour |
| Dark crystal | 100g | 2 | | 0g | | | | 100g | 20 | ABV + colour |
| Carafa III | 350g | 5 | | 250g | | | | 500g | 5 | Colour |

Mash in at 64°C for 60min • Mash out at 76°C for 10min

| HOP | Qty g | AA | Time | g min | Variance score | | | g max | Impacts | Alternatives |
|---|---|---|---|---|---|---|---|---|---|---|
| ❶ Target | 20 | 11 | 60 | 15 | | | | 30 | Bitterness | Fuggles |
| | | | | | | | | | | Galena |
| | | | | | | | | | | Willamette |
| ❷ Target | 10 | 11 | 15 | 0 | | | | 20 | Aroma + bitterness | Fuggles |
| | | | | | | | | | | Galena |
| | | | | | | | | | | Goldings |

| Lactose | 500g | 0 |
|---|---|---|

| YEAST | Temp °C | | Condition / Wks | | | Alternative yeasts | Temp °C | |
|---|---|---|---|---|---|---|---|---|
| | Min | Max | 1st | 2nd | Bot | | MIN | MAX |
| MJ's M42 Strong Ale | 14 | 21 | 1-2 | 2-4 | 2 | Wyeast #1332 Northwest Ale | 17 | 22 |

# ABOUT THIS BREW

| Volume | 23 litres |
|---|---|
| Boil volume | 27 litres |
| Alcohol | 5.6% (4.2% – 5.9%) |
| Bitterness / IBU | 29 IBU (25 – 40 IBU) |
| Colour | 60 EBC (40 – 80 EBC) |
| Original Gravity | 1.057 (1.048 – 1.065) |
| Final Gravity | 1.014 (1.010 – 1.018) |

## EXTRACT RECIPE:

Steep 350g pale chocolate malt, 100g of dark crystal and 350g of Carafa II in 27 litres of water at 65°C for half an hour. Remove and then add 2.7kg of light dried malt extract or 3.375kg of Maris Otter pale liquid malt extract, bring to the boil and add hops as normal to the boil.

# OATMEAL STOUT

Arising from the 'nourishing' stouts from the late 1800s, today's oatmeal stouts are noted for its silken-bodied texture due to the addition of oats. The overall impression is of a roasty, malty ale with a distinct oatmeal flavour. The level of sweetness can vary but it's generally rich and velvety.

## CORE RECIPE / MAKE IT YOUR OWN

| MALT | Ideal qty | % | Overall qty kg | Qty min | Variance score | Qty max | max % | Impacts |
|---|---|---|---|---|---|---|---|---|
| Pale malt (Maris Otter) | 4.5kg | 79 | | 3.8kg | | 4.8kg | 80 | ABV + colour |
| Flaked oats | 500g | 9 | | 100g | | 500g | 10 | Mouthfeel |
| Roasted barley | 225g | 4 | 5.675 | 100g | | 300g | 10 | Colour |
| Chocolate malt | 225g | 4 | | 100g | | 400g | 20 | Colour + aroma |
| Medium crystal | 225g | 4 | | 100g | | 500g | 10 | Colour + flavour |

**Mash in** at 64°C for 60min **Mash out** at 76°C for 10min

| HOP | Qty g | AA | Time | g min | Variance score | g max | Impacts | Alternatives |
|---|---|---|---|---|---|---|---|---|
| ❶ Willamette | 50 | 5 | 60 | 45 | | 70 | Aroma + bitterness | Styrian Golding |
| | | | | | | | | Target |
| | | | | | | | | Tettnanger |
| ❷ Challenger | 20 | 7 | 5 | 10 | | 60 | Aroma + bitterness | Perle |
| | | | | | | | | Admiral |
| | | | | | | | | Northdown |
| ❸ Willamette | 20 | 5 | 0 | 10 | | 30 | Aroma | Styrian Golding |
| | | | | | | | | Target |
| | | | | | | | | Tettnanger |

| YEAST | Temp °C Min | Max | Condition / Wks 1st | 2nd | Bot | Alternative yeasts | Temp °C MIN | MAX |
|---|---|---|---|---|---|---|---|---|
| MJ's M42 Strong Ale | 14 | 21 | 1-2 | 1-2 | 2 | Wyeast #1945 NeoBritannia | 17 | 22 |

Mash 67°C
Mash out 74°C
Boil

0
60
70
60

5
0

## ABOUT THIS BREW

| | |
|---|---|
| Volume | 23 litres |
| Boil volume | 27 litres |
| Alcohol | 5.1% (4% – 6%) |
| Bitterness / IBU | 24 IBU (20 – 40 IBU) |
| Colour | 60 EBC (60 – 79 EBC) |
| Original Gravity | 1.052 (1.044 – 1.060) |
| Final Gravity | 1.013 (1.012 – 1.024) |

### EXTRACT RECIPE:

Steep 225g each of pale chocolate malt, dark crystal and black malt in 27 litres of water at 65°C for half an hour. Remove and then add 2.7kg of light dried malt extract or 3.375kg of Maris Otter pale liquid malt extract, bring to the boil and add hops as normal to the boil and coffee to the seconadry fermenter.

# COFFEE STOUT

A classic stout brewed with coffee, this beer combines two of the world's greatest brews. Dark roasted malts are the perfect platform for the roasty bitterness of coffee. They come together alongside notes of chocolate, caramel, berries and a dry, roasty finish to create a decadent cold-weather beer.

//////////////////////////

**ADJUNCTS:** Add 120g of quality coarse coffee grinds to the secondary fermenter.

## CORE RECIPE / MAKE IT YOUR OWN

| MALT | Ideal qty | % | Overall qty kg | Qty min | Variance score | | | Qty max | max % | Impacts |
|---|---|---|---|---|---|---|---|---|---|---|
| Pale malt (Maris Otter) | 4.5kg | 87 | | 4kg | | | | 5.2kg | 80 | ABV |
| Dark crystal | 225g | 4 | 5.175 | 100g | | | | 200g | 10 | ABV + colour |
| Pale chocolate | 225g | 5 | | 200g | | | | 300g | 10 | Colour + flavour |
| Black malt | 225g | 4 | | 200g | | | | 300g | 5 | Colour + flavour |

**Mash in** at 67°C for 60min  **Mash out** at 76°C for 10min

| HOP | Qty g | AA | Time | g min | Variance score | | | g max | Impacts | Alternatives |
|---|---|---|---|---|---|---|---|---|---|---|
| ① East Kent Goldings | 40 | 5.5 | 60 | 40 | | | | 70 | Aroma + bitterness | Fuggles |
| | | | | | | | | | | Progress |
| | | | | | | | | | | First Gold |

| YEAST | Temp °C Min | Temp °C Max | Condition / Wks 1st | 2nd | Bot | Alternative yeasts | Temp °C MIN | Temp °C MAX |
|---|---|---|---|---|---|---|---|---|
| MJ's M15 Empire Ale | 18 | 22 | 1-2 | 2 | 1-2 | Wyeast #1968 London ESB | 17 | 22 |

## ABOUT THIS BREW

| | |
|---|---|
| Volume | 23 litres |
| Boil volume | 27 litres |
| Alcohol | 3.9% (3.5% – 5%) |
| Bitterness / IBU | 18 IBU (15 – 25 IBU) |
| Colour | 60 EBC (40 – 69 EBC) |
| Original Gravity | 1.040 (1.039 – 1.050) |
| Final Gravity | 1.010 (1.010 – 1.016) |

# BREAKFAST STOUT

A smooth, low alcohol stout, a breakfast stout could be considered a cross between an oatmeal stout and a sweet stout. A coffee-like flavour from roasted barley is accompanied by a buttery note from the yeast, leaving the impression of a complete meal in a glass.

**ADJUNCTS:** Lactose added at the end of the boil adds a sweetness to the beer.

| CORE RECIPE | | | | | MAKE IT YOUR OWN | | | | |
|---|---|---|---|---|---|---|---|---|---|
| MALT | Ideal qty | % | Overall qty kg | Qty min | Variance score | Qty max | max % | Impacts | |
| Pale malt (Maris Otter) | 3kg | 81 | | 2.5kg | | 3.5kg | 80 | ABV + colour | |
| Flaked oats | 400g | 11 | 3.7 | 300g | | 400g | 15 | Mouthfeel | |
| Roasted barley | 400g | 8 | | 300g | | 400g | 10 | Colour | |

**Mash in** at 64°C for 60min  **Mash out** at 76°C for 10min

| HOP | Qty g | AA | Time | g min | Variance score | g max | Impacts | Alternatives |
|---|---|---|---|---|---|---|---|---|
| ① Willamette | 30 | 5 | 60 | 15 | | 45 | Aroma + bitterness | Styrian Golding |
| | | | | | | | | Target |
| | | | | | | | | Tettnanger |

| Lactose | 500g | 0 |
|---|---|---|

| YEAST | Temp °C | | Condition / Wks | | | Alternative yeasts | Temp °C | |
|---|---|---|---|---|---|---|---|---|
| | Min | Max | 1st | 2nd | Bot | | MIN | MAX |
| MJ's M15 Empire Ale | 18 | 22 | 1 | 1 | 2 | Wyeast #1084 Irish Ale | 16 | 22 |

# ABOUT THIS BREW

| | |
|---|---|
| Volume | 23 litres |
| Boil volume | 27 litres |
| Alcohol | 8.7% (8 – 12%) |
| Bitterness / IBU | 88 IBU (50 – 90 IBU) |
| Colour | 70 EBC (60 – 80 EBC) |
| Original Gravity | 1.090 (1.075 – 1.115) |
| Final Gravity | 1.022 (1.018 – 1.030) |

## EXTRACT RECIPE:

Steep 225g each of chocolate malt, medium crystal and roasted barley, plus 100g of black malt in 27 litres of water at 65°C for half an hour. Remove and then add 4.8kg of light dried malt extract or 6kg of pale liquid malt extract and bring to the boil and add hops as normal to the boil.

# IMPERIAL STOUT

Imperial stouts were first brewed in England for export to the royal courts of the Russian tsars. This style is noted for its intense, roasty malt flavours sometimes accompanied by dark fruit notes or an aggressive hop bitterness. These intense flavours and high alcohol content still find a way to be harmonious.

**NOTES:** This recipe uses American hops, but for a more English version use 60g of Challenger at the beginning of the boil and 60g of East Kent Goldings at 30 minutes. A yeast starter or two packets of yeast is recommended.

## CORE RECIPE / MAKE IT YOUR OWN

| MALT | Ideal qty | % | Overall qty kg | Qty min | Variance score | Qty max | max % | Impacts |
|---|---|---|---|---|---|---|---|---|
| Pale ale | 8kg | 91 | | 7kg | | 10kg | 80 | ABV + colour |
| Roasted barley | 225g | 3 | 8.8 | 100g | | 270g | 10 | Flavour + colour |
| Chocolate malt | 225g | 2 | | 100g | | 300g | 10 | Aroma + colour |
| Medium crystal | 250g | 3 | | 100g | | 600g | 10 | Colour + flavour |
| Black malt | 100g | 1 | | 0 | | 150g | 5 | Colour + flavour |

**Mash in** at 67°C for 60min **Mash out** at 76°C for 10min

| HOP | Qty g | AA | Time | g min | Variance score | g max | Impacts | Alternatives |
|---|---|---|---|---|---|---|---|---|
| ① Summit | 50 | 17.5 | 60 | 40 | | 65 | Aroma | Amarillo |
| | | | | | | | | Cascade |
| | | | | | | | | East Kent Goldings |
| ② Cascade | 50 | 5.8 | 15 | 0 | | 60 | Aroma + bitterness | Summit |
| | | | | | | | | Amarillo |
| | | | | | | | | Challenger |

| YEAST | Temp °C Min | Temp °C Max | Condition / Wks 1st | 2nd | Bot | Alternative yeasts | Temp °C MIN | Temp °C MAX |
|---|---|---|---|---|---|---|---|---|
| MJ's M42 Strong Ale | 16 | 22 | 2 | 3m | 2-4 | Wyeast #1728 Scottish Ale | 13 | 21 |

## ABOUT THIS BREW

| | |
|---|---|
| Volume | 23 litres |
| Boil volume | 27 litres |
| Alcohol | 5.2% (4% – 6%) |
| Bitterness / IBU | 21 IBU (17 – 28 IBU) |
| Colour | 30 EBC (16 – 35 EBC) |
| Original Gravity | 1.054 (1.044 – 1.060) |
| Final Gravity | 1.013 (1.010 – 1.014) |

### EXTRACT RECIPE:

Steep 350g of caramel pils, 100g of roasted barley and 50g each of biscuit malt and pale chocolate malt in 27 litres of water at 65°C for half an hour. Remove and then add 2.1kg of light dried malt extract or 3kg of pale liquid malt extract, along with 3.75kg of pale liquid malt extract and bring to the boil and add hops as normal to the boil.

# IRISH RED ALE

Subtle and easy drinking, the Irish red ale is noted for its deep copper-red colour created by a blend of malts. While there is some variation to the style – ranging from quite malt-forward with fruity esters to rather neutral – they're all relatively low in hops which leads to a crowd-pleasing drinkability.

## CORE RECIPE / MAKE IT YOUR OWN

| MALT | Ideal qty | % | Overall qty kg | Qty-min | Variance score | Qty max | max % | Impacts |
|---|---|---|---|---|---|---|---|---|
| Pale malt | 5kg | 90 | | 4kg | | 5.2kg | 90 | ABV + colour |
| Caramel pils | 350g | 6 | | 100g | | 500g | 20 | Body + flavour |
| Roasted barley | 100g | 2 | 5.55 | 100g | | 140g | 10 | Colour + flavour |
| Biscuit malt | 50g | 1 | | 50g | | 300g | 10 | Colour + flavour |
| Pale chocolate | 50g | 1 | | 50g | | 100g | 10 | Colour + flavour |

⟩ **Mash in** at 64°C for 60min   **Mash out** at 76°C for 10min

| HOP | Qty g | AA | Time | g min | Variance score | g max | Impacts | Alternatives |
|---|---|---|---|---|---|---|---|---|
| ❶ Fuggles | 35 | 4.8 | 60 | 30 | | 45 | Aroma + bitterness | Styrian Golding |
| | | | | | | | | Willamette |
| | | | | | | | | Tettnanger |
| ❷ Challenger | 20 | 7 | 5 | 20 | | 45 | Aroma + bitterness | Perle |
| | | | | | | | | Admiral |
| | | | | | | | | Northdown |

| YEAST | Temp °C Min | Temp °C Max | Condition / Wks 1st | 2nd | Bot | Alternative yeasts | Temp °C MIN | Temp °C MAX |
|---|---|---|---|---|---|---|---|---|
| MJ's M42 Strong | 16 | 22 | 1-2 | 2 | 2 | Wyeast #1272 American Ale II | 15 | 22 |

## ABOUT THIS BREW

| Volume | 23 litres |
|---|---|
| Boil volume | 27 litres |
| Alcohol | 5% (4% – 6%) |
| Bitterness / IBU | 23 IBU (17 – 28 IBU) |
| Colour | 10 EBC (10 – 25 EBC) |
| Original Gravity | 1.051 (1.044 – 1.060) |
| Final Gravity | 1.013 (1.010 – 1.014) |

### EXTRACT RECIPE:

Steep 300g of light crystal and 100g golden naked oats in 27 litres of water at 65°C for half an hour. Remove and then add 2.4kg of light dried malt extract or 3kg of pale liquid malt extract and bring to the boil and add hops and honey as normal.

# IRISH DRAFT ALE

More of a variant on an Irish red than a style, these are sociable session beers with a low alcohol content but substantial body. This beer pours a deep red colour and tan head over a caramel-like malt character with roasty and fruity notes. A small dose of oats adds creaminess to the mouthfeel and a hint of grain to the flavour.

/ / / / / / / / / / / / / / / / / / / /

**ADJUNCTS:** 500g of honey added to the end of the boil lightens the body and boosts the gravity of this recipe.

## CORE RECIPE / MAKE IT YOUR OWN

| MALT | Ideal qty | % | Overall qty kg | Qty min | Variance score | Qty max | max % | Impacts |
|---|---|---|---|---|---|---|---|---|
| Pale ale (Maris Otter) | 4kg | 91 | | 3.5kg | | 4.5kg | 90 | ABV + colour |
| Light crystal | 300g | 7 | 4.4 | 100g | | 400g | 10 | Aroma + colour |
| Golden naked oats | 100g | 2 | | 50g | | 300g | 10 | Flavour + mouthfeel |

⊂⊃ **Mash in** at 67°C for 60min ▬ **Mash out** at 76°C for 10min

| HOP | Qty g | AA | Time | g min | Variance score | g max | Impacts | Alternatives |
|---|---|---|---|---|---|---|---|---|
| ❶ Cluster | 30 | 7 | 60 | 25 | | 35 | Aroma | Galena |
| | | | | | | | | Eroica |
| | | | | | | | | Fuggles |

| Honey | 500g | | 0 |
|---|---|---|---|

| YEAST | Temp °C Min | Temp °C Max | Condition / Wks 1st | Condition / Wks 2nd | Condition / Wks Bot | Alternative yeasts | Temp °C MIN | Temp °C MAX |
|---|---|---|---|---|---|---|---|---|
| MJ's M15 Empire Ale | 16 | 22 | 1-2 | 1-2 | 2 | Wyeast #1084 Irish Ale | 17 | 22 |

## ABOUT THIS BREW

| | |
|---|---|
| Volume | 23 litres |
| Boil volume | 27 litres |
| Alcohol | 3.2% (2.5% – 3.2%) |
| Bitterness / IBU | 17 IBU (10 – 20 IBU) |
| Colour | 18 EBC (17 – 33 EBC) |
| Original Gravity | 1.035 (1.030 – 1.035) |
| Final Gravity | 1.010 (1.010 – 1.013) |

### EXTRACT RECIPE:

Steep 400 of medium crystal in 27 litres of water at 65°C for half an hour. Remove and then add 1.8kg of light dried malt extract or 2.25kg of pale liquid malt extract and bring to the boil and add hops as normal to the boil.

# SCOTTISH 60/

The Scottish 60/ may also be known as a Scottish light. This low-gravity session beer is sparingly hopped and given a long, cool fermentation to produce a beer with good clarity and a clean, malty flavour and aroma. It has a modest alcohol content but is actually the darkest Scottish ale.

Mash 67°C
Mash out 74°C
Boil

0
60
70
60

1

## CORE RECIPE

## MAKE IT YOUR OWN

| MALT | Ideal qty | % | Overall qty kg | Qty min | Variance score | Qty max | max % | Impacts |
|---|---|---|---|---|---|---|---|---|
| Pale malt (Maris Otter) | 3kg | 88 | 3.4 | 2.8kg | | 3.2kg | 90 | ABV + colour |
| Medium crystal | 400g | 6 | | 100g | | 500g | 20 | Body + flavour |

**Mash in** at 64°C for 60min ⬤ **Mash out** at 76°C for 10min

| HOP | Qty g | AA | Time | g min | Variance score | g max | Impacts | Alternatives |
|---|---|---|---|---|---|---|---|---|
| ① East Kent Goldings | 35 | 5.5 | 60 | 30 | | 45 | Aroma + bitterness | Fuggles |
| | | | | | | | | Progress |
| | | | | | | | | First Gold |

| YEAST | Temp °C | | Condition / Wks | | | Alternative yeasts | Temp °C | |
|---|---|---|---|---|---|---|---|---|
| | Min | Max | 1st | 2nd | Bot | | MIN | MAX |
| MJ'sM15 Empire Ale | 16 | 22 | 1-2 | 1-2 | 2 | Wyeast #1728 Scottish Ale | 13 | 21 |

## ABOUT THIS BREW

| | |
|---|---|
| Volume | 23 litres |
| Boil volume | 27 litres |
| Alcohol | 3.9% (3.2% – 3.9%) |
| Bitterness / IBU | 20 IBU (10 – 25 IBU) |
| Colour | 25 EBC (16 – 33 EBC) |
| Original Gravity | 1.040 (1.035 – 1.040) |
| Final Gravity | 1.010 (1.010 – 1.015) |

### EXTRACT RECIPE:

Steep 200g of medium crystal, 250g of oat malt, 100g of amber malt and 50 of roasted barley in 27 litres of water at 65°C for half an hour. Remove and then add 2.1kg of light dried malt extract or 2.6kg of pale liquid malt extract and bring to the boil and add hops as normal to the boil.

# SCOTTISH 70/

Otherwise known as Scottish 'heavy'; the 'heavy' might be a bit of a misnomer: it is stronger than a Scottish light but its sessionability means it's a far cry from a wee heavy. This style is clean and balanced with a malt forward character that is usually rich and caramelly.

## CORE RECIPE / MAKE IT YOUR OWN

| MALT | Ideal qty | % | Overall qty kg | Qty min | Variance score | Qty max | max % | Impacts |
|---|---|---|---|---|---|---|---|---|
| Pale malt (Maris Otter) | 3.4kg | 85 | | 3.3kg | | 3.8kg | 90 | ABV + colour |
| Medium crystal | 200g | 5 | 4 | 100g | | 250g | 10 | Colour + flavour |
| Oat malt | 250g | 6 | | 100g | | 250g | 10 | Mouthfeel |
| Amber malt | 100g | 3 | | 100g | | 200g | 10 | Colour + flavour |
| Roasted barley | 50g | 1 | | 50g | | 100g | 5 | Colour + flavour |

**Mash in** at 64°C for 60min  **Mash out** at 76°C for 10min

| HOP | Qty g | AA | Time | g min | Variance score | g max | Impacts | Alternatives |
|---|---|---|---|---|---|---|---|---|
| ❶ Fuggles | 20 | 4.8 | 60 | 10 | | 25 | Aroma + bitterness | Styrian Golding, Willamette, Tettnanger |
| ❷ Fuggles | 15 | 4.8 | 30 | 10 | | 25 | Aroma + bitterness | Styrian Golding, Willamette, Tettnanger |
| ❸ Fuggles | 7 | 4.8 | 15 | 0 | | 15 | Aroma | Styrian Golding, Willamette, Tettnanger |

| YEAST | Temp °C Min | Temp °C Max | Condition / Wks 1st | 2nd | Bot | Alternative yeasts | Temp °C MIN | Temp °C MAX |
|---|---|---|---|---|---|---|---|---|
| MJ's M15 Empire Ale | 16 | 22 | 1-2 | 1-2 | 2 | Wyeast #1728 Scottish Ale | 13 | 21 |

## ABOUT THIS BREW

| | |
|---|---|
| Volume | 23 litres |
| Boil volume | 27 litres |
| Alcohol | 4.3% (3.9% – 5% |
| Bitterness / IBU | 28 IBU (15 – 30 IBU) |
| Colour | 20 EBC (19 – 33 EBC) |
| Original Gravity | 1.045 (1.040 – 1.054) |
| Final Gravity | 1.011 (1.010 – 1.016) |

### EXTRACT RECIPE:

Steep 400 of medium crystal in 27 litres of water at 65°C for half an hour. Remove and then add 1.8kg of light dried malt extract or 2.25kg of pale liquid malt extract and bring to the boil and add hops as normal to the boil.

# SCOTTISH 80/

Satisfying without being too rich, a Scottish 80/- export – or could be seen as a Scottish export – is a malt-focused ale with enough hops to balance and support the malt. While the overall feel of the beer is malty and rich, its clean, somewhat fruity yeast and balancing bitterness lends to a enjoyable drinkability

| CORE RECIPE | | | | MAKE IT YOUR OWN | | | | |
|---|---|---|---|---|---|---|---|---|
| **MALT** | Ideal qty | % | Overall qty kg | Qty min | Variance score | Qty max | max % | Impacts |
| **Pale malt (Golden Promise)** | 4kg | 89 | 4.5 | 3.7kg | | 4.6kg | 90 | ABV + colour |
| **Medium crystal** | 500g | 11 | | 400g | | 900g | 20 | Flavour + colour |

**Mash in** at 64°C for 60min ▬ **Mash out** at 76°C for 10min

| **HOP** | Qty g | AA | Time | g min | Variance score | g max | Impacts | Alternatives |
|---|---|---|---|---|---|---|---|---|
| ➀ **Fuggles** | 50 | 4.8 | 60 | 30 | | 55 | Aroma + bitterness | Styrian Golding |
| | | | | | | | | Willamette |
| | | | | | | | | Goldings |

| **YEAST** | Temp °C | | Condition / Wks | | | Alternative yeasts | Temp °C | |
|---|---|---|---|---|---|---|---|---|
| | Min | Max | 1st | 2nd | Bot | | MIN | MAX |
| **MJ's M15 Empire Ale** | 16 | 22 | 1-2 | 1-2 | 2 | Wyeast #1728 Scottish Ale | 13 | 21 |

## ABOUT THIS BREW

| | |
|---|---|
| Volume | 23 litres |
| Boil volume | 27 litres |
| Alcohol | 8.4% (6.5% – 10%) |
| Bitterness / IBU | 21 IBU (17 – 35 IBU) |
| Colour | 32 EBC (27 – 50 EBC) |
| Original Gravity | 1.087 (1.070 – 1.130) |
| Final Gravity | 1.022 (1.018 – 1.056) |

### EXTRACT RECIPE:

Steep 400g medium crystal, 200g of biscuit malt and 50g of roasted barley in 27 litres of water for half an hour. Remove and then add 4.8kg of light dried malt extract or 6kg of Maris Otter pale liquid malt extract, bring to the boil and add hops as normal to the boil.

# WEE HEAVY

Finding its roots in strong ales from the 1700s, the wee heavy is the very strongest of all Scottish ales with a ruby-brown hue, profound maltiness and high alcohol content. The wee heavy showcases complex toffee and vinous notes and a restrained hop character. This style is perfect for aging.

| CORE RECIPE | | | | | MAKE IT YOUR OWN | | | | |
|---|---|---|---|---|---|---|---|---|---|
| MALT | Ideal qty | % | Overall qty kg | Qty min | Variance score | Qty max | max % | Impacts | |
| Pale malt (Golden Promise) | 8 | 92 | | 7kg | | 11kg | 90 | ABV | |
| Medium crystal | 400g | 6 | 8.65 | 300g | | 900g | 10 | Colour + flavour | |
| Biscuit malt | 200g | 2 | | 100g | | 600g | 10 | ABV + colour | |
| Roasted barley | 50g | 1 | | 50g | | 150g | 5 | Colour | |

⬭ **Mash in** at 64°C for 60min ▬ **Mash out** at 76°C for 10min

| HOP | Qty g | AA | Time | g min | Variance score | g max | Impacts | Alternatives |
|---|---|---|---|---|---|---|---|---|
| ⓘ Northern Brewer | 30 | 9 | 60 | 25 | | 45 | Bitterness | Perle<br>Nugget<br>Chinook |

| YEAST | Temp °C | | Condition / Wks | | | Alternative yeasts | Temp °C | |
|---|---|---|---|---|---|---|---|---|
| | Min | Max | 1st | 2nd | Bot | | MIN | MAX |
| MJ's M42 Strong Ale | 14 | 21 | 2 | 4-6 | 2-4 | Wyeast #1728 Scottish Ale | 13 | 21 |

## ABOUT THIS BREW

| | |
|---|---|
| Volume | 23 litres |
| Boil volume | 27 litres |
| Alcohol | 4.7% |
| Bitterness / IBU | 33 IBU (plus heather) |
| Colour | 15 EBC |
| Original Gravity | 1.049 |
| Final Gravity | 1.012 |

### EXTRACT RECIPE:

Steep 350g pale chocolate malt, 100g of dark crystal and 350g of Carafa II in 27 litres of water for half an hour. Remove and then add 2.7kg of light dried malt extract or 3.375kg of Maris Otter pale liquid malt extract, bring to the boil and add hops as normal to the boil.

# HEATHER ALE

The Heather Ale is an ancient un-hopped ale that was first made in Scotland some four thousand years ago. Since hops were hard to come by in the brutal north, brewers foraged for heather as a way to add flavour and balance to the sweet wort. Modern versions use hops and are light and delicate with floral notes on a clean, smooth finish.

**ADJUNCTS:** Don't add more than 100g of heather tips through out. We recommend 50g at the beginning of the boil and 50g at 0 minutes.

## CORE RECIPE / MAKE IT YOUR OWN

| MALT | Ideal qty | % | Overall qty kg | Qty min | Variance score | Qty max | max % | Impacts |
|---|---|---|---|---|---|---|---|---|
| Pale malt (Maris Otter) | 4kg | 82 | | 3.5kg | | 5kg | 90 | ABV + colour |
| Cara Malt | 400g | 9 | 4.8 | 100g | | 400g | 10 | Colour |
| CaraAmber | 400g | 9 | | 100g | | 400g | 10 | Colour + body |

**Mash in** at 64°C for 60min — **Mash out** at 76°C for 10min

| HOP | Qty g | AA | Time | g min | Variance score | g max | Impacts Aroma/Bitternes | Alternatives |
|---|---|---|---|---|---|---|---|---|
| ❶ First Gold | 40 | 7.5 | 60 | 20 | | 70 | Aroma + bitterness | East Kent Goldings / Fuggles |
| ❷ First Gold | 20 | 7.5 | 0 | 10 | | 70 | Aroma | East Kent Goldings / Fuggles |

| YEAST | Temp °C Min | Temp °C Max | Condition / Wks 1st | Condition / Wks 2nd | Condition / Wks Bot | Alternative yeasts | Temp °C MIN | Temp °C MAX |
|---|---|---|---|---|---|---|---|---|
| MJ's M42 Strong Ale | 14 | 21 | 1-2 | 1-2 | 2 | Wyeast #1728 Scottish Ale | 13 | 21 |

Mash 67°C
Mash out 74°C
60
70
60
Boil

GERMAN

## ABOUT THIS BREW

| | |
|---|---|
| Volume | 23 litres |
| Boil volume | 27 litres |
| Alcohol | 3.9% (3.2% – 3.9%) |
| Bitterness / IBU | 41 IBU (35 – 45 IBU) |
| Colour | 6 EBC (6 – 12 EBC) |
| Original Gravity | 1.055 (1.044 – 1.056) |
| Final Gravity | 1.014 (1.013 – 1.017) |

### EXTRACT RECIPE:

Steep 400g of Carahell in 27 litres of water at 65°C for half an hour. Remove and then add 3.75kg of light Pilsner malt extract or 3kg or liquid Pilsner malt extract and bring to the boil and add hops as normal to the boil.

# BOHEMIAN PILSNER

This style was first brewed in 1842 in Pilsen, Czech Republic and had a massive influence on both historic and modern-day beer brewing. Expect a fuller mouthfeel and a more complex malt character that is both balanced and refreshing. A strong yet unassuming bitterness boosts its drinkability.

**NOTES:** A traditional multistep mash: Protein rest: 50°C for 20 minutes. Beta sacch' rest: 65°C for 30 minutes. Alpha sacch' rest: 70°C for 30 minutes. Mashout: 76°C for 10 minutes

| CORE RECIPE | | | | MAKE IT YOUR OWN | | | | | |
|---|---|---|---|---|---|---|---|---|---|
| MALT | Ideal qty | % | Overall qty kg | Qty min | Variance score | Qty max | max % | Impacts | |
| **Bohemian Pilsner malt** | 5kg | 93 | 5.4 | 4.7kg | | 5kg | 100 | ABV + colour | |
| **Carahell** | 400g | 7 | | 100g | | 500g | 10 | Colour + flavour | |

**Mash in** at 64°C for 60min **Mash out** at 76°C for 10min

| HOP | Qty g | AA | Time | g min | Variance score | g max | Impacts | Alternatives |
|---|---|---|---|---|---|---|---|---|
| ❶ **Perle** | 30 | 8.3 | 60 | 25 | | 35 | Aroma + bitterness | Challenger |
| | | | | | | | | Northern Brewer |
| ❷ **Saaz** | 30 | 3.8 | 30 | 10 | | 55 | Aroma + bitterness | Sterling |
| | | | | | | | | Lublin |
| | | | | | | | | Sladek |
| ❸ **Saaz** | 30 | 3.8 | 15 | 10 | | 40 | Aroma | Sterling |

| YEAST | Temp °C | | Condition / Wks | | | Alternative yeasts | Temp °C | |
|---|---|---|---|---|---|---|---|---|
| | Min | Max | 1st | 2nd | Bot | | MIN | MAX |
| **MJ's M76 Bohemian Lager** | 10 | 15 | 1-2 | 4 | 2 | Wyeast #2278 Czech Pils | 13 | 21 |

## ABOUT THIS BREW

| Volume | 23 litres |
|---|---|
| Boil volume | 27 litres |
| Alcohol | 4.7% (4.4% – 5.2%) |
| Bitterness / IBU | 38 IBU (25 – 45 IBU) |
| Colour | 5 EBC (4 – 10 EBC) |
| Original Gravity | 1.049 (1.044 – 1.050) |
| Final Gravity | 1.012 (1.008 – 1.013) |

### EXTRACT RECIPE:

Add 2.7kg of light Pilsner malt extract or 3.375kg or liquid Pilsner malt extract and bring to the boil and add hops as normal to the boil.

# GERMAN PILSENER

Soft water creates a suitable platform for the spicy, herbal, floral hop character that comes from the noble hops of Hallertauer, Saaz or Tettnanger. Expect a light golden colour with a rich, dense head. A crisp bitter finish extends beyond a lovely malt profile. Clean, refreshing and bitter, the Pils is purely pure.

**NOTES:** A traditional multistep mash: Protein rest: 50°C for 20 minutes. Beta sacch' rest: 65°C for 30 minutes. Alpha sacch' rest: 70°C for 30 minutes. Mashout: 76°C for 10 minutes

## CORE RECIPE — MAKE IT YOUR OWN

| MALT | Ideal qty | % | Overall qty kg | Qty min | Variance score | Qty max | max % | Impacts |
|---|---|---|---|---|---|---|---|---|
| Pilsner malt | 4.5kg | 100 | 5 | 4.3kg | | 4.7kg | 100 | ABV + colour |

**Mash in** at 64°C for 60min — **Mash out** at 76°C for 10min

| HOP | Qty g | AA | Time | g min | Variance score | g max | Impacts | Alternatives |
|---|---|---|---|---|---|---|---|---|
| ❶ Tettnang | 50 | 4.5 | 60 | 25 | | 60 | Aroma + bitterness | Hallertau |
| | | | | | | | | Liberty |
| ❷ German Spalt Select | 25 | 5.5 | 30 | 15 | | 40 | Aroma + bitterness | Liberty |
| | | | | | | | | Tettnanger |
| | | | | | | | | Hallertau |
| ❸ Hallertau | 15 | 4.3 | 15 | 10 | | 50 | Aroma | Tettnanger |

| YEAST | Temp °C Min | Temp °C Max | Condition / Wks 1st | Condition / Wks 2nd | Condition / Wks Bot | Alternative yeasts | Temp °C MIN | Temp °C MAX |
|---|---|---|---|---|---|---|---|---|
| MJ's M76 Bavarian Lager | 8 | 14 | 1-2 | 4 | 2 | Wyeast #2206 Bavarian Lager | 13 | 21 |

0

60
70
60

**①**

15

**②**

0

## ABOUT THIS BREW

| | |
|---|---|
| Volume | 23 litres |
| Boil volume | 27 litres |
| Alcohol | 4.7% (4.7% – 5.4%) |
| Bitterness / IBU | 19 IBU (16 – 22 IBU) |
| Colour | 12 EBC (6 – 10 EBC) |
| Original Gravity | 1.049 (1.045 – 1.051) |
| Final Gravity | 1.012 (1.008 – 1.012) |

### EXTRACT RECIPE:

Steep 250g of Carapils in 27 litres of water at 65°C for half an hour. Remove and then add 2.7kg of dried Pilsner malt extract or 3.4kg or liquid Pilsner malt extract and bring to the boil and add hops as normal to the boil.

# MUNICH HELLES

The Munich Helles was first brewed at Munich's Spaten brewery in 1894 as an answer to the Bohemian Pilsener. A Helles is often crystal clear and, since the word helles means 'light', is a light golden colour. A clean malt profile is balanced out by spicy/floral noble hops and a balancing bitterness.

**NOTES:** A traditional multistep mash: Protein rest: 50°C for 20 minutes. Beta sacch' rest: 65°C for 30 minutes. Alpha sacch' rest: 70°C for 30 minutes. Mashout: 76°C for 10 minutes.

## CORE RECIPE / MAKE IT YOUR OWN

| MALT | Ideal qty | % | Overall qty kg | Qty min | Variance score | | | Qty max | max % | Impacts |
|---|---|---|---|---|---|---|---|---|---|---|
| Pilsner malt | 4.5kg | 95 | 4.75 | 4.2kg | | | | 4.5kg | 90 | ABV + colour |
| Carapils | 250g | 5 | | 100g | | | | 200g | 10 | Colour + flavour |

**Mash in** at 64°C for 60min ▬ **Mash out** at 76°C for 10min

| HOP | Qty g | AA | Time | g min | Variance score | | | g max | Impacts | Alternatives |
|---|---|---|---|---|---|---|---|---|---|---|
| ❶ Hallertau | 30 | 4.5 | 60 | 25 | | | | 35 | Aroma + bitterness | Liberty |
| | | | | | | | | | | Mt. Hood |
| | | | | | | | | | | Tettnanger |
| ❷ Hersbrucker | 30 | 14.5 | 15 | 5 | | | | 10 | Aroma + bitterness | Mt. Hood |
| | | | | | | | | | | Strisselpalt |

| YEAST | Temp °C | | Condition / Wks | | | Alternative yeasts | Temp °C | |
|---|---|---|---|---|---|---|---|---|
| | Min | Max | 1st | 2nd | Bot | | MIN | MAX |
| MJ's M76 Bavarian Lager | 8 | 14 | 1-2 | 4 | 2 | Wyeast #2308 Munich Lager | 9 | 15 |

## ABOUT THIS BREW

| | |
|---|---|
| Volume | 23 litres |
| Boil volume | 27 litres |
| Alcohol | 6.9% (6.3% – 7.4% |
| Bitterness / IBU | 35 IBU (23 – 35 IBU) |
| Colour | 12 EBC (12 – 22 EBC) |
| Original Gravity | 1.071 (1.064 – 1.072) |
| Final Gravity | 1.018 (1.011 – 1.018) |

### EXTRACT RECIPE:

Steep 250g of Carahell in 27 litres of water for half an hour. Remove and then add 4.2kg of dried Pilsner malt extract or 5.25kg of liquid Pilsner malt extract, bring to the boil and add hops as normal to the boil.

# MAIBOCK

The "mai" means May in German, and thus is often a seasonal brew tapped in the spring. Also called a Helles Bock, it displays more balance than the traditional Bock. A Maibock often has more hops and a moderately dry finish but still has a focus for fine German malts.

///////////////////////////////

**NOTES:** A traditional multistep mash: Protein rest: 50°C for 20 minutes. Beta sacch' rest: 65°C for 30 minutes. Alpha sacch' rest: 70°C for 30 minutes. Mashout: 76°C for 10 minutes.

| CORE RECIPE | | | | MAKE IT YOUR OWN | | | | | |
|---|---|---|---|---|---|---|---|---|---|
| MALT | Ideal qty | % | Overall qty kg | Qty min | Variance score | Qty max | max % | Impacts | |
| **Pilsen malt** | 6kg | 97 | 7.25 | 6.5kg | | 7.1kg | 100 | ABV + colour | |
| **Carahell** | 250g | 3 | | 100g | | 300g | 10 | Mouthfeel | |

**Mash in** at 64°C for 60min **Mash out** at 76°C for 10min

| HOP | Qty g | AA | Time | g min | Variance score | g max | Impacts | Alternatives |
|---|---|---|---|---|---|---|---|---|
| ① Perle | 15 | 8.3 | 60 | 10 | | 15 | Aroma + bitterness | Challenger |
| | | | | | | | | Northern Brewer |
| ② Hersbrucker | 15 | 14.5 | 60 | 10 | | 15 | Aroma + bitterness | Mt. Hood |
| | | | | | | | | Strisselpalt |
| ③ Hersbrucker | 10 | 14.5 | 15 | 0 | | 10 | Aroma | Mt. Hood |
| | | | | | | | | Strisselpalt |

| YEAST | Temp °C | | Condition / Wks | | | Alternative yeasts | Temp °C | |
|---|---|---|---|---|---|---|---|---|
| | Min | Max | 1st | 2nd | Bot | | MIN | MAX |
| **MJ's M76 Bavarian Lager** | 8 | 14 | 1-2 | 6-8 | 2 | Wyeast #2124 Bohemian Lager | 9 | 14 |

Mash 67°C — 0
Mash out 74°C — 60 / 70 / 60 / ① ②
Boil
③ 15
0

## ABOUT THIS BREW

| | |
|---|---|
| Volume | 23 litres |
| Boil volume | 27 litres |
| Alcohol | 9.9% (7% – 10%) |
| Bitterness / IBU | 17 IBU (16 – 26 IBU) |
| Colour | 33 EBC (12 – 47 EBC) |
| Original Gravity | 1.103 (1.072 – 1.113) |
| Final Gravity | 1.024 (1.016 – 1.024) |

### EXTRACT RECIPE:

Steep 1kg of dark Munich malt and 250g Caramunich II in 27 litres of water at 65°C for half an hour. Remove and then add 6kg of dried Pilsner malt extract or 7.5kg or liquid Pilsner malt extract and bring to the boil and add hops as normal to the boil.

# DOPPELBOCK

Doppelbocks rank among the world's strongest beers. Rich and filling, these lagers used to sustain German monks during Lenten fasts. Deep copper-brown in colour, the doppelbock has a rich mouthfeel, slightly sweet with just enough hops to strike a balance, warming all the way down.

**NOTES:** A traditional multistep mash: Protein rest: 50°C for 20 minutes. Beta sacch' rest: 65°C for 30 minutes. Alpha sacch' rest: 70°C for 30 minutes. Mashout: 76°C for 10 minutes.

| CORE RECIPE | | | | | MAKE IT YOUR OWN | | | | | |
|---|---|---|---|---|---|---|---|---|---|---|
| MALT | Ideal qty | % | Overall qty kg | Qty min | Variance score | | | Qty max | max % | Impacts |
| Munich malt | 7kg | 68 | | 5kg | | | | 7.5kg | 90 | ABV + colour |
| Vienna malt | 2kg | 20 | 10.25 | 500g | | | | 2.8kg | 50 | Flavour |
| Dark Munich malt | 1kg | 10 | | 300g | | | | 1.3kg | 20 | Colour + flavour |
| Caramunich II | 250g | 2 | | 0 | | | | 500g | 10 | Flavour + aroma |

**Mash in** at 64°C for 60min  **Mash out** at 76°C for 10min

| HOP | Qty g | AA | Time | g min | Variance score | | | g max | Impacts | Alternatives |
|---|---|---|---|---|---|---|---|---|---|---|
| ⓵ Perle | 35 | 8.3 | 60 | 30 | | | | 45 | Aroma + bitterness | Styrian Golding |
| | | | | | | | | | | Willamette |
| | | | | | | | | | | Tettnanger |

| YEAST | Temp °C | | Condition / Wks | | | Alternative yeasts | Temp °C | |
|---|---|---|---|---|---|---|---|---|
| | Min | Max | 1st | 2nd | Bot | | MIN | MAX |
| MJ's M76 Bavarian Lager | 8 | 14 | 1-2 | 8-12 | 2-4 | Wyeast #2206 Bavarian Lager | 7 | 13 |

# ABOUT THIS BREW

| | |
|---|---|
| Volume | 23 litres |
| Boil volume | 27 litres |
| Alcohol | 6.6% (6.3% – 7.2%) |
| Bitterness / IBU | 25 IBU (20 – 27 IBU) |
| Colour | 60 EBC (28 – 44 EBC) |
| Original Gravity | 1.069 (1.064 – 1.072) |
| Final Gravity | 1.017 (1.013 – 1.019) |

## EXTRACT RECIPE:

Steep 500g of Munich malt and 500g Carafa I in 27 litres of water at 65°C for half an hour. Remove and then add 3.6kg of dried Pilsner malt extract or 4.5kg or liquid Pilsner malt extract and bring to the boil and add hops as normal to the boil.

# DUNKLES BOCK

A darker version of the Bock, which originated in 14th-century Northern Germany, this is a darker, richer German lager, which plays up the toasty qualities of Munich malts but is not as sweet as a Doppelbock. Complex, rich and smooth, it finishes with a clean lager character.

## CORE RECIPE / MAKE IT YOUR OWN

| MALT | Ideal qty | % | Overall qty kg | Qty min | Variance score | Qty max | max % | Impacts |
|---|---|---|---|---|---|---|---|---|
| Pilsner malt | 4kg | 57 | | 4kg | | 4.8kg | 70 | ABV + colour |
| Carapils | 2kg | 29 | 7 | 1.6kg | | 2.8kg | 50 | Body + flavour |
| Munich malt | 500g | 7 | | 400g | | 900g | 20 | Colour + flavour |
| Carafa I | 500g | 7 | | 200g | | 500g | 10 | Colour + aroma |

**Mash in** at 64°C for 60min **Mash out** at 76°C for 10min

| HOP | Qty g | AA | Time | g min | Variance score | g max | Impacts | Alternatives |
|---|---|---|---|---|---|---|---|---|
| ❶ Magnum | 20 | 12 | 60 | 10 | | 30 | Aroma + bitterness | Horizon |
| | | | | | | | | Newport |
| ❷ Spalt | 10 | 4 | 15 | 10 | | 30 | Aroma + bitterness | Liberty |
| | | | | | | | | Tettnanger |
| | | | | | | | | Hallertau |
| ❸ Spalt | 10 | 4 | 5 | 10 | | 40 | Aroma | Liberty |
| | | | | | | | | Tettnanger |
| | | | | | | | | Hallertau |

| YEAST | Temp °C Min | Max | Condition / Wks 1st | 2nd | Bot | Alternative yeasts | Temp °C MIN | MAX |
|---|---|---|---|---|---|---|---|---|
| MJ's M76 Bavarian Lager | 8 | 14 | 1-2 | 8-12 | 2-4 | Wyeast #2206 Bavarian Lager | 7 | 13 |

Mash 67°C

Mash out 74°C

Boil

## ABOUT THIS BREW

| | |
|---|---|
| Volume | 23 litres |
| Boil volume | 27 litres |
| Alcohol | 6.6% (6.3% – 7.2%) |
| Bitterness / IBU | 23 IBU (20 – 27 IBU) |
| Colour | 26 EBC (26 – 42 EBC) |
| Original Gravity | 1.068 (1.064 – 1.072) |
| Final Gravity | 1.017 (1.013 – 1.019) |

### EXTRACT RECIPE:

Steep 500 of Caramunich, 500. dark Munich in 27 litres of water at 65°C for half an hour. Remove and then add 3.6kg of dried malt extract or 4.5kg or liquid malt extract and bring to the boil and add hops as normal to the boil.

# BOCK

Historically brewed in the winter and lagered until spring, bocks are the original liquid bread. 17th-century monks needed something to help them through their fasts and these strong lagers were the nourishment of choice. Delicately hopped for just enough balance, bocks are noted for malts and a smooth, full body.

**NOTES:** A traditional multistep mash: Protein rest: 50°C for 20 minutes. Beta sacch' rest: 65°C for 30 minutes. Alpha sacch' rest: 70°C for 30 minutes. Mashout: 76°C for 10 minutes.

## CORE RECIPE / MAKE IT YOUR OWN

| MALT | Ideal qty | % | Overall qty kg | Qty min | Variance score | Qty max | max % | Impacts |
|---|---|---|---|---|---|---|---|---|
| Munich malt | 2.5kg | 36 | 7 | 2kg | | 2.7kg | 90 | ABV + colour |
| Vienna malt | 2.5kg | 36 | | 2kg | | 2.7kg | 50 | Flavour |
| Dark Munich malt | 1.5kg | 21 | | 1kg | | 1.5kg | 50 | Colour + flavour |
| Caramunich | 500g | 7 | | 400g | | 600g | 10 | Flavour + aroma |

**Mash in** at 64°C for 60min **Mash out** at 76°C for 10min

| HOP | Qty g | AA | Time | g min | Variance score | g max | Impacts | Alternatives |
|---|---|---|---|---|---|---|---|---|
| ⓘ Perle | 20 | 8.3 | 60 | 30 | | 35 | Aroma + bitterness | Styrian Golding |
| | | | | | | | | Willamette |
| | | | | | | | | Tettnanger |

| YEAST | Temp °C Min | Temp °C Max | Condition / Wks 1st | 2nd | Bot | Alternative yeasts | Temp °C MIN | Temp °C MAX |
|---|---|---|---|---|---|---|---|---|
| MJ's M76 Bavarian Lager | 8 | 14 | 1-2 | 6-8 | 2 | Wyeast #2206 Bavarian Lager | 8 | 13 |

## ABOUT THIS BREW

| | |
|---|---|
| Volume | 23 litres |
| Boil volume | 27 litres |
| Alcohol | 5.2% (4.8% – 6%) |
| Bitterness / IBU | 28 IBU (20 – 30 IBU) |
| Colour | 11 EBC (8 – 14 EBC) |
| Original Gravity | 1.054 (1.048 – 1.056) |
| Final Gravity | 1.013 (1.010 – 1.015) |

### EXTRACT RECIPE:

Steep 500g of Carapils and 300g of Caramunich II in 27 litres of water for half an hour. Remove and then add 2.7kg of dried Pilsner malt extract or 3.375kg of liquid Pilsner malt extract, bring to the boil and add hops as normal to the boil.

# DORTMUNDER EXPORT

As the Pilsner style was taking the European continent by storm in the late 19th century, the industrial German city of Dortmund made their own similar version to capitalise on its popularity. The Dortmunder Export is a slightly stronger German lager that is smooth, well-balanced with a moderate hop and malt character.

## CORE RECIPE / MAKE IT YOUR OWN

| MALT | Ideal qty | % | Overall qty kg | Qty min | Variance score | Qty max | max % | Impacts |
|---|---|---|---|---|---|---|---|---|
| Pilsner malt | 4.5kg | 85 | | 4kg | | 4.7kg | 90 | ABV + colour |
| Carapils | 500g | 9 | 5.3 | 200g | | 700g | 10 | Body + flavour |
| CaraMunich II | 300g | 6 | | 100g | | 300g | 10 | Flavour + aroma |

**Mash in** at 64°C for 60min **Mash out** at 76°C for 10min

| HOP | Qty g | AA | Time | g min | Variance score | g max | Impacts | Alternatives |
|---|---|---|---|---|---|---|---|---|
| ① Tettnang | 40 | 4.5 | 60 | 35 | | 40 | Aroma + bitterness | Hallertau |
| | | | | | | | | Liberty |
| | | | | | | | | Fuggle |
| ② Hallertau | 20 | 4.3 | 15 | 10 | | 60 | Aroma + bitterness | Liberty |
| | | | | | | | | Mt. Hood |
| | | | | | | | | Tettnanger |
| ③ Saaz | 50 | 3.8 | 5 | 40 | | 70 | Aroma | Sladek |
| | | | | | | | | Lublin |
| | | | | | | | | Sterling |

| YEAST | Temp °C Min | Temp °C Max | Condition / Wks 1st | Condition / Wks 2nd | Condition / Wks Bot | Alternative yeasts | Temp °C MIN | Temp °C MAX |
|---|---|---|---|---|---|---|---|---|
| MJ's M76 Bavarian Lager | 14 | 21 | 1-2 | 6-8 | 2 | Wyeast #2206 Bavarian Lager | 8 | 13 |

Mash 67°C
Mash out 74°C

0
60
70
60

Boil

② 15

③ 5

0

## ABOUT THIS BREW

| | |
|---|---|
| Volume | 23 litres |
| Boil volume | 27 litres |
| Alcohol | 4.7% (4.7% – 5.4%) |
| Bitterness / IBU | 21 IBU (20 – 35 IBU) |
| Colour | 8 EBC (6 – 14 EBC) |
| Original Gravity | 1.049 (1.045 – 1.051) |
| Final Gravity | 1.012 (1.008 – 1.012) |

### EXTRACT RECIPE:

Steep 200g of Caramunich III in 27 litres of water at 65°C for half an hour. Remove and then add 2.7kg of dried Pilsner malt extract or 3.4kg or liquid Pilsner malt extract and bring to the boil and add hops as normal to the boil.

# KELLERBIER

A Kellerbier was traditionally conditioned in and served straight from the cellar (keller) under a brewery. While more of a technique than a style, a Kellerbier is any unfiltered and unpasteurised German lager. It has a bit more body than others due to suspended yeast and will sometimes display diacetyl or other byproduct flavours.

**NOTES:** A traditional multistep mash: Protein rest: 50°C for 20 minutes. Beta sacch' rest: 65°C for 30 minutes. Alpha sacch' rest: 70°C for 30 minutes. Mashout: 76°C for 10 minutes.

## CORE RECIPE / MAKE IT YOUR OWN

| MALT | Ideal qty | % | Overall qty kg | Qty min | Variance score | | | | Qty max | max % | Impacts |
|---|---|---|---|---|---|---|---|---|---|---|---|
| Pilsner | 4kg | 83 | | 3.7kg | | | | | 4kg | 90 | ABV + colour |
| Vienna malt | 700g | 15 | 4.8 | 500g | | | | | 800g | 40 | Colour + flavour |
| CaraMunich III | 100g | 2 | | 100g | | | | | 200g | 10 | Colour + aroma |

**Mash in** at 64°C for 60min **Mash out** at 76°C for 10min

| HOP | Qty g | AA | Time | g min | Variance score | | | | g max | Impacts | Alternatives |
|---|---|---|---|---|---|---|---|---|---|---|---|
| ① Hersbrucker | 10 | 14.5 | 60 | 10 | | | | | 20 | Aroma + bitterness | Mt. Hood |
| | | | | | | | | | | | Strisselpalt |
| ② Hersbrucker | 15 | 14.5 | 5 | 10 | | | | | 25 | Aroma | Styrian Golding |
| | | | | | | | | | | | Willamette |

| YEAST | Temp °C | | Condition / Wks | | | Alternative yeasts | Temp °C | |
|---|---|---|---|---|---|---|---|---|
| | Min | Max | 1st | 2nd | Bot | | MIN | MAX |
| MJ's M76 Bavarian Lager | 14 | 21 | 1-2 | 6-8 | 2 | Wyeast #2206 Bavarian Lager | 8 | 13 |

## ABOUT THIS BREW

| Volume | 23 litres |
|---|---|
| Boil volume | 27 litres |
| Alcohol | 4.9% (4.2% – 5.9%) |
| Bitterness / IBU | 24 IBU (22 – 32 IBU) |
| Colour | 39 EBC (33 – 58 EBC) |
| Original Gravity | 1.051 (1.046 – 1.052) |
| Final Gravity | 1.013 (1.010 – 1.016) |

### EXTRACT RECIPE:

Steep 300g Carafa I and 200g Cara 45L in 27 litres of water for half an hour. Remove and then add 2.7kg of dried Pilsner malt extract or 3.375kg of liquid Pilsner malt extract, bring to the boil and add hops as normal to the boil.

# SCHWARZBIER

A regional speciality from Saxony and Franconia, the schwarzbier may look like a porter but is another creature entirely. While literally meaning 'black beer' it's not truly black but is, instead, a very dark brown. The schwarzbier has hints of roastiness with a smooth, clean maltiness and is exceptionally drinkable.

**NOTES:** A traditional multistep mash: Protein rest: 50°C for 20 minutes. Beta sacch' rest: 65°C for 30 minutes. Alpha sacch' rest: 70°C for 30 minutes. Mashout: 76°C for 10 minutes.

## CORE RECIPE / MAKE IT YOUR OWN

| MALT | Ideal qty | % | Overall qty kg | Qty min | Variance score | Qty max | max % | Impacts |
|---|---|---|---|---|---|---|---|---|
| Pilsner malt | 3.5kg | 70 | 5 | 3.2kg | | 3.6kg | 80 | ABV + colour |
| Carafa Special | 300g | 6 | | 300g | | 400g | 5 | Colour + aroma |
| Munich malt | 1kg | 20 | | 600g | | 1kg | 50 | Flavour + aroma |
| Belgian Cara 45 | 200g | 4 | | 100g | | 300g | 5 | Colour + flavour |

**Mash in** at 64°C for 60min — **Mash out** at 76°C for 10min

| HOP | Qty g | AA | Time | g min | Variance score | g max | Impacts | Alternatives |
|---|---|---|---|---|---|---|---|---|
| ❶ Tettnang | 35 | 4.5 | 60 | 30 | | 50 | Aroma + bitterness | Fuggles |
| | | | | | | | | Progress |
| | | | | | | | | First Gold |
| ❷ Hallertau | 20 | 4.5 | 15 | 10 | | 20 | Aroma + bitterness | Chinook |
| | | | | | | | | Galena |
| | | | | | | | | Nugget |
| ❸ Tettnang | 7 | 4.5 | 15 | 5 | | 10 | Aroma + bitterness | Fuggles |
| ❹ Hallertau | 7 | 4.5 | 1 | 5 | | 10 | Aroma | Fuggles |
| ❺ Tettnang | 7 | 4.5 | 1 | 5 | | 10 | Aroma | Fuggles |

| YEAST | Temp °C Min | Temp °C Max | Condition / Wks 1st | 2nd | Bot | Alternative yeasts | Temp °C MIN | Temp °C MAX |
|---|---|---|---|---|---|---|---|---|
| MJ's M84 Bohemian Lager | 10 | 15 | 2 | 4 | 2-4 | Wyeast #2124 Bohemian Lager | 9 | 14 |

0
60
70
60
① 1

0

## ABOUT THIS BREW

| Volume | 23 litres |
|---|---|
| Boil volume | 27 litres |
| Alcohol | (9% – 14%) |
| Bitterness / IBU | (25 – 35 IBU) |
| Colour | (36 – 60 EBC) |
| Original Gravity | (1.078 – 1.120) |
| Final Gravity | (1.020 – 1.035) |

### EXTRACT RECIPE:

Steep 1kg of dark Munich malt and 250g Caramunich II in 27 litres of water at 65°C for half an hour. Remove and then add 6kg of dried Pilsner malt extract or 7.5kg or liquid Pilsner malt extract and bring to the boil and add hops as normal to the boil.

# EISBOCK

Eisbock is an unusual beer made with a special technique: A finished Doppelbock is placed in a below-freezing environment. Any remaining water will freeze and be removed so the beer left behind will be highly concentrated. The result is a strong, rich, intensely malty German lager. It's very hard to achieve in a homebrew setting, but hey, we're completists.

//////////////////////////////////////

**NOTES:** See dopplebock recipe for traditional multistep mash. Once it has fermented and been racked, lager it near freezing for for a month. Rack again and freeze as low as possible until ice crystals form. Draw the liquid out of the slush. The colder the beer, the more concentrated the beer is.

## CORE RECIPE / MAKE IT YOUR OWN

| MALT | Ideal qty | % | Overall qty kg | Qty min | Variance score | | Qty max | max % | Impacts |
|---|---|---|---|---|---|---|---|---|---|
| **Munich malt** | 7kg | 68 | | 5kg | | | 7.5kg | 90 | ABV + colour |
| **Vienna malt** | 2kg | 20 | 10.25 | 500g | | | 2.8kg | 50 | Flavour |
| **Dark Munich malt** | 1kg | 10 | | 300g | | | 1.3kg | 20 | Colour + flavour |
| **Caramunich II** | 250g | 2 | | 0 | | | 500g | 10 | Flavour + aroma |

⟶ **Mash in** at 64°C for 60min ▬▬ **Mash out** at 76°C for 10min

| HOP | Qty g | AA | Time | g min | Variance score | | g max | Impacts | Alternatives |
|---|---|---|---|---|---|---|---|---|---|
| ① **Perle** | 35 | 8.3 | 60 | 30 | | | 45 | Aroma + bitterness | Styrian Golding |
| | | | | | | | | | Willamette |
| | | | | | | | | | Tettnanger |

| YEAST | Temp °C | | Condition / Wks | | | Alternative yeasts | Temp °C | |
|---|---|---|---|---|---|---|---|---|
| | Min | Max | 1st | 2nd | Bot | | MIN | MAX |
| **MJ's M76 Bavarian Lager** | 8 | 14 | 1-2 | 8-12 | 2-4 | Wyeast #2206 Bavarian Lager | 7 | 13 |

## ABOUT THIS BREW

| | |
|---|---|
| Volume | 23 litres |
| Boil volume | 27 litres |
| Alcohol | 4.9% (4.5% – 5.5% |
| Bitterness / IBU | 25 IBU (18 – 30 IBU) |
| Colour | 25 EBC (20 – 32 EBC) |
| Original Gravity | 1.051 (1.046 – 1.052) |
| Final Gravity | 1.013 (1.010 – 1.014) |

### EXTRACT RECIPE:

Steep 300g Caramunich I in 27 litres of water for half an hour. Remove and then add 3.3kg of dried Vienna malt extract or 4.1kg of liquid Vienna malt extract, bring to the boil and add hops as normal to boil.

# VIENNA LAGER

Originating in its namesake Vienna, the Vienna Lager has found popularity throughout the world and especially in Mexico due to Austrian immigrants to the country in the 1800's. The Vienna lager is crisp and refreshing with a fairly full body. Moderate-strength, this lager tastes somewhat toasty and finishes clean and dry.

## CORE RECIPE / MAKE IT YOUR OWN

| MALT | Ideal qty | % | Overall qty kg | Qty min | Variance score | Qty max | max % | Impacts |
|---|---|---|---|---|---|---|---|---|
| Vienna malt | 3kg | 58 | | 2.5kg | | 3kg | 60 | ABV + colour |
| Munich II | 2kg | 38 | 5.2 | 1.5kg | | 2kg | 50 | Flavour |
| Caramunich I | 200g | 4 | | 100g | | 300g | 10 | Colour |

Mash in at 64°C for 60min ▬ Mash out at 76°C for 10min

| HOP | Qty g | AA | Time | g min | Variance score | g max | Impacts | Alternatives |
|---|---|---|---|---|---|---|---|---|
| ❶ Styrian Goldings | 35 | 5.3 | 60 | 25 | | 43 | Aroma + bitterness | Fuggle |
| | | | | | | | | Willamette |
| ❷ Hallertau | 20 | 4.3 | 15 | 10 | | 35 | Aroma + bitterness | Liberty |
| | | | | | | | | Tettnang |
| | | | | | | | | Mt Hood |

| YEAST | Temp °C Min | Temp °C Max | Condition / Wks 1st | Condition / Wks 2nd | Condition / Wks Bot | Alternative yeasts | Temp °C MIN | Temp °C MAX |
|---|---|---|---|---|---|---|---|---|
| MJ's M76 Bavarian Lager | 8 | 14 | 1-2 | 6-8 | 2 | Wyeast #2206 Bavarian Lager | 7 | 13 |

Mash 67°C

Mash out 74°C

0

60
70
60

❶

Boil

❷ 15

0

# ABOUT THIS BREW

| | |
|---|---|
| Volume | 23 litres |
| Boil volume | 27 litres |
| Alcohol | 5.3% (4.8% – 5.7%) |
| Bitterness / IBU | 25 IBU (20 – 28 IBU) |
| Colour | 20 EBC (12 – 27 EBC) |
| Original Gravity | 1.055 (1.050 – 1.057) |
| Final Gravity | 1.014 (1.012 – 1.016) |

### EXTRACT RECIPE:

Steep 500g of dark Munich and 250g of Caramunich III in 27 litres of water at 65°C for half an hour. Remove and then add 3kg of dried Pilsner malt extract or 3.75kg or liquid Pilsner malt extract and bring to the boil and add hops as normal to the boil.

# MÄRZEN

Very similar to the Vienna Lager, the Märzen, sometimes recognised as an Oktoberfest, is noted for its bready yet clean malt flavours. The hops character is a bit more muted than a British bitter but if quaffability is important, then this style is hard to beat.

## CORE RECIPE / MAKE IT YOUR OWN

| MALT | Ideal qty | % | Overall Qty kg | min | Variance score | max | max % | Impacts |
|---|---|---|---|---|---|---|---|---|
| Bohemian Pilsner | 2kg | 37 | | 1.8kg | | 2.1kg | 90 | ABV + colour |
| Munich | 2kg | 37 | 5.45 | 1.8kg | | 2.1kg | 50 | Colour + flavour |
| Dark Munich | 1.2kg | 22 | | 800g | | 1.4kg | 10 | Colour + flavour |
| Caramunich III | 250g | 4 | | 100g | | 400g | 10 | Colour + aroma |

**Mash in** at 64°C for 60min **Mash out** at 76°C for 10min

| HOP | Qty g | AA | Time | g min | Variance score | g max | Impacts | Alternatives |
|---|---|---|---|---|---|---|---|---|
| ① Tradition | 40 | 6 | 60 | 30 | | 45 | Aroma + bitterness | Liberty |
| | | | | | | | | Hallertau |

| YEAST | Temp °C Min | Temp °C Max | Condition / Wks 1st | 2nd | Bot | Alternative yeasts | Temp °C MIN | Temp °C MAX |
|---|---|---|---|---|---|---|---|---|
| MJ's M76 Bavarian Lager | 8 | 14 | 1-2 | 4-6 | 2 | Wyeast #2633 Octoberfest Lager Blend | 8 | 14 |

## ABOUT THIS BREW

| | |
|---|---|
| Volume | 23 litres |
| Boil volume | 27 litres |
| Alcohol | 5.1% (4.5% – 6%) |
| Bitterness / IBU | 16 IBU (10 – 20 IBU) |
| Colour | 17 EBC (28 – 38 EBC) |
| Original Gravity | 1.053 (1.046 – 1.056) |
| Final Gravity | 1.013 (1.010 – 1.014) |

### EXTRACT RECIPE:

Add 3.75kg of liquid rye malt extract, bring to the boil and add hops as normal to the boil.

# ROGGENBIER

A signature brew of Bavaria, this is a medium-bodied, effervescent beer exploding with yeast and wheat malt character. Traditional versions will be cloudy, malty, and spicy, with a smooth mouthfeel and dense, whipped-cream head. Serve in a tall glass 'mit hefe' — swirl the bottle to make sure you get all the yeast!

## CORE RECIPE / MAKE IT YOUR OWN

| MALT | Ideal qty | % | Overall qty kg | Qty min | Variance score | Qty max | max % | Impacts |
|---|---|---|---|---|---|---|---|---|
| Pilsner malt | 2.5kg | 48 | | 2kg | | 2.6kg | 60 | ABV + colour |
| Rye malt | 1.5kg | 29 | 5.2 | 1kg | | 2kg | 50 | Flavour + colour |
| Vienna malt | 1kg | 19 | | 800g | | 1.3kg | 40 | Flavour + aroma |
| Caramunich malt II | 200g | 4 | | 100g | | 250g | 20 | Colour |

**Mash in** at 64°C for 60min **Mash out** at 76°C for 10min

| HOP | Qty g | AA | Time | g min | Variance score | g max | Impacts | Alternatives |
|---|---|---|---|---|---|---|---|---|
| ❶ Hersbrucker | 10 | 14.5 | 60 | 10 | | 20 | Aroma + bitterness | Mt. Hood / Strisselpalt |
| ❷ Hersbrucker | 20 | 14.5 | 0 | 15 | | 35 | Aroma | Mt. Hood / Strisselpalt |

| YEAST | Temp °C Min | Temp °C Max | Condition / Wks 1st | Condition / Wks 2nd | Condition / Wks Bot | Alternative yeasts | Temp °C MIN | Temp °C MAX |
|---|---|---|---|---|---|---|---|---|
| MJ's M20 Bavarian Wheat | 18 | 30 | 1-2 | 4-6 | 2 | Wyeast #3638 Bavarian Wheat | 17 | 23 |

## ABOUT THIS BREW

| Volume | 23 litres |
|---|---|
| Boil volume | 27 litres |
| Alcohol | 4.9% (4.3% – 5.6%) |
| Bitterness / IBU | 13 IBU (8 – 15 IBU) |
| Colour | 6 EBC (4 – 16 EBC) |
| Original Gravity | 1.051 (1.044 – 1.052) |
| Final Gravity | 1.013 (1.010 – 1.014) |

### EXTRACT RECIPE:

Add 3kg of wheat malt extract or 3.75 kg wheat liquid malt extract and bring to the boil and add hops as normal to the boil.

# RASPBERRY WHEAT

Meet the Raspberry Wheat: mild, approachable and fruity, this beer straddles several styles and adds natural raspberry extract to create a highly drinkable beer with mass appeal. Medium-bodied with the flavour profile of a Bavarian Hefeweizen, it is laced with a tart, fruity raspberry aroma and flavour.

/ / / / / / / / / / / / / / / / / / / / / / / / / / / / / /

**ADJUNCTS:** Natural raspberry extract added to taste at bottling lets you tone down the fruit or turn it way up, as you prefer. We'd recommend around 120g.

| CORE RECIPE | | | | MAKE IT YOUR OWN | | | | | |
|---|---|---|---|---|---|---|---|---|---|
| **MALT** | Ideal qty | % | Overall qty kg | Qty min | Variance score | Qty max | max % | Impacts | |
| **White wheat malt** | 2.4kg | 50 | 4.8 | 2.1kg | | 2.6kg | 60 | ABV + colour | |
| **Pilsner** | 2.4kg | 50 | | 2.1kg | | 2.6kg | 60 | ABV + colour | |

**Mash in** at 64°C for 60min **Mash out** at 76°C for 10min

| HOP | Qty g | AA | Time | g min | Variance score | g max | Impacts | Alternatives |
|---|---|---|---|---|---|---|---|---|
| ➊ **Hersbrucker** | 8 | 14.5 | 60 | 5 | | 10 | Aroma + bitterness | Mt. Hood |
| | | | | | | | | Strisselpalt |

| YEAST | Temp °C | | Condition / Wks | | | Alternative yeasts | Temp °C | |
|---|---|---|---|---|---|---|---|---|
| | Min | Max | 1st | 2nd | Bot | | MIN | MAX |
| **MJ's M20 Bavarian Wheat** | 18 | 30 | 2 | 0 | 2 | Wyeast #3333 German Wheat | 18 | 25 |

# ABOUT THIS BREW

| | |
|---|---|
| Volume | 23 litres |
| Boil volume | 27 litres |
| Alcohol | 4.4% (4.3% – 5.6%) |
| Bitterness / IBU | 13 IBU (8 – 15 IBU) |
| Colour | 6 EBC (4 – 16 EBC) |
| Original Gravity | 1.078 (1.064 – 1.090) |
| Final Gravity | 1.011 (1.010 – 1.014) |

### EXTRACT RECIPE:

Add 3kg of wheat malt extract or 3.75 kg wheat liquid malt extract and bring to the boil and add hops as normal to the boil.

# HEFEWEIZEN

A signature brew of Bavaria, this is a medium-bodied, effervescent beer exploding with yeast and wheat malt character. Traditional versions will be cloudy, malty, and spicy, with a smooth mouthfeel and dense, whipped-cream head. Serve in a tall glass 'mit hefe' — swirl the bottle to make sure you get all the yeast!

**NOTES:** A traditional multistep mash: Protein rest: 50°C for 20 minutes. Beta sacch' rest: 65°C for 30 minutes. Alpha sacch' rest: 70°C for 30 minutes. Mashout: 76°C for 10 minutes.

## CORE RECIPE / MAKE IT YOUR OWN

| MALT | Ideal qty | % | Overall qty kg | Qty min | Variance score | Qty max | max % | Impacts |
|---|---|---|---|---|---|---|---|---|
| Pale wheat malt | 2.5kg | 56 | 4.5 | 2.3kg | | 3.1kg | 60 | ABV + colour |
| Pilsner malt | 2kg | 44 | | 1.9kg | | 2.6kg | 60 | ABV + colour |

**Mash in** at 64°C for 60min — **Mash out** at 76°C for 10min

| HOP | Qty g | AA | Time | g min | Variance score | g max | Impacts | Alternatives |
|---|---|---|---|---|---|---|---|---|
| ⓘ Tettnang | 25 | 4.5 | 60 | 20 | | 30 | Aroma + bitterness | Styrian Golding / Target / Tettnanger |

| YEAST | Temp °C Min | Temp °C Max | Condition / Wks 1st | 2nd | Bot | Alternative yeasts | Temp °C MIN | Temp °C MAX |
|---|---|---|---|---|---|---|---|---|
| MJ'sM20 Bavarian Wheat | 18 | 30 | 2 | 0 | 2 | Wyeast #3068 Weihenstephan Wheat | 17 | 23 |

## ABOUT THIS BREW

| | |
|---|---|
| Volume | 23 litres |
| Boil volume | 27 litres |
| Alcohol | 9.6% |
| Bitterness / IBU | 21 IBU |
| Colour | 23 EBC |
| Original Gravity | 1.099 |
| Final Gravity | 1.025 |

# WEIZENDOPPELBOCK

This none-to-common beer is the wheat version of a doppelbock out of Bavaria. Pale wheat malt makes up around 50 per cent of the grist. The result is a dark lager, but with the wheaty flavours and aromas from the wheat and the use of a Bavarian weissbier yeast.

## CORE RECIPE / MAKE IT YOUR OWN

| MALT | Ideal qty | % | Overall qty kg | Qty min | Variance score | Qty max | max % | Impacts |
|---|---|---|---|---|---|---|---|---|
| Pale wheat malt | 5.5kg | 55 | | 5kg | | 6kg | 70 | ABV + colour |
| Pilsner malt | 3.5kg | 35 | 10 | 3kg | | 5kg | 50 | Colour + flavour |
| CaraHell | 600g | 6 | | 500g | | 800g | 10 | Colour + flavour |
| Caramunich III | 400g | 4 | | 300g | | 500g | 10 | Colour |

⟞⟝ **Mash in** at 64°C for 60min ▬▬ **Mash out** at 76°C for 10min

| HOP | Qty g | AA | Time | g min | Variance score | g max | Impacts | Alternatives |
|---|---|---|---|---|---|---|---|---|
| ① Hallertau | 60 | 4.3 | 60 | 40 | | 80 | Aroma + bitterness | Liberty |
| | | | | | | | | Mt. Hood |
| | | | | | | | | Tettnanger |
| ② Hallertau | 40 | 4.3 | 5 | 20 | | 70 | Aroma + bitterness | Liberty |
| | | | | | | | | Mt. Hood |
| | | | | | | | | Tettnanger |

| YEAST | Temp °C Min | Temp °C Max | Condition / Wks 1st | 2nd | Bot | Alternative yeasts | Temp °C MIN | Temp °C MAX |
|---|---|---|---|---|---|---|---|---|
| MJ's M20 Bavarian Wheat | 18 | 30 | 1-2 | 6-8 | 2 | Wyeast #3638 Bavarian Wheat | 17 | 23 |

## ABOUT THIS BREW

| | |
|---|---|
| Volume | 23 litres |
| Boil volume | 27 litres |
| Alcohol | 7.6% (6.5% – 8%) |
| Bitterness / IBU | 27 IBU (15 – 30 IBU) |
| Colour | 28 EBC (26 – 50 EBC) |
| Original Gravity | 1.078 (1.064 – 1.090) |
| Final Gravity | 1.020 (1.015 – 1.02) |

### EXTRACT RECIPE:

Steep 250g of CaraAroma in 27 litres of water for half an hour. Remove and then add 4.2kg of wheat malt extract or 5.25kg wheat liquid malt extract, bring to the boil and add hops as normal to the boil.

# WEIZENBOCK

First created at Schneider Weisse Brauhaus in 1907, the weizenbock is a German wheat beer brewed to bock strength, with intense malt flavors. It has the same banana and clove yeast character that can be found in a Hefeweizen, but with intensely rich maltiness and an ABV approaching 9%.

Mash 67°C

Mash out 74°C

60
70
60

Boil

0

60
70
60

5

0

## CORE RECIPE — MAKE IT YOUR OWN

| MALT | Ideal qty | % | Overall qty kg | Qty min | Variance score | Qty max | max % | Impacts |
|---|---|---|---|---|---|---|---|---|
| Pale wheat malt | 3.6kg | 46 | | 2.6kg | | 4.6kg | 60 | ABV + flavour |
| Munich malt | 3kg | 38 | 7.85 | 2kg | | 4kg | 60 | ABV + colour |
| Pilsner malt | 1kg | 13 | | 500g | | 2kg | 40 | ABV + colour |
| CaraAroma | 250g | 3 | | 200g | | 700g | 10 | Aroma |

**Mash in** at 64°C for 60min    **Mash out** at 76°C for 10min

| HOP | Qty g | AA | Time | g min | Variance score | g max | Impacts | Alternatives |
|---|---|---|---|---|---|---|---|---|
| ① Perle | 25 | 8.3 | 60 | 10 | | 27 | Aroma + bitterness | Styrian Golding |
| | | | | | | | | Target |
| | | | | | | | | Tettnanger |
| ② Hersbrucker | 15 | 14.5 | 15 | 5 | | 25 | Aroma + bitterness | Perle |
| | | | | | | | | Admiral |
| | | | | | | | | Northdown |

| YEAST | Temp °C Min | Temp °C Max | Condition / Wks 1st | Condition / Wks 2nd | Condition / Wks Bot | Alternative yeasts | Temp °C MIN | Temp °C MAX |
|---|---|---|---|---|---|---|---|---|
| MJ's M20 Bavarian Wheat | 18 | 30 | 1-2 | 6-8 | 2 | Wyeast #3638 Bavarian Wheat | 17 | 23 |

## ABOUT THIS BREW

| Volume | 23 litres |
|---|---|
| Boil volume | 27 litres |
| Alcohol | 5% (4.3% – 5.6%) |
| Bitterness / IBU | 15 IBU (10 – 18 IBU) |
| Colour | 33 EBC (26 – 47 EBC) |
| Original Gravity | 1.051 (1.044 – 1.056) |
| Final Gravity | 1.014 (1.010 – 1.014) |

### EXTRACT RECIPE:

Steep 400g of Caramunich II and 400g of Caramel 120L, and 500g of dark Munich malt in 27 litres of water at 65°C for half an hour. Remove and then add 2.4kg of dried wheat malt extract or 3kg or liquid wheat malt extract and bring to the boil and add hops as normal to the boil.

# DUNKELWEIZEN

Its name means 'dark wheat', and that's just what it is. An amber-coloured version of a German Hefeweizen, Dunkelweizen has the same spicy yeast and creamy wheat character of its pale counterpart, but with as much rich maltiness as a dark Bavarian lager. This recipe produces a beer with a hazy mahogany colour, medium-to-full body and spicy, bready aromas and flavours.

**NOTES:** A traditional multistep mash: Protein rest: 50°C for 20 minutes. Beta sacch' rest: 65°C for 30 minutes. Alpha sacch' rest: 70°C for 30 minutes. Mashout: 76°C for 10 minutes.

## CORE RECIPE / MAKE IT YOUR OWN

| MALT | Ideal qty | % | Overall qty kg | Qty min | Variance score | Qty max | max % | Impacts |
|---|---|---|---|---|---|---|---|---|
| Dark wheat malt | 2.2kg | 44 | | 2.2kg | | 2.8kg | 50 | ABV + colour |
| Pilsner malt | 1.5kg | 30 | | 1kg | | 2kg | 50 | ABV + colour |
| Dark Munich malt | 500g | 10 | 5 | 100g | | 800g | 20 | Colour + flavour |
| Caramunich II | 400g | 8 | | 200g | | 800g | 15 | Colour + flavour |
| Caramel 120L | 400g | 8 | | 300g | | 800g | 10 | Colour + flavour |

**Mash in** at 64°C for 60min **Mash out** at 76°C for 10min

| HOP | Qty g | AA | Time | g min | Variance score | g max | Impacts | Alternatives |
|---|---|---|---|---|---|---|---|---|
| ➊ Tettnang | 30 | 4.5 | 60 | 25 | | 35 | Aroma + bitterness | Styrian Golding |
| | | | | | | | | Willamette |
| | | | | | | | | Tettnanger |

| YEAST | Temp °C Min | Temp °C Max | Condition / Wks 1st | Condition / Wks 2nd | Condition / Wks Bot | Alternative yeasts | Temp °C MIN | Temp °C MAX |
|---|---|---|---|---|---|---|---|---|
| MJ's M20 Bavarian Wheat | 18 | 30 | 1-2 | 1-2 | 2 | Wyeast #3068 Weihenstephan Wheat | 17 | 24 |

# ABOUT THIS BREW

| | |
|---|---|
| Volume | 23 litres |
| Boil volume | 27 litres |
| Alcohol | 5.6% (4.2% – 5.9%) |
| Bitterness / IBU | 29 IBU (25 – 40 IBU) |
| Colour | 60 EBC (40 – 80 EBC) |
| Original Gravity | 1.057 (1.048 – 1.065) |
| Final Gravity | 1.014 (1.010 – 1.018) |

## EXTRACT RECIPE:

Steep 250g dark Munich malt, 250g of caramel/crystal 80 and 100g of Carafa II in 27 litres of water for half an hour. Remove and then add 3kg of dried malt extract or 3.75kg of liquid malt extract, bring to the boil and add hops as normal to the boil.

# DUNKEL

This classic dark brown lager originated in Munich and today is one of the most popular styles in Germany.  An intensely rich dark lager, the dunkel focuses on Munich malt, which imparts a wonderfully malty flavor with notes of dense bread, while the use of lager yeast keeps fruitiness to a minimum.

////////////////////////

**NOTES:** Maintain the cool temperature for secondary fermentation.

## CORE RECIPE / MAKE IT YOUR OWN

| MALT | Ideal qty | % | Overall qty kg | Qty min | Variance score | | | Qty max | max % | Impacts |
|---|---|---|---|---|---|---|---|---|---|---|
| Vienna malt | 2.5kg | 45 | | 2.2kg | | | | 2.6kg | 50 | ABV + colour |
| Munich malt | 2.5kg | 45 | 5.6 | 2.2kg | | | | 2.6kg | 50 | ABV + colour |
| Dark Munich malt | 250g | 4 | | 100g | | | | 400g | 10 | Colour + flavour |
| Caramel 80 | 250g | 4 | | 100g | | | | 400g | 20 | Colour + flavour |
| Carafa II | 100g | 2 | | 50g | | | | 200g | 10 | Colour + aroma |

**Mash in** at 64°C for 60min        **Mash out** at 76°C for 10min

| HOP | Qty g | AA | Time | g min | Variance score | | | g max | Impacts | Alternatives |
|---|---|---|---|---|---|---|---|---|---|---|
| ❶ Tradition | 35 | 6 | 60 | 30 | | | | 40 | Aroma + bitterness | Styrian Golding |
| | | | | | | | | | | Target |
| | | | | | | | | | | Tettnanger |

| YEAST | Temp °C Min | Temp °C Max | Condition / Wks 1st | Condition / Wks 2nd | Condition / Wks Bot | Alternative yeasts | Temp °C MIN | Temp °C MAX |
|---|---|---|---|---|---|---|---|---|
| MJ's M76 Bavarian Lager | 8 | 14 | 1-2 | 4 | 2 | Wyeast #2206 Bavarian Lager | 8 | 15 |

Mash 67°C

Mash out 74°C · 60 · 70 · 60

Boil

0

## ABOUT THIS BREW

| | |
|---|---|
| Volume | 23 litres |
| Boil volume | 27 litres |
| Alcohol | 5.4% (4.8% – 6%) |
| Bitterness / IBU | 26 IBU (20 – 30 IBU) |
| Colour | 20 EBC (20 – 40 EBC) |
| Original Gravity | 1.056 (1.050 – 1.057) |
| Final Gravity | 1.014 (1.012 – 1.016) |

### EXTRACT RECIPE:

Steep 1.5kg of smoked malt and 600g of Caramunich in 27 litres of water at 65°C for half an hour. Remove and then add 2.4kg of dried malt extract or 3kg or liquid malt extract and bring to the boil and add hops as normal to the boil.

# RAUCHBIER

German for 'smoke beer', this lager style features a rich smoke flavour and aroma. This speciality of the Bavarian city of Bamberg has a noticeable wood-fire smokiness due to the malts being smoked over beechwood. Generally brewed as a Märzen, a Rauchbier has a subtle bitterness and clean, malty finish.

**NOTES:** A traditional multistep mash: Protein rest: 50°C for 20 minutes. Beta sacch' rest: 65°C for 30 minutes. Alpha sacch' rest: 70°C for 30 minutes. Mashout: 76°C for 10 minutes.

## CORE RECIPE / MAKE IT YOUR OWN

| MALT | Ideal qty | % | Overall qty.kg | Qty min | Variance score | Qty max | max % | Impacts |
|---|---|---|---|---|---|---|---|---|
| Pilsner malt | 1.5kg | 27 | | 1kg | | 1.7kg | 50 | ABV + colour |
| Munich malt | 2kg | 36 | 4 | 1kg | | 2kg | 50 | ABV + colour |
| Smoked malt | 1.5kg | 27 | | 1kg | | 1.7kg | 40 | Aroma |
| Caramunich | 600g | 10 | | 200g | | 700g | 15 | Aroma + flavour |

⟹ **Mash in** at 64°C for 60min ━━ **Mash out** at 76°C for 10min

| HOP | Qty g | AA | Time | g min | Variance score | g max | Impacts | Alternatives |
|---|---|---|---|---|---|---|---|---|
| ① Perle | 30 | 8.3 | 60 | 25 | | 35 | Aroma + bitterness | Styrian Golding |
| | | | | | | | | Willamette |
| | | | | | | | | Tettnanger |

| YEAST | Temp °C Min | Temp °C Max | Condition / Wks 1st | 2nd | Bot | Alternative yeasts | Temp °C MIN | Temp °C MAX |
|---|---|---|---|---|---|---|---|---|
| MJ's M15 Empire Ale | 16 | 22 | 1-2 | 4 | 2 | Wyeast #2206 Bavarian Lager | 8 | 13 |

# ABOUT THIS BREW

| | |
|---|---|
| Volume | 23 litres |
| Boil volume | 27 litres |
| Alcohol | 5.6% (4.2% – 5.9%) |
| Bitterness / IBU | 29 IBU (25 – 40 IBU) |
| Colour | 60 EBC (40 – 80 EBC) |
| Original Gravity | 1.057 (1.048 – 1.065) |
| Final Gravity | 1.014 (1.010 – 1.018) |

## EXTRACT RECIPE:

Add 2.7kg of dried Pilsner malt extract or 3.375kg of liquid Pilsner malt extract, bring to the boil and add hops as normal to the boil.

# KÖLSCH

A beer from Cologne, the Kölsch is another hybrid style that is made with ale yeast and then lagered. The clean, dry finish is suggestive of traditional German lagers yet this style has a subtle fruitiness due to the yeast. Crisp and delicate, the Kölsch is a pleasant drink.

///////////////////////////////////////

**NOTES:** A traditional multistep mash: Protein rest: 50°C for 20 minutes. Beta sacch' rest: 65°C for 30 minutes. Alpha sacch' rest: 70°C for 30 minutes. Mashout: 76°C for 10 minutes.

| CORE RECIPE | | | | MAKE IT YOUR OWN | | | | | |
|---|---|---|---|---|---|---|---|---|---|
| **MALT** | Ideal qty | % | Overall qty kg | Qty min | Variance score | Qty max | max % | Impacts | |
| Pilsner malt | 4.5kg | 100 | 4.5 | 4.3kg | | 4.8kg | 100 | ABV + colour | |

⊂⊃ **Mash in** at 64°C for 60min ▬ **Mash out** at 76°C for 10min

| HOP | Qty g | AA | Time | g min | Variance score | g max | Impacts | Alternatives |
|---|---|---|---|---|---|---|---|---|
| ❶ Tradition | 15 | 6 | 60 | 10 | | 20 | Aroma + bitterness | Styrian Golding |
| | | | | | | | | Target |
| | | | | | | | | Tettnanger |
| ❷ Hersbrucker | 15 | 14.5 | 30 | 10 | | 20 | Aroma + bitterness | Perle |
| | | | | | | | | Admiral |
| | | | | | | | | Northdown |

| YEAST | Temp °C | | Condition / Wks | | | Alternative yeasts | Temp °C | |
|---|---|---|---|---|---|---|---|---|
| | Min | Max | 1st | 2nd | Bot | | MIN | MAX |
| MJ's M54 California Lager | 18 | 20 | 1-2 | 1-2 | 2 | Wyeast #2565 Kolsch | 13 | 17 |

0
60
70
60
① 
② 30
③ 15
0

## ABOUT THIS BREW

| | |
|---|---|
| Volume | 23 litres |
| Boil volume | 27 litres |
| Alcohol | 4.9% (4.5% – 5.2%) |
| Bitterness / IBU | 48 IBU (35 – 50 IBU) |
| Colour | 22 EBC (20 – 33 EBC) |
| Original Gravity | 1.051 (1.046 – 1.054) |
| Final Gravity | 1.013 (1.010 – 1.015) |

### EXTRACT RECIPE:

Steep 500 of Caramunich II in 27 litres of water at 65°C for half an hour. Remove and then add 2.7kg of dried Pilsner malt extract or 3.375kg or liquid Pilsner malt extract and bring to the boil and add hops as normal to the boil.

# ALTBIER

Hailing from Düsseldorf, the Altbier is an old style which traces its lineage to the days before lager brewing in Germany. Alts are amber in colour with a rich maltiness and spicy bitterness. It's fermented with ale yeast yet undergoes a lagering period for a clean, smooth finish.

**NOTES:** A traditional multistep mash: Protein rest: 50°C for 20 minutes. Beta sacch' rest: 65°C for 30 minutes. Alpha sacch' rest: 70°C for 30 minutes. Mashout: 76°C for 10 minutes.

## CORE RECIPE / MAKE IT YOUR OWN

| MALT | Ideal qty | % | Overall qty kg | Qty min | Variance score | Qty max | max % | Impacts |
|---|---|---|---|---|---|---|---|---|
| Munich malt | 1.8kg | 35 | | 1.5kg | | 2kg | 50 | ABV + colour |
| Dark Munich malt | 1kg | 20 | 5.1 | 800g | | 1.3kg | 40 | Colour + flavour |
| Pilsner malt | 1.8kg | 35 | | 1.5kg | | 2kg | 50 | ABV + colour |
| Caramunich II | 500g | 10 | | 500g | | 800g | 10 | Colour + flavour |

**Mash in** at 64°C for 60min  **Mash out** at 76°C for 10min

| HOP | Qty g | AA | Time | g min | Variance score | g max | Impacts | Alternatives |
|---|---|---|---|---|---|---|---|---|
| ❶ Perle | 15 | 8.3 | 60 | 10 | | 17 | Aroma + bitterness | Styrian Golding |
| | | | | | | | | Willamette |
| | | | | | | | | Tettnanger |
| ❷ Perle | 15 | 8.3 | 30 | 10 | | 17 | Aroma + bitterness | Styrian Golding |
| | | | | | | | | Willamette |
| | | | | | | | | Tettnanger |
| ❸ Hersbrucker | 30 | 14.5 | 15 | 15 | | 30 | Aroma | Styrian Golding |
| | | | | | | | | Willamette |
| | | | | | | | | Tettnanger |

| YEAST | Temp °C Min | Temp °C Max | Condition / Wks 1st | 2nd | Bot | Alternative yeasts | Temp °C MIN | Temp °C MAX |
|---|---|---|---|---|---|---|---|---|
| MJ's M54 California Lager | 18 | 20 | 1-2 | 1-2 | 2 | Wyeast #1007 German Ale | 13 | 19 |

## ABOUT THIS BREW

| Volume | 23 litres |
|---|---|
| Boil volume | 27 litres |
| Alcohol | 6.3% |
| Bitterness / IBU | 50 IBU |
| Colour | 40 EBC |
| Original Gravity | 1.065 |
| Final Gravity | 1.016 |

### EXTRACT RECIPE:

Steep 250g CaraAmber malt, 250g of Carafa I and 500g of wheat malt in 27 litres of water for half an hour. Remove and then add 3.3kg of dried malt extract or 4.1kg of liquid malt extract, bring to the boil and add hops as normal to the boil.

# STICKE

Essentially a double-Altbier, the Sticke is a seasonal variant from Düsseldorf's Altbier breweries. This special reserve style has even richer malts and higher alcohol content than its Altbier sibling. Hop bitterness in the Sticke is overall higher resulting in a bigger and bolder beer that is only occasionally available.

**NOTES:** A traditional multistep mash: Protein rest: 50°C for 20 minutes. Beta sacch' rest: 65°C for 30 minutes. Alpha sacch' rest: 70°C for 30 minutes. Mashout: 76°C for 10 minutes.

## CORE RECIPE / MAKE IT YOUR OWN

| MALT | Ideal qty | % | Overall qty kg | Qty min | Variance score | Qty max | max % | Impacts |
|---|---|---|---|---|---|---|---|---|
| Munich malt | 5.5kg | 85 | | 5kg | | 6kg | 80 | ABV + colour |
| Pale wheat malt | 500g | 7 | 6.5 | 300g | | 600g | 10 | Head retention |
| CaraAmber | 250g | 4 | | 100g | | 300g | 5 | Colour + aroma |
| Carafa I | 250g | 4 | | 100g | | 300g | 5 | Colour + aroma |

**Mash in** at 64°C for 60min   **Mash out** at 76°C for 10min

| HOP | Qty g | AA | Time | g min | Variance score | g max | Impacts | Alternatives |
|---|---|---|---|---|---|---|---|---|
| ❶ Tradition | 50 | 6 | 60 | 30 | | 50 | Aroma + bitterness | Hallertauer |
| | | | | | | | | Liberty |
| ❷ Hersbrucker | 15 | 14.5 | 30 | 10 | | 20 | Aroma + bitterness | Perle |
| | | | | | | | | Admiral |
| | | | | | | | | Northdown |
| ❸ Hersbrucker | 15 | 14.5 | 5 | 10 | | 20 | Aroma | Styrian Golding |
| | | | | | | | | Target |
| | | | | | | | | Tettnanger |

| YEAST | Temp °C | | Condition / Wks | | | Alternative yeasts | Temp °C | |
|---|---|---|---|---|---|---|---|---|
| | Min | Max | 1st | 2nd | Bot | | MIN | MAX |
| MJ's M54 California Lager | 18 | 20 | 1-2 | 4 | 2 | Wyeast #1007 German Ale | 13 | 19 |

## ABOUT THIS BREW

| Volume | 23 litres |
|---|---|
| Boil volume | 27 litres |
| Alcohol | 3% (2.8% – 3.8%) |
| Bitterness / IBU | 6 IBU (3 – 8 IBU) |
| Colour | 5 EBC (4 – 6 EBC) |
| Original Gravity | 1.029 (1.028 – 1.032) |
| Final Gravity | 1.006 (1.003 – 1.006) |

### EXTRACT RECIPE:

Add 1.8kg of dried wheat malt extract or 2.25kg of liquid wheat malt extract and bring to the boil and add hops as normal to the boil.

# BERLINER WEISSE

Made famous in Berlin, the Berliner Weisse is a cloudy, sour beer measuring at about 3% ABV. It's made with a blend of barley and wheat malts and gets its sour character thanks to a *lactobacillus* culture. It's popular to add syrups like raspberry to balance out the tartness.

**NOTES:** The easiest way to make a Berliner Weisse at home with a Wyeast or WhiteLabs Berliner Weisse Blend that mixes a German weizen yeast and Lactobacillus bacteria. The Wyeast strain also has some Brettanomyces.

| CORE RECIPE | | | | MAKE IT YOUR OWN | | | | | |
|---|---|---|---|---|---|---|---|---|---|
| MALT | Ideal qty | % | Overall qty kg | Qty min | Variance score | Qty max | max % | Impacts | |
| Pilsner malt | 1.7kg | 55 | | 1.5kg | | 1.7kg | 60 | ABV + colour | |
| Pale wheat | 1.2kg | 39 | 4.1 | 1kg | | 1.3kg | 50 | Colour + flavour | |
| CaraHell | 200g | 6 | | 100g | | 250g | 10 | Colour | |

**Mash in** at 64°C for 60min **Mash out** at 76°C for 10min

| HOP | Qty g | AA | Time | g min | Variance score | g max | Impacts | Alternatives |
|---|---|---|---|---|---|---|---|---|
| ⓘ Hallertau | 10 | 4.5 | 60 | 5 | | 15 | Aroma + bitterness | Liberty |
| | | | | | | | | Mt. Hood |
| | | | | | | | | Tettnanger |

| YEAST | Temp °C | | Condition / Wks | | | Alternative yeasts | Temp °C | |
|---|---|---|---|---|---|---|---|---|
| | Min | Max | 1st | 2nd | Bot | | MIN | MAX |
| N/A | - | - | 1-2 | 4m | 2 | Wyeast #3191-PC Berliner Weisse Blend | 20 | 22 |

## ABOUT THIS BREW

| | |
|---|---|
| Volume | 23 litres |
| Boil volume | 27 litres |
| Alcohol | 4% (4.2% – 4.8%) |
| Bitterness / IBU | 9 IBU (5 – 12 IBU) |
| Colour | 6 EBC (6 – 8 EBC) |
| Original Gravity | 1.041 (1.036 – 1.056) |
| Final Gravity | 1.010 (1.006 – 1.010) |

### EXTRACT RECIPE:

Steep 350g pale chocolate malt, 100g of dark crystal and 350g of Carafa II in 27 litres of water for half an hour. Remove and then add 2.7kg of light dried malt extract or 3.375kg of Maris Otter pale liquid malt extract, bring to the boil and add hops as normal to the boil.

# GOSE

Originating from around Leipzig, Germany, the gose is a sour wheat beer noted for its tartness due to the addition of *lactobacillus* bacteria after the boil. The gose stands out thanks to a bit of salt and coriander, which results in a refreshingly salty, herbal character balanced by a tart citrus.

**NOTES:** The easiest way to make a Gose at home with a Wyeast or WhiteLabs Berliner Weisse Blend that mixes a German weizen yeast and Lactobacillus bacteria. The Wyeast strain also has some Brettanomyces.
**ADJUNCTS:** Add 20-30g of Kosher or sea salt and 10g of crushed coriander seeds to the boil with 10 minutes left. ●

| CORE RECIPE | | | | MAKE IT YOUR OWN | | | | | |
|---|---|---|---|---|---|---|---|---|---|
| MALT | Ideal qty | % | Overall qty kg | Qty min | Variance score | Qty max | max % | Impacts | |
| Pale wheat malt | 2kg | 48 | | 1.5kg | | 2.5kg | 60 | ABV + colour | |
| Pilsner malt | 2kg | 48 | 4.15 | 1.5kg | | 2.5kg | 60 | Mouthfeel | |
| Acidulated malt | 100g | 3 | | 50g | | 100g | 10 | Flavour | |
| Rice Hulls | 50g | 1 | | 50g | | 100g | 5 | Mashing | |

⟹ **Mash in** at 64°C for 60min ▬ **Mash out** at 76°C for 10min

| HOP | Qty g | AA | Time | g min | Variance score | g max | Impacts | Alternatives |
|---|---|---|---|---|---|---|---|---|
| ❶ Saaz | 20 | 3.8 | 60 | 10 | | 30 | Aroma + bitterness | Sladek |
| | | | | | | | | Lublin |
| | | | | | | | | Sterling |

| Lactose | 500g | | 0 | |
|---|---|---|---|---|

| YEAST | Temp °C | | Condition / Wks | | | Alternative yeasts | Temp °C | |
|---|---|---|---|---|---|---|---|---|
| | Min | Max | 1st | 2nd | Bot | | MIN | MAX |
| N/A | - | - | 1-2 | 1-2 | 2 | Wyeast #3191-PC Berliner Weisse Blend | 20 | 22 |

STYLES

BELGIAN

## ABOUT THIS BREW

| | |
|---|---|
| Volume | 23 litres |
| Boil volume | 27 litres |
| Alcohol | 6.5% (6% – 7.5%) |
| Bitterness / IBU | 30 IBU (15 – 30 IBU) |
| Colour | 8 EBC 8 – 15 EBC) |
| Original Gravity | 1.068 (1.062 – 1.075) |
| Final Gravity | 1.017 (1.008 – 1.018) |

### EXTRACT RECIPE:

Steep 400g of caramel 10 in 27 litres of water at 65°C for half an hour. Remove and then add 3.3kg of light dried malt extract or 4kg of pale liquid malt extract and bring to the boil and add hops as normal to the boil.

# BELGIAN BLOND

Created to compete with the popularity of the Pils on the Continent, the Belgian blond unsurprisingly has a lager-like character. The use of Belgian yeast gives a distinctive spicy and fruity character yet it is much more subtle than other classic Belgian styles. A dry finish furthers its appeal.

**ADJUNCTS:** 500g of soft candi sugar is added to the boil 15 minutes before the end.
**NOTES:** A traditional multistep mash: Protein rest: 50°C for 20 minutes. Beta sacch' rest: 65°C for 30 minutes. Alpha sacch' rest: 70°C for 30 minutes. Mashout: 76°C for 10 minutes.

## CORE RECIPE / MAKE IT YOUR OWN

| MALT | Ideal qty | % | Overall qty kg | Qty min | Variance score | | | | Qty max | max % | Impacts |
|---|---|---|---|---|---|---|---|---|---|---|---|
| Pilsner malt | 5.5kg | 89 | 4 | 5.3kg | | | | | 6.3kg | 90 | ABV + colour |
| Caramel 10 | 400g | 3 | | 200g | | | | | 500g | 10 | Colour + flavour |

**Mash in** at 64°C for 60min **Mash out** at 76°C for 10min

| HOP | Qty g | AA | Time | g min | Variance score | | | | g max | Impacts | Alternatives |
|---|---|---|---|---|---|---|---|---|---|---|---|
| ① Hersbrucker | 15 | 14.5 | 60 | 10 | | | | | 20 | Aroma + bitterness | Mt. Hood |
| | | | | | | | | | | | Strisselpalt |
| ② Saaz | 15 | 3.8 | 45 | 10 | | | | | 20 | Aroma + bitterness | Sterling |
| | | | | | | | | | | | Lublin |
| | | | | | | | | | | | Sladek |
| ③ Hersbrucker | 15 | 14.5 | 5 | 10 | | | | | 30 | Aroma | Mt. Hood |
| | | | | | | | | | | | Strisselpalt |

| Soft candi sugar | 500g | | | | 15 | | | | | | |
|---|---|---|---|---|---|---|---|---|---|---|---|

| YEAST | Temp °C | | Condition / Wks | | | Alternative yeasts | Temp °C | |
|---|---|---|---|---|---|---|---|---|
| | Min | Max | 1st | 2nd | Bot | | MIN | MAX |
| MJ's M41 Belgian Ale | 18 | 28 | 1-2 | 1-2 | 2 | Wyeast #1762 Belgian Abbey II | 18 | 24 |

## ABOUT THIS BREW

| Volume | 23 litres |
|---|---|
| Boil volume | 27 litres |
| Alcohol | 6.4% (6.3% – 7.6% |
| Bitterness / IBU | 24 IBU (15 – 25 IBU) |
| Colour | 33 EBC (20 – 33 EBC) |
| Original Gravity | 1.067 (1.062 – 1.075) |
| Final Gravity | 1.017 (1.008 – 1.018) |

### EXTRACT RECIPE:

Steep 250g of Cara 45 and 100g of Belgian Special B in 27 litres of water for half an hour. Remove and then add 3.3kg of light dried malt extract or 4kg of pale liquid malt extract, bring to the boil and add hops as normal to the boil.

# DUBBEL

Dating back to monastic breweries from the middle ages, dubbels are still one of the most celebrated Belgian Trappist style ales. The dubbel generally displays a gleaming russet colour and has a complex flavour and aroma: spice, florals, dried fruits and plums. Moderately sweet and medium-full bodied, the dubbel finishes dry.

**ADJUNCTS:** Dark candi sugar needs to be added 15 minutes before the end of the boil.

## CORE RECIPE / MAKE IT YOUR OWN

| MALT | Ideal qty | % | Overall qty kg | Qty min | Variance score | Qty max | max % | Impacts |
|---|---|---|---|---|---|---|---|---|
| Belgian pale malt | 5.5kg | 87 | | 5.3kg | | 6kg | 90 | ABV + colour |
| Belgian Cara 45 | 250g | 4 | 6.35 | 100g | | 600g | 10 | Mouthfeel |
| Belgian Special B | 100g | 2 | | 100g | | 200g | 10 | Colour + flavour |

**Mash in** at 64°C for 60min  **Mash out** at 76°C for 10min

| HOP | Qty g | AA | Time | g min | Variance score | g max | Impacts | Alternatives |
|---|---|---|---|---|---|---|---|---|
| ❶ Tradition | 30 | 6 | 60 | 15 | | 30 | Aroma + bitterness | Hallertauer / Liberty |
| ❷ Hersbrucker | 10 | 14.5 | 10 | 5 | | 20 | Aroma | Mt. Hood / Strisselpalt |

| Dark candi sugar | 500g | | 15 |
|---|---|---|---|

| YEAST | Temp °C Min | Max | Condition / Wks 1st | 2nd | Bot | Alternative yeasts | Temp °C MIN | MAX |
|---|---|---|---|---|---|---|---|---|
| MJ's M41 Belgian Ale | 18 | 28 | 1-2 | 2-4 | 2 | Wyeast #1214 Belgian Ale | 17 | 22 |

Mash 67°C — 0
Mash out 74°C — 60 70 60
Boil — 15
— 10
— 0

0

60
70
60

15

0

## ABOUT THIS BREW

| | |
|---|---|
| Volume | 23 litres |
| Boil volume | 27 litres |
| Alcohol | 7.6% (7.5% − 9.5%) |
| Bitterness / IBU | 28 IBU (20 − 40 IBU) |
| Colour | 9 EBC (8 − 14 EBC) |
| Original Gravity | 1.078 (1.075 − 1.085) |
| Final Gravity | 1.014 (1.008 − 1.014) |

### EXTRACT RECIPE:

Steep 500g of Cara B in 27 litres of water at 65°C for half an hour. Remove and then add 3.9kg of dried Pilsner malt extract or 4.8kg or liquid Pilsner malt extract and bring to the boil and add hops and candi sugar as normal to the boil.

# TRIPEL

The famed Westmalle Trappist brewery is widely regarded as the creator of the popular Belgian tripel style. The tripel is higher in alcohol than the dubbel but lighter in colour and body. Spicy and fruity with a gentle sweetness and hints of alcohol lead to a dry and mildly bitter finish.

**ADJUNCTS:** 500g of clear candi sugar is added to the boil 15 minutes from the end.
**NOTES:** A traditional multistep mash: Protein rest: 50°C for 20 minutes. Beta sacch' rest: 65°C for 30 minutes. Alpha sacch' rest: 70°C for 30 minutes. Mashout: 76°C for 10 minutes.

## CORE RECIPE / MAKE IT YOUR OWN

| MALT | Ideal qty | % | Overall qty kg | Qty min | Variance score | Qty max | max % | Impacts |
|---|---|---|---|---|---|---|---|---|
| Belgian Pilsner malt | 6.5kg | 93 | 7.5 | 6.2kg | | 7kg | 90 | ABV + colour |
| Belgian Cara 8 | 500g | 7 | | 500g | | 800g | 10 | Colour + flavour |

**Mash in** at 64°C for 60min **Mash out** at 76°C for 10min

| HOP | Qty g | AA | Time | g min | Variance score | g max | Impacts | Alternatives |
|---|---|---|---|---|---|---|---|---|
| ❶ Tradition | 45 | 6 | 60 | 40 | | 70 | Aroma + bitterness | Hallertauer |
| | | | | | | | | Liberty |
| ❷ Saaz | 30 | 3.8 | 15 | 10 | | 50 | Aroma + bitterness | Sterling |
| | | | | | | | | Lublin |
| | | | | | | | | Sladek |

| Clear candi sugar | 500g | 15 |
|---|---|---|

| YEAST | Temp °C Min | Max | Condition / Wks 1st | 2nd | Bot | Alternative yeasts | Temp °C MIN | MAX |
|---|---|---|---|---|---|---|---|---|
| MJ's M41 Belgian Ale | 18 | 28 | 1-2 | 1-2 | 2 | Wyeast #3787 Trappist High Gravity | 18 | 25 |

## ABOUT THIS BREW

| Volume | 23 litres |
|---|---|
| Boil volume | 27 litres |
| Alcohol | 5.6% (4.2% – 5.9%) |
| Bitterness / IBU | 29 IBU (25 – 40 IBU) |
| Colour | 60 EBC (40 – 80 EBC) |
| Original Gravity | 1.057 (1.048 – 1.065) |
| Final Gravity | 1.014 (1.010 – 1.018) |

### EXTRACT RECIPE:

Add 3.9kg of dried Pilsner malt extract or 4.8kg of liquid Pilsner malt extract, bring to the boil and add hops and candi syrup as normal to the boil.

# GOLDEN STRONG

The Belgian golden strong is a complex beer noted for its very high strength that was brewed to compete with the Pils. As such, the golden strong is crisp and dry while still being full of fruity and spicy flavour. Many commercial examples have names referencing the devil because of its strength.

**ADJUNCTS:** 900g of candi syrup is added to the boil 15 minutes before the end.

**NOTES:** A traditional multistep mash: Protein rest: 50°C for 20 minutes. Beta sacch' rest: 65°C for 30 minutes. Alpha sacch' rest: 70°C for 30 minutes. Mashout: 76°C for 10 minutes.

| CORE RECIPE | | | | MAKE IT YOUR OWN | | | | | |
|---|---|---|---|---|---|---|---|---|---|
| **MALT** | Ideal qty | % | Overall qty kg | Qty min | Variance score | Qty max | max % | Impacts | |
| Pilsner malt | 6.5kg | 98 | 6.6 | 6kg | | 7.5kg | 98 | ABV + colour | |
| Belgian pale malt | 100g | 2 | | 100g | | 500g | 5 | Mouthfeel | |

**Mash in** at 64°C for 60min  **Mash out** at 76°C for 10min

| HOP | Qty g | AA | Time | g min | Variance score | g max | Impacts | Alternatives |
|---|---|---|---|---|---|---|---|---|
| ❶ Saaz | 60 | 3.8 | 60 | 55 | | 90 | Aroma + bitterness | Sladek |
| | | | | | | | | Lublin |
| | | | | | | | | Sterling |
| ❷ Saaz | 30 | 3.8 | 15 | 30 | | 60 | Aroma | Sladek |
| | | | | | | | | Lublin |
| | | | | | | | | Sterling |

| Candi syrup | 900g | 15 |
|---|---|---|

| YEAST | Temp °C | | Condition / Wks | | | Alternative yeasts | Temp °C | |
|---|---|---|---|---|---|---|---|---|
| | Min | Max | 1st | 2nd | Bot | | MIN | MAX |
| MJ's M41 Belgian Ale | 18 | 28 | 2 | 3m | 2 | Wyeast #3787 Trappist High Gravity | 17 | 22 |

Mash 67°C

Mash out 74°C

0

60
70
60

❶

Boil

30

❷

15

0

## ABOUT THIS BREW

| | |
|---|---|
| Volume | 23 litres |
| Boil volume | 27 litres |
| Alcohol | 4.3% |
| Bitterness / IBU | 47 IBU |
| Colour | 7 EBC |
| Original Gravity | 1.044 |
| Final Gravity | 1.011 |

### EXTRACT RECIPE:

Steep 350g of torrified wheat in 27 litres of water for half an hour. Remove and then add 2.7kg of light dried malt extract or 3.375kg of pale liquid malt extract, bring to the boil and add hops as normal to the boil.

# PETIT SAISON

This session-strength saison pours tawny-gold and perfumes the air with tangy yeast and pungent hop aromas. The flavour is lightly earthy with spicy, flowery hops and a grainy, bready malt character; the finish is dry.

## CORE RECIPE

| MALT | Ideal qty | % | Overall qty kg | Qty min | Variance score | Qty max | max % | Impacts |
|---|---|---|---|---|---|---|---|---|
| Belgian Pilsner malt | 2.5kg | 57 | | 2kg | | 3g | 80 | ABV + colour |
| Vienna malt | 1.5kg | 35 | 4.35 | 1kg | | 2g | 60 | Colour + flavour |
| Torrified wheat | 350g | 8 | | 300g | | 700g | 40 | Head retention + flavour |

Mash in at 64°C for 60min ▬▬ Mash out at 76°C for 10min

## MAKE IT YOUR OWN

| HOP | Qty g | AA | Time | g min | Variance score | g max | Impacts | Alternatives |
|---|---|---|---|---|---|---|---|---|
| ❶ East Kent Goldings | 30 | 5.5 | 60 | 30 | | 70 | Aroma + bitterness | Fuggles |
| | | | | | | | | Progress |
| | | | | | | | | First Gold |
| ❷ Styrian Goldings | 7 | 5.3 | 10 | 5 | | 15 | Aroma | Fuggles |
| | | | | | | | | Willamette |
| | | | | | | | | Styrian Bobek |
| ❸ Saaz | 7 | 3.8 | 10 | 5 | | 15 | Aroma | Sterling |
| | | | | | | | | Lublin |
| | | | | | | | | Sladek |
| ❹ Styrian Goldings | 20 | 5.3 | 2 | 20 | | 70 | Aroma | Fuggles |
| | | | | | | | | Willamette |
| | | | | | | | | Styrian Bobek |
| ❺ Saaz | 20 | 3.8 | 2 | 20 | | 70 | Aroma | Sterling |
| | | | | | | | | Lublin |
| | | | | | | | | Sladek |

| YEAST | Temp °C Min | Temp °C Max | Condition / Wks 1st | 2nd | Bot | Alternative yeasts | Temp °C MIN | Temp °C MAX |
|---|---|---|---|---|---|---|---|---|
| MJ's M29 French Saison | 26 | 32 | 1 | 1 | 2 | Wyeast #3711 French Saison | 18 | 25 |

## ABOUT THIS BREW

| | |
|---|---|
| Volume | 23 litres |
| Boil volume | 27 litres |
| Alcohol | 5.4% (5% – 7% |
| Bitterness / IBU | 34 IBU (20 – 35 IBU) |
| Colour | 14 EBC (10 – 28 EBC) |
| Original Gravity | 1.056 (1.048 – 1.065) |
| Final Gravity | 1.014 (1.002 – 1.012) |

### EXTRACT RECIPE:

Steep 400g of crystal/caramel 20 malt in 27 litres of water for half an hour. Remove and then add 3kg of light dried malt extract or 3.75kg of pale liquid malt extract, bring to the boil and add hops as normal to the boil.

# SAISON

First made by Belgian farmers in the 1700s, the saison was brewed to provide refreshment during harvest. This rustic style is noted for its spicy, tangy and dry yeast character and sometimes a bit of funk from Brettanomyces. Assertively hopped with a refreshing finish, the saison is a highly versatile style.

## CORE RECIPE / MAKE IT YOUR OWN

| MALT | Ideal qty | % | Overall qty kg | Qty min | Variance score | Qty max | max % | Impacts |
|---|---|---|---|---|---|---|---|---|
| Belgian pale malt | 5kg | 93 | 5.4 | 4.5kg | | 5.7kg | 95 | ABV + colour |
| Caramel 20 | 400g | 7 | | 100g | | 900g | 10 | Mouthfeel |

**Mash in** at 64°C for 60min **Mash out** at 76°C for 10min

| HOP | Qty g | AA | Time | g min | Variance score | g max | Impacts | Alternatives |
|---|---|---|---|---|---|---|---|---|
| ❶ Hersbrucker | 15 | 14.5 | 60 | 5 | | 20 | Aroma + bitterness | Mt. Hood |
| | | | | | | | | Strisselpalt |
| ❷ Hersbrucker | 20 | 14.5 | 10 | 10 | | 30 | Aroma + bitterness | Mt. Hood |
| | | | | | | | | Strisselpalt |

| YEAST | Temp °C Min | Temp °C Max | Condition / Wks 1st | 2nd | Bot | Alternative yeasts | Temp °C MIN | Temp °C MAX |
|---|---|---|---|---|---|---|---|---|
| MJ's M29 French Saison | 26 | 32 | 1-2 | 2-4 | 2 | Wyeast #3724 Belgian Saison | 21 | 30 |

## ABOUT THIS BREW

| Volume | 23 litres |
|---|---|
| Boil volume | 27 litres |
| Alcohol | 5.2% (5% – 6.5%) |
| Bitterness / IBU | 8 IBU (0 – 10 IBU) |
| Colour | 10 EBC (6 – 14 EBC) |
| Original Gravity | 1.054 (1.040 – 1.054) |
| Final Gravity | 1.013 (1.001 – 1.010) |

# LAMBIC

Traditionally crafted around the city of Brussels, Lambics are famed for their intensely sour character that gains complexity with age. Made with unmalted wheat in the malt bill, straight lambics are spontaneously fermented and aged in oak. They are generally served 'young' and uncarbonated at their home brewery.

**NOTES:** The easiest way to make a Lambic at home with a Wyeast or WhiteLabs Belgian Lambic Blend that Lactobacillus and Pediococcus culture with some Brettanomyces strains.

| CORE RECIPE | | | | MAKE IT YOUR OWN | | | | | |
|---|---|---|---|---|---|---|---|---|---|
| MALT | Ideal qty | % | Overall qty kg | Qty min | Variance score | Qty max | max % | Impacts | |
| Pale malt | 4kg | 75 | 5.3 | 3.8kg | | 4.8kg | 60 | ABV + colour | |
| Unmalted wheat | 1.3kg | 25 | | 1kg | | 1.5 | 40 | Mouthfeel | |

**Mash in** at 64°C for 60min ▬▬ **Mash out** at 76°C for 10min

| HOP | Qty g | AA | Time | g min | Variance score | g max | Impacts | Alternatives |
|---|---|---|---|---|---|---|---|---|
| ❶ Saaz (old) | 20 | 3.8 | 60 | 10 | | 80 | Aroma + bitterness | Sterling |
| | | | | | | | | Lublin |
| | | | | | | | | Sladek |

| YEAST | Temp °C | | Condition / Wks | | | Alternative yeasts | Temp °C | |
|---|---|---|---|---|---|---|---|---|
| | Min | Max | 1st | 2nd | Bot | | MIN | MAX |
| N/A | - | - | 12m | 12m | 2 | Wyeast #3278 Belgian Lambic Blend | 17 | 24 |

## ABOUT THIS BREW

| | |
|---|---|
| Volume | 23 litres |
| Boil volume | 27 litres |
| Alcohol | (5% – 8%) |
| Bitterness / IBU | (0 – 10 IBU) |
| Colour | (6 – 14 EBC) |
| Original Gravity | (1.040 – 1.060) |
| Final Gravity | (1.000 – 1.006) |

# GUEUZE

The most famed of Belgian sour ales, the gueuze is traditionally made by blending one, two and three-year-old lambics. While noticeably sour due to its spontaneous fermentation, a fine Gueuze should not taste like vinegar rather still have a lovely bouquet, silky mouthfeel and effervescent carbonation.

/////////////////////////////

**NOTES:** A gueuze is traditionally made by mixing different aged lambics, often one one-year old and one three-year old bottle. We offer the same recipe as the lambic here, but note the ABV is higher.

| CORE RECIPE | | | | MAKE IT YOUR OWN | | | | | |
|---|---|---|---|---|---|---|---|---|---|
| **MALT** | Ideal qty | % | Overall qty kg | Qty min | Variance score | Qty max | max % | Impacts | |
| **Pale malt** | 4kg | 75 | 5.3 | 3.8kg | | 4.8kg | 60 | ABV + colour | |
| **Unmalted wheat** | 1.3kg | 25 | | 1kg | | 1.5 | 40 | Mouthfeel | |

⊂══⊃ **Mash in** at 64°C for 60min ■■■ **Mash out** at 76°C for 10min

| HOP | Qty g | AA | Time | g min | Variance score | g max | Impacts | Alternatives |
|---|---|---|---|---|---|---|---|---|
| ① **Saaz (old)** | 20 | 3.8 | 60 | 10 | | 80 | Aroma + bitterness | Sterling |
| | | | | | | | | Lublin |
| | | | | | | | | Sladek |

| YEAST | Temp °C | | Condition / Wks | | | Alternative yeasts | Temp °C | |
|---|---|---|---|---|---|---|---|---|
| | Min | Max | 1st | 2nd | Bot | | MIN | MAX |
| **N/A** | - | - | 12m | 12m | 2 | Wyeast #3278 Belgian Lambic Blend | 17 | 24 |

0

60
70
60

① 1

0

## ABOUT THIS BREW

| | |
|---|---|
| Volume | 23 litres |
| Boil volume | 27 litres |
| Alcohol | 5.4% (5% – 7%) |
| Bitterness / IBU | 45 IBU (varies) |
| Colour | 60 EBC (6 – 14 EBC) |
| Original Gravity | 1.056 (1.040 – 1.060) |
| Final Gravity | 1.010 (1.000 – 1.010) |

# FRUIT LAMBIC

The most popular fruit lambics are kriek (with cherries) and framboise (with raspberries). We're describing the cherry here, but the same applies to all fruit additions. Reddish-brown in colour and blessed with a cherry pie aroma, followed by a tart, acidic bite that comes from a combination of cherries and bacteria, the sour character of this beer subdued and the cherries more pronounced when young. However, sourness increases with age.

////////////////////////////

**ADJUNCTS & NOTES:** Two cans of cherry puree are added to the secondary fermentation. Primary fermentation can be extended to 12 months before the cherry addition. Secondary fermentation on the cherries can be extended for up to 12 months before packaging. We have found it helpful to rack the beer again when secondary fermentation is complete to separate it from the fruit; allow it to settle a week or so before bottling. We also add fresh yeast at bottling to ensure even carbonation - one pack of general purpose ale yeast like US-05 or Nottingham will do the trick. This beer will keep for many years in the bottle.

## CORE RECIPE / MAKE IT YOUR OWN

| MALT | Ideal qty | % | Overall qty kg | Qty min | Variance score | | | Qty max | max % | Impacts |
|---|---|---|---|---|---|---|---|---|---|---|
| **Pale malt** | 4kg | 70 | | 3kg | | | | 4.5kg | 80 | ABV + colour |
| **Flaked wheat** | 1.5kg | 25 | 5.75 | 1kg | | | | 3kg | 10 | ABV + flavour |
| **Rice hulls** | 250g | 4 | | 200g | | | | 400g | 10 | Body |

**Mash in** at 64°C for 60min **Mash out** at 76°C for 10min

| HOP | Qty g | AA | Time | g min | Variance score | | | g max | Impacts | Alternatives |
|---|---|---|---|---|---|---|---|---|---|---|
| ❶ Hersbrucker (old) | 30 | 14.5 | 60 | 20 | | | | 70 | Aroma + bitterness | Mt. Hood Strisselpalt |

| YEAST | Temp °C | | Condition / Wks | | | Alternative yeasts | Temp °C | |
|---|---|---|---|---|---|---|---|---|
| | Min | Max | 1st | 2nd | Bot | | MIN | MAX |
| **N/A** | - | - | 6m | 6m | 2-4 | Wyeast #3278 Belgian Lambic Blend | 17 | 24 |

## ABOUT THIS BREW

| | |
|---|---|
| Volume | 23 litres |
| Boil volume | 27 litres |
| Alcohol | 5.5% (4.6% – 6.5%) |
| Bitterness / IBU | 23 IBU (10 – 25 IBU) |
| Colour | 21 EBC (20 – 32 EBC) |
| Original Gravity | 1.057 (1.048 – 1.057) |
| Final Gravity | 1.014 (1.002 – 1.012) |

# FLANDERS RED ALE

The Flanders red is an ale originating from West Flanders in Belgium. It has a deep burgundy colour reminiscent of a red wine. It's aged for at least two years in oak barrels where it picks up bacteria like *lactobacillus*, which sours the beer and leaves an acetic yet fruity complexity.

**NOTES:** A traditional multistep mash: 50°C for 20 minutes, 62°C for 40 minutes, 72°C for 30 minutes, 76°C for 5 minutes.

**ADJUNCTS:** Can be bottled and consumed after just a month or two in secondary if you wish, but under most conditions it will need 12 to 18 months to develop authentic sourness; your mileage may vary, so sample periodically and package when you like the flavour. Blend mature batch with young batches of the same beer at packaging for increased complexity. The addition of cherries after about three months will add to the flavour.

## CORE RECIPE / MAKE IT YOUR OWN

| MALT | Ideal qty | % | Overall qty kg | Qty min | Variance score | Qty max | max % | Impacts |
|---|---|---|---|---|---|---|---|---|
| Vienna malt | 3kg | 52 | | 2.8kg | | 4kg | 70 | ABV + colour |
| Pale malt | 2kg | 34 | 5.8 | 1.5kg | | 2kg | 50 | ABV + colour |
| Wheat malt | 300g | 5 | | 400g | | 1kg | 10 | Body |
| Caramunich III | 500g | 9 | | 300g | | 500g | 20 | Colour |

**Mash in** at 64°C for 60min　**Mash out** at 76°C for 10min

| HOP | Qty g | AA | Time | g min | Variance score | g max | Impacts | Alternatives |
|---|---|---|---|---|---|---|---|---|
| ⓘ East Kent Goldings | 40 | 5.5 | 60 | 20 | | 40 | Aroma + bitterness | Styrian Golding<br>Target<br>Tettnang |

| YEAST | Temp °C Min | Temp °C Max | Condition / Wks 1st | 2nd | Bot | Alternative yeasts | Temp °C MIN | Temp °C MAX |
|---|---|---|---|---|---|---|---|---|
| MJ's M47 Belgian Abbey | 18 | 25 | 1-2 | 12m | 2-4 | Wyeast #3763 Roselare Blend | 18 | 30 |

## ABOUT THIS BREW

| | |
|---|---|
| Volume | 23 litres |
| Boil volume | 27 litres |
| Alcohol | 4.9% (4% – 8%) |
| Bitterness / IBU | 23 IBU (20 – 25 IBU) |
| Colour | 33 EBC (28 – 47 EBC) |
| Original Gravity | 1.051 (1.040 – 1.074) |
| Final Gravity | 1.013 (1.008 – 1.012) |

# OUD BRUIN

Like the Flanders red, the oud bruin traces its origins to Flemish Belgium. It's different, however, in that it isn't aged on wood rather in steel casks. It's noted for its complex fruity maltiness while well-aged versions can carry a sherry-like, sweet-and-sour quality thanks to *lactobacillus*.

/ / / / / / / / / / / / / / / / / / / / / / / / / / /

**NOTES:** A traditional multistep mash: 50°C for 20 minutes, 62°C for 40 minutes, 72°C for 30 minutes, 76°C for 5 minutes.
**ADJUNCTS:** Can be bottled and consumed after just a month or two in secondary if you wish, but under most conditions it will need 12 to 18 months to develop authentic sourness; your mileage may vary, so sample periodically and package when you like the flavour.
Blend mature batch with young batches of the same beer at packaging for increased complexity. Rack to six-gallon carboy with whole/frozen cherries or raspberries after 1 year in secondary to make oud bruin kriek or frambozen.

## CORE RECIPE / MAKE IT YOUR OWN

| MALT | Ideal qty | % | Overall qty kg | Qty min | Variance score | | | | Qty max | max % | Impacts |
|---|---|---|---|---|---|---|---|---|---|---|---|
| Belgian Pilsner malt | 4kg | 80 | | 3kg | | | | | 6kg | 90 | ABV + colour |
| Flaked maize | 250g | 5 | | 250g | | | | | 1kg | 10 | ABV |
| Belgian Cara 45 | 350g | 7 | 5.05 | 250g | | | | | 1kg | 10 | Colour + flavour |
| Caramel 120 | 350g | 7 | | 100g | | | | | 600g | 10 | Colour + flavour |
| Carafa III | 50g | 1 | | 50g | | | | | 100g | 5 | Colour |

⊂⊃ **Mash in** at 64°C for 60min ▬▬ **Mash out** at 76°C for 10min

| HOP | Qty g | AA | Time | g min | Variance score | | | | g max | Impacts | Alternatives |
|---|---|---|---|---|---|---|---|---|---|---|---|
| ① Tradition | 35 | 6 | 60 | 30 | | | | | 35 | Aroma + bitterness | Hallertauer Liberty |

| YEAST | Temp °C Min | Temp °C Max | Condition / Wks 1st | Condition / Wks 2nd | Condition / Wks Bot | Alternative yeasts | Temp °C MIN | Temp °C MAX |
|---|---|---|---|---|---|---|---|---|
| MJ's M47 Belgian Abbey | 18 | 25 | 1-2 | 12m | 2-4 | Wyeast #3763 Roselare Blend | 18 | 30 |

# ABOUT THIS BREW

| | |
|---|---|
| Volume | 23 litres |
| Boil volume | 27 litres |
| Alcohol | 4.8% (4.5% – 5.5%) |
| Bitterness / IBU | 19 IBU (10 – 20 IBU) |
| Colour | 6 EBC (4 – 8 EBC) |
| Original Gravity | 1.050 (1.044 – 1.052) |
| Final Gravity | 1.012 (1.008 – 1.012) |

## EXTRACT RECIPE:

Add 3kg of dried wheat malt extract or 3.75kg of liquid wheat malt extract, bring to the boil and add hops as normal to the boil.

# WITBIER

This 400-year-old Belgian style has found modern popularity thanks to Hoegaarden. Literally 'white beer', this Belgian wheat ale got its name because of its cloudy haze. A smooth mouthfeel and grainy malts meet a dry and spicy Belgian yeast character with notes of coriander and orange. The witbier is exceedingly refreshing.

//////////////////////////////////

**ADJUNCTS:** Coriander and orange peel is added to the boil five minutes before the end. ●
**NOTES: NOTES:** Multi step mash: Protien rest: 50°C for 20 minutes, Sacch' rest: 66°C for 20 minutes, Mashout: 76°C for 10 minutes.

## CORE RECIPE / MAKE IT YOUR OWN

| MALT | Ideal qty | % | Overall qty kg | Qty min | Variance score | Qty max | max % | Impacts |
|---|---|---|---|---|---|---|---|---|
| Pilsner malt | 2.5kg | 50 | 5 | 2.3kg | | 2.7kg | 60 | ABV + flavour |
| Flaked wheat | 2.5kg | 50 | | 2.3kg | | 2.7kg | 60 | ABV + flavour |

**Mash in** at 64°C for 60min  **Mash out** at 76°C for 10min

| HOP | Qty g | AA | Time | g min | Variance score | g max | | Alternatives |
|---|---|---|---|---|---|---|---|---|
| ❶ Saaz | 30 | 3.8 | 60 | 15 | | 30 | Aroma + bitterness | Sterling |
| | | | | | | | | Lublin |
| | | | | | | | | Sladek |
| ❷ Saaz | 30 | 3.8 | 15 | 15 | | 30 | Aroma + bitterness | Sterling |
| | | | | | | | | Lublin |
| | | | | | | | | Sladek |

| Coriander | 30g | | 5 |
|---|---|---|---|
| Orange peel | 30g | | 5 |

| YEAST | Temp °C Min | Temp °C Max | Condition / Wks 1st | Condition / Wks 2nd | Condition / Wks Bot | Alternative yeasts | Temp °C MIN | Temp °C MAX |
|---|---|---|---|---|---|---|---|---|
| MJ's M21 Belgian Wit | 18 | 25 | 1-2 | 1-2 | 2 | Wyeast #3944 Belgian Wit | 17 | 23 |

Mash 67°C
Mash out 74°C
60
70
60
❶
Boil
❷ 15
5
0

Mash
67°C

Mash out
76°C

0

60
70
60

❶
❷

Boil

❸ 10

0

## ABOUT THIS BREW

| Volume | 23 litres |
|---|---|
| Boil volume | 27 litres |
| Alcohol | 4% |
| Bitterness / IBU | 30 IBU |
| Colour | 4 EBC |
| Original Gravity | 1.041 |
| Final Gravity | 1.010 |

### EXTRACT RECIPE:

Add 2.7kg of dried Pilsner malt extract or 3kg of liquid Pilsner malt extract, bring to the boil and add hops as normal to the boil.

# PATERSBIER

This recipe is based on one of the rarest beers in the world, brewed in the Belgian town Malle solely for consumption by the reverent Cistercian brothers. This ale is not served or sold to the public. Made only from Pilsner malt, hops, and yeast, the complexity that results from these simple ingredients is staggering: perfumey floral hops, ripe pear fruit, sour apple, spicy cloves, candied citrus and a slight biscuit character on the drying finish... a monks' session beer.

**ADJUNCTS:** A traditional multistep mash: 57°C for 15 minutes, 62°C for 35 minutes, 74°C for 25 minutes, 76°C for 5 minutes. If you wish to achieve a level of carbonation similar to the commercial examples of this beer, add an additional 30-60g of plain table sugar to the priming solution.

## CORE RECIPE / MAKE IT YOUR OWN

| MALT | Ideal qty | % | Overall qty kg | Qty min | Variance score | | | | Qty max | max % | Impacts |
|---|---|---|---|---|---|---|---|---|---|---|---|
| Belgian pilsner malt | 4kg | 100 | 4 | 3.5kg | | | | | 4.5kg | 100 | ABV + colour |

**Mash in** at 64°C for 60min  **Mash out** at 76°C for 10min

| HOP | Qty g | AA | Time | g min | Variance score | | | | g max | Impacts | Alternatives |
|---|---|---|---|---|---|---|---|---|---|---|---|
| ❶ Tradition | 30 | 6 | 60 | 20 | | | | | 40 | Aroma + bitterness | Hallertauer |
| | | | | | | | | | | | Liberty |
| ❷ Saaz | 15 | 3.8 | 60 | 10 | | | | | 25 | Aroma + bitterness | Sterling |
| | | | | | | | | | | | Lublin |
| | | | | | | | | | | | Sladek |
| ❸ Saaz | 15 | 3.8 | 15 | 10 | | | | | 35 | Aroma | Sterling |
| | | | | | | | | | | | Lublin |
| | | | | | | | | | | | Sladek |

| YEAST | Temp °C Min | Max | Condition / Wks 1st | 2nd | Bot | Alternative yeasts | Temp °C MIN | MAX |
|---|---|---|---|---|---|---|---|---|
| MJ's M47 Belgian Abbey | 18 | 25 | 1-2 | 1-2 | 2 | Wyeast #3787 Trappist High Gravity | 13 | 21 |

## ABOUT THIS BREW

| | |
|---|---|
| Volume | 23 litres |
| Boil volume | 27 litres |
| Alcohol | 6.9% (6% – 8.5%) |
| Bitterness / IBU | 22 IBU (18 – 28 IBU) |
| Colour | 13 EBC (12 – 35 EBC) |
| Original Gravity | 1.072 (1.060 – 1.080) |
| Final Gravity | 1.016 (1.008 – 1.016) |

### EXTRACT RECIPE:

Steep 250g of aromatic malt and 250g of honey malt in 27 litres of water at 65°C for half an hour. Remove and then add 3.9kg of light dried malt extract or 4.8kg of pale liquid malt extract and bring to the boil and add hops as normal to the boil.

# BIÈRE DE GARDE

Originating in Northern France, the Bière de Garde was brewed in the early spring to be ready for summer. Now brewed year round, this style can range from blonde to deep brown in colour. Highly drinkable, it has a clean, malty profile, smooth body, moderate alcohol content and a dry finish.

//////////////////////////////////

**NOTES:** A traditional multistep mash: 44°C for 20 minutes, 54°C for 20 minutes, 65°C for 30 minutes, 70°C for 30 minutes, Mashout: 76°C for 10 minutes. This lager yeast is fermented at warmer ale temperatures, but needs to be cold conditioned for two months before serving.

| Mash 67°C | Mash out 74°C | Boil |
|---|---|---|
| 0 | 60 70 60 ① | 0 |

## CORE RECIPE / MAKE IT YOUR OWN

| MALT | Ideal qty | % | Overall qty kg | Qty min | Variance score | Qty max | max % | Impacts |
|---|---|---|---|---|---|---|---|---|
| Belgian Pilsner malt | 4.5kg | 64 | | 4kg | | 5kg | 70 | ABV + colour |
| Vienna malt | 2kg | 29 | 7 | 1kg | | 2.5kg | 40 | Aroma + flavour |
| Aromatic malt | 250g | 4 | | 200g | | 500g | 10 | Aroma |
| Honey malt | 250g | 3 | | 200g | | 400g | 10 | Aroma + flavour |

**Mash in** at 64°C for 60min **Mash out** at 76°C for 10min

| HOP | Qty g | AA | Time | g min | Variance score | g max | Impacts | Alternatives |
|---|---|---|---|---|---|---|---|---|
| ① Styrian Goldings | 45 | 5.3 | 60 | 40 | | 60 | Aroma + bitterness | Fuggles / Styrian Bobek / Willamette |

| YEAST | Temp °C Min | Temp °C Max | Condition / Wks 1st | 2nd | Bot | Alternative yeasts | Temp °C MIN | Temp °C MAX |
|---|---|---|---|---|---|---|---|---|
| MJ's M54 California Lager | 18 | 20 | 1-2 | 2 | 2 | Wyeast #2112 California Lager | 13 | 21 |

AMERICAN

## ABOUT THIS BREW

| | |
|---|---|
| Volume | 23 litres |
| Boil volume | 27 litres |
| Alcohol | 4.7% (4.2% – 5.3%) |
| Bitterness / IBU | 20 IBU (10 – 25 IBU) |
| Colour | 4 EBC (4 – 8 EBC) |
| Original Gravity | 1.048 (1.040 – 1.050) |
| Final Gravity | 1.010 (1.004 – 1.010) |

### EXTRACT RECIPE:

Add 2.4kg of dried Pilsner malt extract or 3kg or liquid Pilsner malt extract and bring to the boil and add hops as normal to the boil.

# AMERICAN LAGER

These are among the most difficult beers to brew because their pale colour, low hop rate, and delicate flavour don't hide flaws. The best course of action is to pick a proven recipe and ferment it at the appropriate temperature! Our American Lager's body and flavour are lightened by rice and yields a straw-coloured and clear beer with a snowy head.

**ADJUNCTS:** Rice syrup solids are added to the boil at 60 minutes.

| CORE RECIPE | | | | MAKE IT YOUR OWN | | | | | |
|---|---|---|---|---|---|---|---|---|---|
| MALT | Ideal qty | % | Overall qty kg | Qty min | Variance score | Qty max | max % | Impacts | |
| Pale malt | 4.5kg | 80 | 5 | 3kg | | 4kg | 80 | ABV + colour | |

**Mash in** at 64°C for 60min — **Mash out** at 76°C for 10min

| HOP | Qty g | AA | Time | g min | Variance score | g max | Impacts | Alternatives |
|---|---|---|---|---|---|---|---|---|
| ⓘ **Saaz** | 30 | 3.8 | 60 | 20 | | 35 | Aroma + bitterness | Sterling |
| | | | | | | | | Lublin |
| | | | | | | | | Sladek |

| Rice syrup solids | 500g | | 60 |
|---|---|---|---|

| YEAST | Temp °C | | Condition / Wks | | | Alternative yeasts | Temp °C | |
|---|---|---|---|---|---|---|---|---|
| | Min | Max | 1st | 2nd | Bot | | MIN | MAX |
| **MJ's M84 Bohemian Lager** | 10 | 15 | 1-2 | 4 | 2 | Wyeast #2007 Pilsen Lager | 9 | 13 |

## ABOUT THIS BREW

| Volume | 23 litres |
|---|---|
| Boil volume | 27 litres |
| Alcohol | 4.2% |
| Bitterness / IBU | 41 IBU |
| Colour | 4 EBC |
| Original Gravity | 1.043 |
| Final Gravity | 1.011 |

### EXTRACT RECIPE:

Steep 500g of Carapils in 27 litres of water for half an hour. Remove and then add 2.4kg of dried Pilsner malt extract or 3kg or liquid pilsner malt extract and bring to the boil and add hops as normal to the boil.

# PRE PROHIBITION LAGER

This is a classic American beer, an official 'historical' style that marries highly enzymatic American 6-row malt with enzyme-poor corn that cuts the high malt proteins. This is not the insipid macro-brew of today, being rich, with a sweetness cut by a generous addition of hops.

/ / / / / / / / / / / / / / / / / / / /

**ADJUNCTS:** Flaked maize is added to the mash to increase alcohol content without affecting flavour.

| Mash 67°C | 0 |
|---|---|
| Mash out 74°C | 60 |
| | 70 |
| ① | 60 |
| Boil | |
| ② | 10 |
| | 0 |

## CORE RECIPE / MAKE IT YOUR OWN

| MALT | Ideal qty | % | Overall qty kg | Qty min | Variance score | Qty max | max % | Impacts |
|---|---|---|---|---|---|---|---|---|
| Rahr 6-row pale malt | 3.5kg | 82 | | 3kg | | 4kg | 90 | ABV + colour |
| Carapils | 250g | 6 | 4.25 | 250g | | 500g | 10 | Mouthfeel |
| Flaked maize | 250g | 12 | | 300g | | 700g | 10 | Colour |

▭ **Mash in** at 64°C for 60min ▬ **Mash out** at 76°C for 10min

| HOP | Qty g | AA | Time | g min | Variance score | g max | Impacts | Alternatives |
|---|---|---|---|---|---|---|---|---|
| ① Cluster | 45 | 7 | 60 | 30 | | 50 | Aroma + bitterness | Galena |
| | | | | | | | | Eroica |
| ② Cluster | 15 | 7 | 10 | 10 | | 40 | Aroma + bitterness | Galena |
| | | | | | | | | Eroica |

| YEAST | Temp °C Min | Temp °C Max | Condition / Wks 1st | 2nd | Bot | Alternative yeasts | Temp °C MIN | Temp °C MAX |
|---|---|---|---|---|---|---|---|---|
| MJ's M84 Bohemian Lager | 10 | 15 | 1-2 | 2 | 2 | Wyeast #2007 Pilsen Lager | 8 | 13 |

## ABOUT THIS BREW

| | |
|---|---|
| Volume | 23 litres |
| Boil volume | 27 litres |
| Alcohol | 5% (4.5% – 6.2%) |
| Bitterness / IBU | 42 IBU (30 – 45 IBU) |
| Colour | 20 EBC (10 – 28 EBC) |
| Original Gravity | 1.051 (1.045 – 1.060) |
| Final Gravity | 1.013 (1.010 – 1.015) |

### EXTRACT RECIPE:

Steep 200g of Caramel 60 in 27 litres of water at 65°C for half an hour. Remove and then add 2.7kg of light dried malt extract or 3.375kg of pale liquid malt extract and bring to the boil and add hops as normal to the boil.

# AMERICAN PALE ALE

The American Pale Ale was first created in the early 1980s and is distinguished by its American hop profile of grapefruit, pine, citrus or spice. A nice balance between malt and hops is accompanied by the typical 'punchy' hoppiness and a moderately dry, bitter finish. This is a refreshing and approachable style.

## CORE RECIPE / MAKE IT YOUR OWN

| MALT | Ideal qty | % | Overall qty kg | Qty min | Variance score | Qty max | max % | Impacts |
|---|---|---|---|---|---|---|---|---|
| Pale malt | 4.5kg | 90 | 5 | 4kg | | 5kg | 80 | ABV + colour |
| Caramel 60 | 500g | 10 | | 200g | | 800g | 15 | Colour + flavour |

**Mash in** at 64°C for 60min **Mash out** at 76°C for 10min

| HOP | Qty g | AA | Time | g min | Variance score | g max | Impacts | Alternatives |
|---|---|---|---|---|---|---|---|---|
| ❶ Chinook | 20 | 13 | 60 | 15 | | 20 | Aroma + bitterness | Brewers Gold |
| | | | | | | | | Columbus |
| | | | | | | | | Northern Brewer |
| ❷ Perle | 25 | 8.3 | 20 | 15 | | 30 | Aroma + bitterness | Challenger |
| | | | | | | | | Northern Brewer |
| ❸ Cascade | 60 | 5.8 | 0 | 30 | | 70 | Aroma | Amarillo |
| | | | | | | | | Centennial |
| | | | | | | | | Summit |

| YEAST | Temp °C Min | Temp °C Max | Condition / Wks 1st | Condition / Wks 2nd | Condition / Wks Bot | Alternative yeasts | Temp °C MIN | Temp °C MAX |
|---|---|---|---|---|---|---|---|---|
| MJ's M15 Empire Ale | 18 | 22 | 1-2 | 1-2 | 2 | Wyeast #1056 American Ale | 15 | 22 |

## ABOUT THIS BREW

| | |
|---|---|
| Volume | 23 litres |
| Boil volume | 27 litres |
| Alcohol | 4.5% (4.2% – 5.6%) |
| Bitterness / IBU | 16 IBU (15 – 20 IBU) |
| Colour | 10 EBC (6 – 10 EBC) |
| Original Gravity | 1.046 (1.042 – 1.055) |
| Final Gravity | 1.012 (1.006 – 1.012) |

### EXTRACT RECIPE:

Steep 350g honey malt and 200g of biscuit malt in 27 litres of water for half an hour. Remove and then add 2.4kg of light dried malt extract or 3kg of pale liquid malt extract, bring to the boil and add hops as normal to the boil.

# AMERICAN CREAM ALE

An ale version of the light, fizzy American lager style, the cream ale is a speciality of the eastern US, though examples can be found on the other side of the continent. It is medium-light bodied and smooth, gold in colour and low in bitterness; the speciality grain blend adds some complexity with a clean, sweet malt profile and a hint of buttered toast in the aroma and flavour. It is pretty hard to beat as a summertime thirst-quencher.

| CORE RECIPE | | | | MAKE IT YOUR OWN | | | | | |
|---|---|---|---|---|---|---|---|---|---|
| MALT | Ideal qty | % | Overall qty kg | Qty min | Variance score | Qty max | max % | Impacts | |
| Pale malt | 4kg | 89 | | 3.8kg | | 4.7kg | 90 | ABV + colour | |
| Honey malt | 350g | 8 | 4.47 | 200g | | 400g | 10 | Flavour | |
| Biscuit malt | 120g | 3 | | 100g | | 300g | 5 | Colour | |

**Mash in** at 64°C for 60min  **Mash out** at 76°C for 10min

| HOP | Qty g | AA | Time | g min | Variance score | g max | Impacts | Alternatives |
|---|---|---|---|---|---|---|---|---|
| ① Cluster | 20 | 7 | 60 | 20 | | 25 | Aroma + bitterness | Galena |
| | | | | | | | | Eroica |

| YEAST | Temp °C | | Condition / Wks | | | Alternative yeasts | Temp °C | |
|---|---|---|---|---|---|---|---|---|
| | Min | Max | 1st | 2nd | Bot | | MIN | MAX |
| MJ's M15 Empire Ale | 18 | 22 | 1 | 1 | 2 | Wyeast #1056 American Ale | 15 | 22 |

0

60
70
60

1

0

## ABOUT THIS BREW

| | |
|---|---|
| Volume | 23 litres |
| Boil volume | 27 litres |
| Alcohol | 5.5% (4.5% – 6.2%) |
| Bitterness / IBU | 34 IBU (25 – 40 IBU) |
| Colour | 22 EBC (20 – 33 EBC) |
| Original Gravity | 1.056 (1.045 – 1.060) |
| Final Gravity | 1.014 (1.010 – 1.015) |

### EXTRACT RECIPE:

Steep 500g of caramel 60 in 27 litres of water at 65°C for half an hour. Remove and then add 3kg of light dried malt extract or 3.75kg of pale liquid malt extract and bring to the boil and add hops as normal to the boil.

# AMERICAN AMBER ALE

One of the few styles that American brewers can legitimately call their own. Originating in California and the Pacific Northwest, this reddish-amber beer has a brings together brisk American hop flavours over a firm malty base. This style makes for a refreshing pint that is flavourful enough to enjoy year-round.

| CORE RECIPE | | | | MAKE IT YOUR OWN | | | | |
|---|---|---|---|---|---|---|---|---|
| MALT | Ideal qty | % | Overall qty kg | Qty min | Variance score | Qty max | max % | Impacts |
| Pale malt | 4kg | 73 | | 3kg | | 4.2kg | 80 | ABV + colour |
| Munich malt | 1kg | 18 | 5.5 | 100g | | 500g | 10 | ABV + flavour |
| Caramel 60L | 500g | 9 | | 500g | | 800g | 10 | Body + colour |

**Mash in** at 64°C for 60min  **Mash out** at 76°C for 10min

| HOP | Qty g | AA | Time | g min | Variance score | g max | Impacts | Alternatives |
|---|---|---|---|---|---|---|---|---|
| ① Cascade | 55 | 5.8 | 60 | 45 | | 60 | Aroma + bitterness | Amarillo |
| | | | | | | | | Centennial |
| | | | | | | | | Summit |
| ② Cascade | 30 | 5.8 | 1 | 20 | | 60 | Aroma | Amarillo |
| | | | | | | | | Centennial |
| | | | | | | | | Summit |

| YEAST | Temp °C | | Condition / Wks | | | Alternative yeasts | Temp °C | |
|---|---|---|---|---|---|---|---|---|
| | Min | Max | 1st | 2nd | Bot | | MIN | MAX |
| MJ's M15 Empire Ale | 18 | 22 | 1-2 | 1-2 | 2 | Wyeast #1056 American Ale | 22 | 25 |

## ABOUT THIS BREW

| | |
|---|---|
| Volume | 23 litres |
| Boil volume | 27 litres |
| Alcohol | 4.8% (4.3% – 6.2%) |
| Bitterness / IBU | 37 IBU (20 – 40 IBU) |
| Colour | 40 EBC (33 – 69 EBC) |
| Original Gravity | 1.049 (1.045 – 1.060) |
| Final Gravity | 1.012 (1.010 – 1.016) |

### EXTRACT RECIPE:

Steep 350g caramel 60, 250g of caramel 80L, 120g of pale chocolate malt and 120g of black malt in 27 litres of water for half an hour. Remove and then add 2.4kg of dried malt extract or 3.3kg of pale liquid malt extract, bring to the boil and add hops as normal to the boil.

# AMERICAN BROWN ALE

This American brown ale is about to become your new favourite beer. Dense layers of malt, caramel, baking chocolate, and a hint of light-roast coffee give way to reveal a hop character you'll be surprised to find if you're used to drinking English brown ale. The finish is complex but balanced.

| CORE RECIPE | | | | MAKE IT YOUR OWN | | | | |
|---|---|---|---|---|---|---|---|---|
| **MALT** | Ideal qty | % | Overall qty kg | Qty min | Variance score | Qty max | max % | Impacts |
| Pale malt | 4kg | 82 | | 4kg | | 5kg | 90 | ABV + colour |
| Caramel 60L | 350g | 7 | | 200g | | 700g | 15 | Colour + flavour |
| Caramel 80L | 250g | 5 | 4.84 | 200g | | 700g | 10 | Colour + flavour |
| Pale chocolate malt | 120g | 3 | | 100g | | 400g | 20 | Colour + aroma |
| Black malt | 120g | 3 | | 100g | | 300g | 10 | Colour + flavour |

Mash in at 64°C for 60min  Mash out at 76°C for 10min

| HOP | Qty g | AA | Time | g min | Variance score | g max | Impacts | Alternatives |
|---|---|---|---|---|---|---|---|---|
| ❶ East Kent Goldings | 30 | 5.5 | 60 | 10 | | 35 | Aroma + bitterness | Fuggles |
| | | | | | | | | Progress |
| | | | | | | | | First Gold |
| ❷ Liberty | 30 | 4 | 30 | 10 | | 35 | Aroma + bitterness | Hallertau |
| | | | | | | | | Tettnanger |
| | | | | | | | | Mt. Hood |
| ❸ Willamette | 30 | 5 | 15 | 10 | | 40 | Aroma | Styrian Golding |
| | | | | | | | | Target |
| | | | | | | | | Tettnanger |

| YEAST | Temp °C | | Condition / Wks | | | Alternative yeasts | Temp °C | |
|---|---|---|---|---|---|---|---|---|
| | Min | Max | 1st | 2nd | Bot | | MIN | MAX |
| MJ's  M15 Empire Ale | 18 | 22 | 1-2 | 1-2 | 2 | Wyeast #1332 Northwest Ale | 18 | 23 |

Mash 67°C
Mash out 74°C
Boil
0
60
70
60
30
15
0

## ABOUT THIS BREW

| Volume | 23 litres |
|---|---|
| Boil volume | 27 litres |
| Alcohol | 4.8% (4.5% – 5.5%) |
| Bitterness / IBU | 39 IBU (30 – 45 IBU) |
| Colour | 24 EBC (20 – 28 EBC) |
| Original Gravity | 1.049 (1.048 – 1.054) |
| Final Gravity | 1.012 (1.011 – 1.014) |

## EXTRACT RECIPE:

Steep 800g of caramel 60 in 27 litres of water at 65°C for half an hour. Remove and then add 3kg of light dried malt extract or 3.75kg of pale liquid malt extract and bring to the boil and add hops as normal to the boil.

# CALIFORNIA COMMON

California Common was an accidental discovery: residents of Gold Rush-era San Francisco wanted to drink Pilsner-style beers, but local brewers were hampered by primitive refrigeration techniques. The result was a hybrid style – an amber coloured beer with lager yeast but fermented at ale temperatures, and possibly America's first original contribution to the beer world. This style finishes dry and slightly crisp with a lingering bitterness. A subtle fruitiness may be present, but the California Common (or you may have seen it called a steam seer) is clean.

| CORE RECIPE | | | | MAKE IT YOUR OWN | | | | | |
|---|---|---|---|---|---|---|---|---|---|
| MALT | Ideal qty | % | Overall qty kg | Qty min | Variance score | Qty max | max % | Impacts | |
| Pale malt | 4kg | 83 | 4.8 | 4kg | | 4.4kg | 90 | ABV + colour | |
| Caramel 60 | 800g | 17 | | 500g | | 800g | 20 | Mouthfeel | |

Mash in at 64°C for 60min ▬ Mash out at 76°C for 10min

| HOP | Qty g | AA | Time | g min | Variance score | g max | Impacts | Alternatives |
|---|---|---|---|---|---|---|---|---|
| ❶ Northern Brewer | 20 | 9 | 60 | 15 | | 25 | Aroma + bitterness | Chinook |
| | | | | | | | | Columbus |
| | | | | | | | | Nugget |
| ❷ Northern Brewer | 15 | 9 | 15 | 10 | | 25 | Aroma + bitterness | Chinook |
| | | | | | | | | Columbus |
| | | | | | | | | Nugget |
| ❸ Northern Brewer | 15 | 9 | 5 | 10 | | 25 | Aroma | Chinook |
| | | | | | | | | Columbus |
| | | | | | | | | Nugget |
| ❹ Northern Brewer | 30 | 9 | 0 | 20 | | 40 | Aroma | Chinook |
| | | | | | | | | Columbus |
| | | | | | | | | Nugget |

| YEAST | Temp °C | | Condition / Wks | | | Alternative yeasts | Temp °C | |
|---|---|---|---|---|---|---|---|---|
| | Min | Max | 1st | 2nd | Bot | | MIN | MAX |
| MJ's M54 California Lager | 18 | 20 | 1-2 | 2-4 | 2 | Wyeast #2112 California Lager | 13 | 21 |

## ABOUT THIS BREW

| | |
|---|---|
| Volume | 23 litres |
| Boil volume | 27 litres |
| Alcohol | 57% (4.8% – 6.5%) |
| Bitterness / IBU | 44 IBU (25 – 50 IBU) |
| Colour | 60 EBC (44 – 70 EBC) |
| Original Gravity | 1.059 (1.048 – 1.065) |
| Final Gravity | 1.015 (1.012 – 1.016) |

### EXTRACT RECIPE:

Steep 400g of crystal 45 malt, 200g of roasted barley, 200g of black malt in 27 litres of water at 65°C for half an hour. Remove and then add 3kg of dried malt extract or 3.75kg or liquid malt extract and bring to the boil and add hops as normal to boil.

# AMERICAN PORTER

As with many American versions of traditional English styles, the American porter is an assertive interpretation of the 300-year-old English type. The American porter varies from one brewery's beer to the next but it is generally robust and strong with a fuller body, more hops and bitterness and a drier finish.

## CORE RECIPE

| MALT | Ideal qty | % | Overall qty kg |
|---|---|---|---|
| Pale malt | 5kg | 85 | |
| Crystal 45 | 400g | 7 | 5.8 |
| Roasted barley | 200g | 4 | |
| Black malt | 200g | 4 | |

## MAKE IT YOUR OWN

| Qty min | Variance score | Qty max | max % | Impacts |
|---|---|---|---|---|
| 4kg | | 5.5kg | 80 | ABV + colour |
| 300g | | 800g | 20 | Colour + flavour |
| 100g | | 400g | 10 | Colour + flavour |
| 100g | | 300g | 10 | Colour + aroma |

**Mash in** at 64°C for 60min • **Mash out** at 76°C for 10min

| HOP | Qty g | AA | Time | g min | Variance score | g max | Impacts | Alternatives |
|---|---|---|---|---|---|---|---|---|
| ① Nugget | 20 | 13.3 | 60 | 10 | | 25 | Aroma + bitterness | Cluster |
| | | | | | | | | Target |
| | | | | | | | | Brewers Gold |
| ② Willamette | 30 | 5 | 15 | 20 | | 45 | Aroma + bitterness | Styrian Golding |
| | | | | | | | | Target |
| | | | | | | | | Tettnanger |
| ③ Willamette | 20 | 5 | 15 | 20 | | 50 | Aroma | Styrian Golding |
| | | | | | | | | Target |
| | | | | | | | | Tettnanger |

| YEAST | Temp °C Min | Temp °C Max | Condition / Wks 1st | Condition / Wks 2nd | Condition / Wks Bot | Alternative yeasts | Temp °C MIN | Temp °C MAX |
|---|---|---|---|---|---|---|---|---|
| MJ's M44 US West Coast | 18 | 23 | 1-2 | 4 | 2 | Wyeast #1332 Northwest Ale | 17 | 22 |

Mash 67°C · Mash out 74°C · Boil

0 · 60 · 70 · 60 · 15 · 0

## ABOUT THIS BREW

| | |
|---|---|
| Volume | 23 litres |
| Boil volume | 27 litres |
| Alcohol | 6.3% (5% – 7%) |
| Bitterness / IBU | 47 IBU (35 – 75 IBU) |
| Colour | 70 EBC (60 – 80 EBC) |
| Original Gravity | 1.065 (1.050 – 1.075) |
| Final Gravity | 1.016 (1.010 – 1.022) |

### EXTRACT RECIPE:

Steep 350g of black malt, 250g of roasted barley, 250g of caramel 120 and 100g of Carafa II in 27 litres of water at 65°C for half an hour. Remove and then add 3.3kg of dried malt extract or 4.1kg or liquid malt extract and bring to the boil and add hops as normal to the boil.

# AMERICAN STOUT

Drawing inspiration from English and Irish stouts, American homebrewers and craft brewers have reshaped the American version to feature aggressive hopping of American hop varietals. The American stout displays assertive hop bitterness and roast character on top of a fairly strong, full-bodied base with a creamy mouthfeel.

## CORE RECIPE — MAKE IT YOUR OWN

| MALT | Ideal qty | % | Overall qty kg | Qty min | Variance score | Qty max | max % | Impacts |
|---|---|---|---|---|---|---|---|---|
| Pale malt | 5.5kg | 85 | | 4kg | | 6.5kg | 90 | ABV + colour |
| Black malt | 350g | 6 | | 250g | | 450g | 10 | Colour + flavour |
| Roasted barley | 250g | 4 | 6.45 | 200g | | 700g | 10 | Colour |
| Caramel 120 | 250g | 4 | | 200g | | 600g | 20 | Colour + aroma |
| Carafa III | 100g | 1 | | 100g | | 200g | 10 | Colour |

**Mash in** at 64°C for 60min  **Mash out** at 76°C for 10min

| HOP | Qty g | AA | Time | g min | Variance score | g max | Impacts | Alternatives |
|---|---|---|---|---|---|---|---|---|
| ❶ Willamette | 80 | 5 | 60 | 40 | | 130 | Aroma + bitterness | Styrian Golding |
| | | | | | | | | Target |
| | | | | | | | | Tettnanger |
| ❷ Cascade | 30 | 5.8 | 15 | 20 | | 120 | Aroma + bitterness | Perle |
| | | | | | | | | Admiral |
| | | | | | | | | Northdown |
| ❸ Cascade | 30 | 5.8 | 0 | 20 | | 120 | Aroma | Styrian Golding |
| | | | | | | | | Target |
| | | | | | | | | Tettnanger |

| YEAST | Temp °C Min | Temp °C Max | Condition / Wks 1st | 2nd | Bot | Alternative yeasts | Temp °C MIN | Temp °C MAX |
|---|---|---|---|---|---|---|---|---|
| MJ's M44 US West Coast | 18 | 23 | 1-2 | 4 | 2 | Wyeast #1332 Northwest Ale | 18 | 24 |

## ABOUT THIS BREW

| | |
|---|---|
| Volume | 23 litres |
| Boil volume | 27 litres |
| Alcohol | 6.5% (5.5% – 7.5%) |
| Bitterness / IBU | 50 IBU (40 – 70 IBU) |
| Colour | 18 EBC (12 – 30 EBC) |
| Original Gravity | 1.067 (1.056 – 1.075) |
| Final Gravity | 1.017 (1.010 – 1.018) |

### EXTRACT RECIPE:

Steep 800g of caramel 40 in 27 litres of water at 65°C for half an hour. Remove and then add 3.6kg of light dried malt extract or 4.5kg of pale liquid malt extract and bring to the boil and add hops as normal to the boil.

# AMERICAN IPA

A direct descendent of the English IPA, the American IPA is known for being hop-forward with assertive bitterness. American IPAs generally display American or New World hops which have citrus, pine, floral or spicy characteristics. Medium-bodied with a moderate maltiness it has a clean, dry and lingering bitter finish.

## CORE RECIPE / MAKE IT YOUR OWN

| MALT | Ideal qty | % | Overall qty kg | Qty min | Variance score | Qty max | max % | Impacts |
|---|---|---|---|---|---|---|---|---|
| Pale malt | 6kg | 92 | 6.5 | 5kg | | 6.8kg | 90 | ABV + colour |
| Caramel 40 | 500g | 9 | | 300g | | 1kg | 15 | ABV + colour |

**Mash in** at 64°C for 60min ▬ **Mash out** at 76°C for 10min

| HOP | Qty g | AA | Time | g min | Variance score | g max | Impacts | Alternatives |
|---|---|---|---|---|---|---|---|---|
| ❶ Centennial | 30 | 10.5 | 60 | 20 | | 40 | Aroma + bitterness | Amarillo / Cascade / Columbus |
| ❷ Centennial | 30 | 10.5 | 20 | 20 | | 40 | Aroma + bitterness | Amarillo / Cascade / Columbus |
| ❸ Centennial | 60 | 10.5 | 5 | 20 | | 80 | Aroma | Amarillo / Cascade / Columbus |
| ❹ Glacier | 30 | 10.5 | Dry hop | 30 | | 80 | Aroma | Amarillo / Cascade / Columbus |

| YEAST | Temp °C Min | Temp °C Max | Condition / Wks 1st | 2nd | Bot | Alternative yeasts | Temp °C MIN | Temp °C MAX |
|---|---|---|---|---|---|---|---|---|
| MJ's M44 West Coast IPA | 18 | 23 | 1-2 | 2-4 | 2 | Wyeast #1056 American Ale | 15 | 22 |

Mash 67°C
Mash out 74°C
0 / 60 / 70 / 60

Boil

❶
❷ 20
❸ 5
0

❹
Dry hop in secondary 1 week before packaging

## ABOUT THIS BREW

| | |
|---|---|
| Volume | 23 litres |
| Boil volume | 27 litres |
| Alcohol | 4.5% (4% – 5%) |
| Bitterness / IBU | 43 IBU (40 – 60 IBU) |
| Colour | 16 EBC (10 – 26 EBC) |
| Original Gravity | 1.044 (1.045 – 1.055) |
| Final Gravity | 1.012 (1.010 – 1.015) |

### EXTRACT RECIPE:

Steep 500g of caramel 40 in 27 litres of water at 65°C for half an hour. Remove and then add 2.4kg of light dried malt extract or 3kg of pale liquid malt extract and bring to the boil and add hops as normal to the boil.

# SESSION IPA

Bridging the gap between the classic American pale ale and West Coast IPA, this is a deliciously decadent session ale bursting with flavours. It's enticing and inviting appearance will open one's mind to prolonged sessions of sensual sipping pleasure. It pours a golden-amber, the seductive hop aroma gently gives way to a sturdy, yet flexible malt backbone with a delicate touch of silky caramel that supports the combination of juicy tropical and citrus hop flavour that follows, leading to a satisfying finish.

| CORE RECIPE | | | | MAKE IT YOUR OWN | | | | | |
|---|---|---|---|---|---|---|---|---|---|
| **MALT** | Ideal qty | % | Overall qty kg | Qty min | Variance score | Qty max | max % | Impacts | |
| **Pale malt (Maris Otter)** | 4kg | 89 | 4.5 | 3.5kg | | 4.5kg | 90 | ABV + colour | |
| **Caramel 40** | 500g | 11 | | 400g | | 800g | 15 | Colour + flavour | |

Mash in at 64°C for 60min — Mash out at 76°C for 10min

| HOP | Qty g | AA | Time | g min | Variance score | g max | Impacts | Alternatives |
|---|---|---|---|---|---|---|---|---|
| ❶ Centennial | 20 | 10.5 | 60 | 15 | | 30 | Aroma + bitterness | Amarillo |
| | | | | | | | | Cascade |
| | | | | | | | | Columbus |
| ❷ Cascade | 30 | 5.8 | 20 | 20 | | 40 | Aroma + bitterness | Amarillo |
| | | | | | | | | Centennial |
| | | | | | | | | Summit |
| ❸ Cascade | 30 | 5.8 | 10 | 20 | | 40 | Aroma | Amarillo |
| | | | | | | | | Centennial |
| | | | | | | | | Summit |
| ❹ Citra | 60 | 12 | 0 | 40 | | 70 | Aroma | Galaxy |
| | | | | | | | | Tarus |
| ❺ Citra | 30 | 12 | Dry hop | 20 | | 70 | Aroma | Centennial |
| ❻ Cascade | 30 | 5.8 | Dry hop | 20 | | 70 | Aroma | Galaxy |

| YEAST | Temp °C | | Condition / Wks | | | Alternative yeasts | Temp °C | |
|---|---|---|---|---|---|---|---|---|
| | Min | Max | 1st | 2nd | Bot | | MIN | MAX |
| **MJ's M44 West Coast IPA** | 18 | 23 | 2 | 2 | 2 | Wyeast #1272 American Ale II | 13 | 21 |

## ABOUT THIS BREW

| | |
|---|---|
| Volume | 23 litres |
| Boil volume | 27 litres |
| Alcohol | 6.4% |
| Bitterness / IBU | 29 IBU |
| Colour | 60 EBC |
| Original Gravity | 1.057 |
| Final Gravity | 1.014 |

# WEST COAST IPA

Boldly flavoured and colourfully hopped variant of IPA, which showcases the hop varieties of the US West Coast. There is plenty of tropical fruit (mango, lychee, papaya), resin/pine (a pine forest after a shower of rain perhaps) and the hint of allium (chive, leek, even garlic). The finish is dry and appetising.

### EXTRACT RECIPE:

Steep 500g of caramel 40 in 27 litres of water at 65°C for half an hour. Remove and then add 3.6kg of light dried malt extract or 4.5kg of pale liquid malt extract and bring to the boil and add hops as normal to the boil.

## CORE RECIPE / MAKE IT YOUR OWN

| MALT | Ideal qty | % | Overall qty kg | Qty min | Variance score | Qty max | max % | Impacts |
|---|---|---|---|---|---|---|---|---|
| Pale malt | 4kg | 62 | | 3.5kg | | 4.7kg | 80 | ABV + colour |
| Pale malt (Maris Otter) | 2kg | 30 | 6.5 | 1kg | | 3kg | 80 | ABV + colour |
| Caramel 60 | 500g | 8 | | 100g | | 600g | 15 | Colour |

▭▭▭ **Mash in** at 64°C for 60min ▬▬▬ **Mash out** at 76°C for 10min

| HOP | Qty g | AA | Time | g min | Variance score | g max | Impacts | Alternatives |
|---|---|---|---|---|---|---|---|---|
| ❶ Summit | 30 | 17.5 | 60 | 30 | | 50 | Aroma + bitterness | Amarillo / Cascade / Columbus |
| ❷ Cascade | 20 | 5.8 | 20 | 20 | | 40 | Aroma + bitterness | Amarillo / Centennial / Summit |
| ❸ Cascade | 60 | 5.8 | 10 | 30 | | 70 | Aroma | Amarillo / Centennial / Summit |
| ❹ Cascade | 120 | 5.8 | Dry hop | 80 | | 120 | Aroma | Amarillo / Centennial |

| YEAST | Temp °C Min | Temp °C Max | Condition / Wks 1st | 2nd | Bot | Alternative yeasts | Temp °C MIN | Temp °C MAX |
|---|---|---|---|---|---|---|---|---|
| MJ's M44 West Coast IPA | 18 | 23 | 1-2 | 2-3 | 2-3 | Wyeast #1272 American Ale II | 17 | 22 |

Mash 67°C

Mash out 74°C

Boil

❶ 60 / 70 / 60

❷ 20

❸ 10

❹ Dry hop in secondary 1 week before packaging

## ABOUT THIS BREW

| Volume | 23 litres |
| --- | --- |
| Boil volume | 27 litres |
| Alcohol | 7% (5.5% – 8%) |
| Bitterness / IBU | 69 IBU (50 – 75 IBU) |
| Colour | 20 EBC (12 – 26 EBC) |
| Original Gravity | 1.073 (1.056 – 1.075) |
| Final Gravity | 1.018 (1.010 – 1.018) |

# RYE IPA

Hefty in all respects, this IPA is full-bodied, hoppy, strong, and unique. When you take a sip, the beer opens with a bit of spicy hop flavour from the Mount. Hood first wort hops. The next thing that hits you is the bitterness from the Columbus. The flavour finishes with a back of the throat spiciness from the rye.

## CORE RECIPE / MAKE IT YOUR OWN

| MALT | Ideal qty | % | Overall qty kg | Qty min | Variance score | Qty max | max % | Impacts |
| --- | --- | --- | --- | --- | --- | --- | --- | --- |
| Pale malt | 5kg | 67 | | 4kg | | 5kg | 70 | ABV + colour |
| Rye malt | 1.4kg | 19 | | 1kg | | 1.6kg | 30 | Flavour + spice |
| Crystal 60 | 500g | 6 | 7.4 | 500g | | 800g | 10 | Colour + flavour |
| Carapils | 250g | 4 | | 200g | | 400g | 20 | Colour |
| White wheat malt | 250g | 4 | | 200g | | 400g | 10 | Flavour + head retention |

**Mash in** at 64°C for 60min · **Mash out** at 76°C for 10min

| HOP | Qty g | AA | Time | g min | Variance score | g max | Impacts | Alternatives |
| --- | --- | --- | --- | --- | --- | --- | --- | --- |
| ❶ Mt Hood | 30 | 6 | 60 | 15 | | 30 | Aroma + bitterness | Strisselpalt |
| | | | | | | | | Hallertau |
| | | | | | | | | Hersbruker |
| ❷ Columbus | 30 | 15 | 60 | 15 | | 30 | Aroma + bitterness | Chinook |
| | | | | | | | | Galena |
| | | | | | | | | Nugget |
| ❸ Mt Hood | 30 | 6 | 30 | 20 | | 40 | Aroma + bitterness | Strisselpalt |
| | | | | | | | | Hallertau |
| | | | | | | | | Hersbruker |
| ❹ Mt Hood | 30 | 6 | 0 | 20 | | 40 | Aroma | Strisselpalt |
| | | | | | | | | Hallertau |
| | | | | | | | | Hersbruker |
| ❺ Columbus | 30 | 15 | Dry hop | 20 | | 60 | Aroma | Chinook |
| | | | | | | | | Galena |
| | | | | | | | | Nugget |

| YEAST | Temp °C Min | Temp °C Max | Condition / Wks 1st | Condition / Wks 2nd | Condition / Wks Bot | Alternative yeasts | Temp °C MIN | Temp °C MAX |
| --- | --- | --- | --- | --- | --- | --- | --- | --- |
| MJ's M44 West Coast IPA | 18 | 23 | 1-2 | 4 | 2 | Wyeast #1272 American Ale II | 17 | 24 |

## ABOUT THIS BREW

| Volume | 23 litres |
|---|---|
| Boil volume | 27 litres |
| Alcohol | 5.6% (5.5% – 9%) |
| Bitterness / IBU | 25 IBU (50 – 90 IBU) |
| Colour | 50 EBC (40 – 80 EBC) |
| Original Gravity | 1.062 (1.050 – 1.085) |
| Final Gravity | 1.016 (1.010 – 1.018) |

### EXTRACT RECIPE:

Steep 250g caramel 80, 170g of Carafa III and 170 of chocolate malt in 27 litres of water for half an hour. Remove and then add 3.3kg of light dried malt extract or 4.1kg of Maris Otter pale liquid malt extract, bring to the boil and add hops as normal to the boil.

# BLACK IPA

An ebony-hued tipple topped with a beige head and surrounded by an aromatic citrus-and-pine force field, backed by a smooth roastiness redolent of cocoa and French roast coffee. Full-bodied, hop-bitter, and boozy, this beer is compelling enough to both fuel and quash the argument of its stylistic integrity, and it goes great with a blue-cheese stuffed sirloin burger or steak.

//////////////////////////////////////////

**ADJUNCTS:** 500g of corn sugar is added at the end of the boil to increase alcoholic strength. ●

## CORE RECIPE      MAKE IT YOUR OWN

| MALT | Ideal qty | % | Overall qty kg | Qty min | Variance score | Qty max | max % | Impacts |
|---|---|---|---|---|---|---|---|---|
| Pale malt | 5.5kg | 90 | | 5kg | | 6.5kg | 80 | ABV + colour |
| Caramel 80L | 250g | 4 | 6.09 | 250g | | 500g | 10 | Colour + flavour |
| Carafa III | 170g | 3 | | 100g | | 300g | 10 | Colour |
| Chocolate malt | 170g | 3 | | 100g | | 300g | 10 | Colour + aroma |

═══ **Mash in** at 64°C for 60min ═══ **Mash out** at 76°C for 10min

| HOP | Qty g | AA | Time | g min | Variance score | g max | Impacts | Alternatives |
|---|---|---|---|---|---|---|---|---|
| ❶ Summit | 25 | 17.5 | 60 | 15 | | 30 | Aroma + bitterness | Amarillo |
| | | | | | | | | Cascade |
| ❷ Chinook | 30 | 13 | 15 | 15 | | 35 | Aroma + bitterness | Brewers Gold |
| | | | | | | | | Columbus |
| ❸ Centennial | 30 | 10.5 | 10 | 15 | | 35 | Aroma | Amarillo |
| | | | | | | | | Cascade |
| ❹ Cascade | 30 | 5.8 | 5 | 20 | | 40 | Aroma | Amarillo |
| | | | | | | | | Centennial |
| ❺ Centennial | 30 | 10.5 | 0 | 20 | | 40 | Aroma | Amarillo |
| | | | | | | | | Cascade |
| ❻ Cascade | 30 | 5.8 | Dry hop | 30 | | 40 | Aroma | Amarillo |
| | | | | | | | | Centennial |

| Corn sugar | 500g | | 0 | |
|---|---|---|---|---|

| YEAST | Temp °C Min | Temp °C Max | Condition / Wks 1st | 2nd | Bot | Alternative yeasts | Temp °C MIN | Temp °C MAX |
|---|---|---|---|---|---|---|---|---|
| MJ's M44 West Coast IPA | 18 | 23 | 1-2 | 1-2 | 2 | Wyeast #1272 American Ale Yeast II | 15 | 22 |

Mash 67°C
Mash out 74°C
0
60
70
60
①
Boil
② 15
③ 10
④ 5
⑤ 0
⑥
Dry hop in secondary 1 week before packaging

Mash 67°C

Mash out 76°C

0

60
70
60

❶

Boil

❷ 10

❸ 0
## ABOUT THIS BREW

| | |
|---|---|
| Volume | 23 litres |
| Boil volume | 27 litres |
| Alcohol | 8.9% |
| Bitterness / IBU | 74 IBU |
| Colour | 80 EBC |
| Original Gravity | 1.092 |
| Final Gravity | 1.023 |

### EXTRACT RECIPE:

Steep 500g of crystal 60 and 500g of Carafa III in 27 litres of water at 65°C for half an hour. Remove and then add 4.8kg of light dried malt extract or 6kg of pale liquid malt extract and bring to the boil and add hops as normal in boil.

# IMPERIAL BLACK IPA

While not a standard style, the appearance of the imperial black IPA is indicative of modern beer's desire to push the boundaries of what was once known. Dark, hoppy and just overall colossal, it features an intense rush of hops and roastiness over top of a potent, full-bodied ale.

| CORE RECIPE | | | | MAKE IT YOUR OWN | | | | | |
|---|---|---|---|---|---|---|---|---|---|
| MALT | Ideal qty | % | Overall qty kg | Qty min | Variance score | Qty max | max % | Impacts | |
| Pale malt | 8kg | 90 | | 6.5kg | | 8.5kg | 90 | ABV + colour | |
| Crystal 60 | 500g | 5 | 9 | 300g | | 800g | 10 | Colour + flavour | |
| Carafa III | 500g | 5 | | 300g | | 500g | 10 | Colour | |

**Mash in** at 64°C for 60min **Mash out** at 76°C for 10min

| HOP | Qty g | AA | Time | g min | Variance score | g max | Impacts | Alternatives |
|---|---|---|---|---|---|---|---|---|
| ❶ Columbus | 50 | 15 | 60 | 30 | | 80 | Aroma + bitterness | Magnum |
| | | | | | | | | Chinook |
| | | | | | | | | Northern Brewer |
| ❷ Citra | 50 | 12 | 10 | 30 | | 50 | Aroma | Simcoe |
| ❸ Citra | 60 | 12 | 0 | 30 | | 70 | Aroma | Simcoe |

| YEAST | Temp °C | | Condition / Wks | | | Alternative yeasts | Temp °C | |
|---|---|---|---|---|---|---|---|---|
| | Min | Max | 1st | 2nd | Bot | | MIN | MAX |
| MJ's M44 West Coast IPA | 18 | 23 | 2 | 6-8 | 2 | Wyeast #1272 American Ale Yeast II | 15 | 22 |

HB100
174

## ABOUT THIS BREW

| Volume | 23 litres |
|---|---|
| Boil volume | 27 litres |
| Alcohol | 6.1% (5.5% – 7.5%) |
| Bitterness / IBU | 65 IBU (40 – 70 IBU) |
| Colour | 38 EBC (22 – 38 EBC) |
| Original Gravity | 1.063 (1.056 – 1.070) |
| Final Gravity | 1.016 (1.008 – 1.016) |

### EXTRACT RECIPE:

Steep 200g pale chocolate malt, 500g of crystal 60 in 27 litres of water for half an hour. Remove and then add 3.3kg of dried malt extract or 4.1kg of liquid malt extract, bring to the boil and add hops as normal to the boil.

# RED IPA

A modern craft beer variant, the red IPA draws on the hop character of a standard American IPA while incorporating the malt flavours of an American amber ale. A hoppy, fruity character from New World hops couples with a firm bitterness on top of caramel or dark fruit from the malts.

## CORE RECIPE / MAKE IT YOUR OWN

| MALT | Ideal qty | % | Overall qty kg | Qty min | Variance score | Qty max | max % | Impacts |
|---|---|---|---|---|---|---|---|---|
| Pale malt | 5.5kg | 89 | | 4.5kg | | 6kg | 90 | ABV + colour |
| Crystal 60 | 500g | 8 | 6.2 | 300g | | 800g | 15 | Colour + flavour |
| Chocolate malt | 200g | 3 | | 100g | | 400g | 10 | Colour |

**Mash in** at 64°C for 60min     **Mash out** at 76°C for 10min

| HOP | Qty g | AA | Time | g min | Variance score | g max | Impacts | Alternatives |
|---|---|---|---|---|---|---|---|---|
| ① Columbus | 40 | 15 | 60 | 20 | | 60 | Aroma + bitterness | Magnum |
| | | | | | | | | Chinook |
| | | | | | | | | Northern Brewer |
| ② Cascade | 15 | 5.8 | 30 | 10 | | 30 | Aroma + bitterness | Amarillo |
| | | | | | | | | Centennial |
| | | | | | | | | Summit |
| ③ Cascade | 40 | 5.8 | 0 | 20 | | 100 | Aroma | Amarillo |
| | | | | | | | | Centennial |
| | | | | | | | | Summit |
| ④ Cascade | 40 | 5.8 | Dry hop | 20 | | 100 | Aroma | Amarillo |
| | | | | | | | | Centennial |
| | | | | | | | | Summit |

| YEAST | Temp °C Min | Max | Condition / Wks 1st | 2nd | Bot | Alternative yeasts | Temp °C MIN | MAX |
|---|---|---|---|---|---|---|---|---|
| MJ's M44 West Coast IPA | 18 | 23 | 1-2 | 1-2 | 2 | Wyeast #1272 American Ale Yeast II | 15 | 22 |

Mash 67°C

Mash out 74°C

70
60

60

Boil

30

0

Dry hop in secondary 1 week before packaging

Mash 67°C

0

Mash out 74°C

60
70
60

① 

Boil

② 30

③ 20

④ 15

⑤ 10

⑥ 5

0

⑦

Dry hop in secondary 1 week before packaging

## ABOUT THIS BREW

| | |
|---|---|
| Volume | 23 litres |
| Boil volume | 27 litres |
| Alcohol | 6.1% (5.5% – 7%) |
| Bitterness / IBU | 66 IBU (40 – 70 IBU) |
| Colour | 10 EBC (10 – 16 EBC) |
| Original Gravity | 1.063 (1.056 – 1.065) |
| Final Gravity | 1.016 (1.010 – 1.016) |

# WHITE IPA

At first glance, this beer looks like a witbier, but spindrifts of American hop flavour and aromas abound. A traditional witbier grain bill and yeast strain is coupled with US West Coast hops and yields a wonderfully complex India White Ale. A slight spice and tartness from the yeast intermingling with citrus notes from abundant hop additions complement the silky smooth body created by flaked oats and unmalted wheat.

## CORE RECIPE / MAKE IT YOUR OWN

| MALT | Ideal qty | % | Overall qty kg | Qty min | Variance score | Qty max | max % | Impacts |
|---|---|---|---|---|---|---|---|---|
| Pale malt | 3.5kg | 56 | | 3kg | | 4.5kg | 80 | ABV + colour |
| White wheat malt | 2kg | 32 | 6.2 | 2kg | | 2.5kg | 50 | ABV + colour |
| Unmalted wheat | 350g | 6 | | 200g | | 400g | 10 | Body |
| Flaked oats | 350g | 6 | | 200g | | 400g | 5 | Mouthfeel |

**Mash in** at 64°C for 60min **Mash out** at 76°C for 10min

| HOP | Qty g | AA | Time | g min | Variance score | g max | Impacts | Alternatives |
|---|---|---|---|---|---|---|---|---|
| ❶ Summit | 15 | 17.5 | 60 | 10 | | 20 | Aroma + bitterness | Amarillo |
| | | | | | | | | Cascade |
| | | | | | | | | Columbus |
| ❷ Centennial | 15 | 10.5 | 30 | 10 | | 20 | Aroma + bitterness | Amarillo |
| | | | | | | | | Cascade |
| | | | | | | | | Columbus |
| ❸ Amarillo | 15 | 9 | 20 | 10 | | 20 | Aroma + bitterness | Cascade |
| | | | | | | | | Centennial |
| | | | | | | | | Simcoe |
| ❹ Centennial | 15 | 10.5 | 15 | 10 | | 20 | Aroma + bitterness | Amarillo |
| | | | | | | | | Cascade |
| | | | | | | | | Columbus |
| ❺ Amarillo | 30 | 9 | 10 | 20 | | 40 | Aroma | Cascade |
| | | | | | | | | Centennial |
| | | | | | | | | Simcoe |
| ❻ Centennial | 15 | 10.5 | 5 | 10 | | 30 | Aroma | Cascade |
| ❼ Galaxy | 30 | 14.2 | Dry hop | 30 | | 50 | Aroma | Citra |

| YEAST | Temp °C Min | Max | Condition / Wks 1st | 2nd | Bot | Alternative yeasts | Temp °C MIN | MAX |
|---|---|---|---|---|---|---|---|---|
| MJ's M21 Belgian Wit | 18 | 23 | 2 | 2-4 | 2 | Wyeast #3944 Belgian Wit | 16 | 24 |

# DOUBLE IPA

## ABOUT THIS BREW

| | |
|---|---|
| Volume | 23 litres |
| Boil volume | 27 litres |
| Alcohol | 8% (7.5% – 10% |
| Bitterness / IBU | 111 IBU (60 – 120 IBU) |
| Colour | 20 EBC (12 – 24 EBC) |
| Original Gravity | 1.083 (1.056 – 1.070) |
| Final Gravity | 1.014 (1.008 – 1.018) |

### EXTRACT RECIPE:

Steep 350g Caramel Pils malt, 200g of caramel 120 in 27 litres of water for half an hour. Remove and then add 4.5kg of light dried malt extract or 5.6kg of Maris Otter pale liquid malt extract, bring to the boil and add hops as normal to the boil.

The DIPA is generally a more malt, more hops, more alcohol, more everything version of the American IPA and an intense demonstration of American hops. While 'double' does not mean 'double the strength' these are definitely not session beers but rather a creamy, hoppy, and rich American-style IPA.

## CORE RECIPE

| MALT | Ideal qty | % | Overall qty kg | Qty min | Variance score | Qty max | max % | Impacts |
|---|---|---|---|---|---|---|---|---|
| Pale malt (Maris Otter) | 7.5kg | 93 | | 7kg | | 8.5kg | 95 | ABV + colour |
| Caramel Pils | 350g | 4 | 8.05 | 300g | | 500g | 10 | Flavour |
| Caramel 120 | 200g | 3 | | 100g | | 300g | 10 | Colour |

## MAKE IT YOUR OWN

**Mash in** at 64°C for 60min **Mash out** at 76°C for 10min

| HOP | Qty g | AA | Time | g min | Variance score | g max | Impacts | Alternatives |
|---|---|---|---|---|---|---|---|---|
| ❶ Summit | 60 | 17.5 | 60 | 30 | | 65 | Bitterness | Amarillo |
| | | | | | | | | Cascade |
| | | | | | | | | Simcoe |
| ❷ Centennial | 30 | 10.5 | 60 | 20 | | 50 | Bitterness | Amarillo |
| | | | | | | | | Cascade |
| | | | | | | | | Columbus |
| ❸ Cascade | 30 | 5.8 | 30 | 20 | | 50 | Aroma + bitterness | Amarillo |
| | | | | | | | | Centennial |
| | | | | | | | | Summit |
| ❹ Glacier | 60 | 5.6 | 0 | 40 | | 70 | Aroma | Fuggles |
| | | | | | | | | Willamette |
| | | | | | | | | Styrian Golding |
| ❺ Cascade | 60 | 5.8 | Dry hop | 40 | | 70 | Aroma | Amarillo |
| | | | | | | | | Centennial |
| | | | | | | | | Summit |

| YEAST | Temp °C Min | Temp °C Max | Condition / Wks 1st | Condition / Wks 2nd | Condition / Wks Bot | Alternative yeasts | Temp °C MIN | Temp °C MAX |
|---|---|---|---|---|---|---|---|---|
| MJ's M44 West Coast IPA | 18 | 23 | 1-2 | 6-8 | 2 | Wyeast #1056 American Ale | 17 | 22 |

Mash 67°C

Mash out 74°C

❶ 60
❷ 70
60

Boil ❸ 30

❹ 0

❺

Dry hop in secondary 1 week before packaging

## ABOUT THIS BREW

| Volume | 23 litres |
|---|---|
| Boil volume | 27 litres |
| Alcohol | 6.2% |
| Bitterness / IBU | 45 IBU |
| Colour | 14 EBC |
| Original Gravity | 1.064 |
| Final Gravity | 1.016 |

### EXTRACT RECIPE:

Steep 250g of Cara 20 and 110g of caramel 20 in 27 litres of water at 65°C for half an hour. Remove and then add 3.6kg of dried malt extract or 4.5kg or liquid malt extract and bring to the boil and add hops as normal to the boil.

# GRAPEFRUIT IPA

This bright showcase of apricot, peach, cantaloupe and lemon dives into crisp grapefruit flavour. A perfect complement to citrusy hop aroma, this IPA has stripes of ruby red grapefruit and hoppy, lingering bitterness.

/ / / / / / / / / / / / / / / / / / / / / / / / /

**ADJUNCTS:** Add 50g of grapefruit peel when dry hopping.

## CORE RECIPE / MAKE IT YOUR OWN

| MALT | Ideal qty | % | Overall qty kg | Qty min | Variance score | Qty max | max % | Impacts |
|---|---|---|---|---|---|---|---|---|
| Pale malt | 6kg | 94 | 6.36 | 5.5kg | | 7kg | 95 | ABV + colour |
| Cara 20 | 250g | 4 | | 200g | | 500g | 10 | Colour + flavour |
| Caramel 20 | 110g | 2 | | 100g | | 300g | 10 | Colour + flavour |

▭ **Mash in** at 64°C for 60min ▬ **Mash out** at 76°C for 10min

| HOP | Qty g | AA | Time | g min | Variance score | g max | Impacts | Alternatives |
|---|---|---|---|---|---|---|---|---|
| ❶ Chinook | 15 | 13 | 60 | 10 | | 25 | Bitterness | Brewers Gold |
| | | | | | | | | Columbus |
| | | | | | | | | Northern Brewer |
| ❷ Cascade | 15 | 5.8 | 20 | 10 | | 25 | Aroma + bitterness | Amarillo |
| | | | | | | | | Centennial |
| | | | | | | | | Summit |
| ❸ Chinook | 15 | 13 | 20 | 10 | | 25 | Aroma + bitterness | Brewers Gold |
| | | | | | | | | Columbus |
| | | | | | | | | Northern Brewer |
| ❹ Amarillo | 30 | 9 | 5 | 20 | | 45 | Aroma | Amarillo |
| | | | | | | | | Cascade |
| ❺ Chinook | 15 | 13 | 5 | 10 | | 25 | Aroma | Brewers Gold |
| | | | | | | | | Columbus |
| ❻ Cascade | 30 | 5.8 | Dry hop | 20 | | 45 | Aroma | Amarillo |
| ❼ Simcoe | 30 | 13 | Dry hop | 20 | | 35 | | Northern Brewer |
| Grapefruit | 50g | | Dry hop | | | | | |

| YEAST | Temp °C Min | Temp °C Max | Condition / Wks 1st | 2nd | Bot | Alternative yeasts | Temp °C MIN | Temp °C MAX |
|---|---|---|---|---|---|---|---|---|
| MJ's M44 West Coast IPA | 18 | 23 | 1-2 | 2-4 | 2 | Wyeast #1056 American Ale | 16 | 24 |

## ABOUT THIS BREW

| | |
|---|---|
| Volume | 23 litres |
| Boil volume | 27 litres |
| Alcohol | 7.3% |
| Bitterness / IBU | 59 IBU |
| Colour | 20 EBC |
| Original Gravity | 1.076 |
| Final Gravity | 1.019 |

### EXTRACT RECIPE:

Steep 250g of caramel 40 and caramel 80 in 27 litres of water for half an hour. Remove and then add 3.9kg of light dried malt extract or 4.8kg of pale liquid malt extract, bring to the boil and add hops as normal to the boil, adding the corn sugar at 10 minutes from the end.

# MOSIAC IPA

Mosaic is the icon of single-hop complexity and bursts with grapefruit, pineapple-mango and herbal vividness, letting a kaleidoscope of tantalising citrus, pine, tropical fruit, and berry notes decorate each golden-copper hued glass. Meanwhile, the arrangement of malts lends subtle caramel sweetness to a modest, bready backbone. There is also an appetising bitterness for a refreshing, hop-forward finish. Other hops suitable for single hop brews include Chinook, Centennial and Ella.

**ADJUNCTS:** 500g of corn sugar added at 10 minutes form the end adds to the alcohol and sweetness.

| CORE RECIPE | | | | MAKE IT YOUR OWN | | | | |
|---|---|---|---|---|---|---|---|---|
| MALT | Ideal qty | % | Overall qty kg | Qty min | Variance score | Qty max | max % | Impacts |
| Pale malt | 5.5kg | 81 | 6.75 | 5kg | | 6kg | 90 | ABV + colour |
| Vienna malt | 750g | 11 | | 100g | | 500g | 10 | Colour + flavour |
| Caramel 40 | 250g | 4 | | 100g | | 400g | 10 | Colour + aroma |
| Caramel 80 | 250g | 4 | | 100g | | 300g | 20 | Colour + aroma |

**Mash in** at 64°C for 60min  **Mash out** at 76°C for 10min

| HOP | Qty g | AA | Time | g min | Variance score | g max | Impacts | Alternatives |
|---|---|---|---|---|---|---|---|---|
| ① Mosiac | 30 | 12.7 | 60 | 20 | | 40 | Aroma + bitterness | Simcoe |
| ② Mosiac | 30 | 12.7 | 30 | 20 | | 40 | Aroma + bitterness | Simcoe |
| ③ Mosiac | 60 | 12.7 | 0 | 50 | | 70 | Aroma | Simcoe |
| ④ Mosiac | 60 | 12.7 | Dry hop | 50 | | 70 | Aroma | Simcoe |

| Corn sugar | 500g | 10 |
|---|---|---|

| YEAST | Temp °C | | Condition / Wks | | | Alternative yeasts | Temp °C | |
|---|---|---|---|---|---|---|---|---|
| | Min | Max | 1st | 2nd | Bot | | MIN | MAX |
| MJ's M42 Strong Ale | 16 | 22 | 1-2 | 2-4 | 2 | Wyeast #1335 British Ale | 17 | 24 |

Mash 67°C

Mash out 74°C

0

60
70
60

① Boil

② 30

10

③ 0

④ Dry hop in secondary 1 week before packaging

## ABOUT THIS BREW

| | |
|---|---|
| Volume | 23 litres |
| Boil volume | 27 litres |
| Alcohol | 4.5% (4% – 5.5%) |
| Bitterness / IBU | 20 IBU (10 – 25 IBU) |
| Colour | 11 EBC (6 – 12 EBC) |
| Original Gravity | 1.047 (1.040 – 1.055) |
| Final Gravity | 1.012 (1.008 – 1.013) |

### EXTRACT RECIPE:

Steep 350g of caramel 40 in 27 litres of water at 65°C for half an hour. Remove and then add 3kg of liquid rye malt and bring to the boil and add hops as normal to the boil.

# AMERICAN RYE ALE

Until late, using rye has been a bit of a novelty in American brewing. American rye ales all have a notable amount of rye in the grain bill which gives the beer a slick texture and spicy taste. A modest bitterness lets the character of the rye shine through.

## CORE RECIPE / MAKE IT YOUR OWN

| MALT | Ideal qty | % | Overall qty kg | Qty min | Variance score | Qty-max | max % | Impacts |
|---|---|---|---|---|---|---|---|---|
| Pale malt | 3.5kg | 75 | | 3kg | | 4kg | 80 | ABV + colour |
| Rye malt | 800g | 17 | 4.65 | 500g | | 1.3kg | 30 | Flavour |
| Caramel 40L | 350g | 8 | | 100g | | 350g | 10 | Colour |

**Mash in** at 64°C for 60min **Mash out** at 76°C for 10min

| HOP | Qty g | AA | Time | g min | Variance score | g max | Impacts | Alternatives |
|---|---|---|---|---|---|---|---|---|
| ❶ Liberty | 20 | 4 | 60 | 15 | | 35 | Aroma + bitterness | Hallertau |
| | | | | | | | | Tettnanger |
| | | | | | | | | Mt. Hood |
| ❷ Cascade | 30 | 5.8 | 15 | 20 | | 50 | Aroma | Amarillo |
| | | | | | | | | Centennial |
| | | | | | | | | Summit |

| YEAST | Temp °C Min | Temp °C Max | Condition / Wks 1st | 2nd | Bot | Alternative yeasts | Temp °C MIN | Temp °C MAX |
|---|---|---|---|---|---|---|---|---|
| MJ's M15 Empire Ale | 18 | 22 | 2 | 1-2 | 2 | Wyeast #1056 American Ale | 15 | 22 |

Mash 67°C

Mash out 76°C

Boil

❶

0
60
70
60

❷ 15

0

## ABOUT THIS BREW

| | |
|---|---|
| Volume | 23 litres |
| Boil volume | 27 litres |
| Alcohol | 5.7% |
| Bitterness / IBU | 38 IBU |
| Colour | 28 EBC |
| Original Gravity | 1.059 |
| Final Gravity | 1.015 |

### EXTRACT RECIPE:

Steep 350g caramel 60 and 250g of Belgian Special B in 27 litres of water for half an hour. Remove and then add 3.3kg of dried malt extract or 4.1kg of liquid malt extract, bring to the boil and add hops as normal to the boil.

# AMERICAN RED ALE

The American red ale is a bog and bold beer, with floral and citrus aromas. A balanced citrus bite comes from Chinook and Cascade hops followed shortly by mild, fruity esters from the ale yeast.

/ / / / / / / / / / / / / / / / / / / / / / / / / / / / / / / /

**NOTES:** A 90-minute boil is recommended for this recipe. Add the hops as normal from 60 minutes.

## CORE RECIPE / MAKE IT YOUR OWN

| MALT | Ideal qty | % | Overall qty kg | Qty min | Variance score | Qty max | max % | Impacts |
|---|---|---|---|---|---|---|---|---|
| Pale malt | 5.5kg | 90 | | 5kg | | 6kg | 80 | ABV + colour |
| Caramel 60L | 350g | 6 | 6.1 | 200g | | 500g | 10 | Mouthfeel |
| Belgian Special B | 250g | 4 | | 100g | | 300g | 10 | Colour |

**Mash in** at 64°C for 90min ▬ **Mash out** at 76°C for 10min

| HOP | Qty g | AA | Time | g min | Variance score | g max | Impacts | Alternatives |
|---|---|---|---|---|---|---|---|---|
| ❶ Columbus | 15 | 15 | 60 | 10 | | 30 | Bitterness | Chinook |
| | | | | | | | | Galena |
| | | | | | | | | Nugget |
| ❷ Chinook | 15 | 13 | 20 | 10 | | 30 | Aroma + bitterness | Brewers Gold |
| | | | | | | | | Columbus |
| | | | | | | | | Northern Brewer |
| ❸ Cascade | 30 | 5.8 | 5 | 20 | | 40 | Aroma | Amarillo |
| | | | | | | | | Centennial |
| | | | | | | | | Summit |
| ❹ Citra | 30 | 12 | Dry hop | 20 | | 70 | Aroma | Galaxy |
| | | | | | | | | Tarus |
| ❺ Chinook | 30 | 13 | Dry hop | 20 | | 70 | Aroma | Brewers Gold |
| | | | | | | | | Columbus |
| | | | | | | | | Northern Brewer |

| YEAST | Temp °C Min | Temp °C Max | Condition / Wks 1st | 2nd | Bot | Alternative yeasts | Temp °C MIN | Temp °C MAX |
|---|---|---|---|---|---|---|---|---|
| MJ's M15 Empire Ale | 18 | 22 | 1-2 | 2-4 | 2 | Wyeast #1056 American Ale | 15 | 22 |

Mash 67°C · Mash out 74°C · 0 · 60 · 70 · 90

Boil · 60 · 20 · 5 · 0

Dry hop in secondary 1 week before packaging

Mash 67°C  
Mash out 76°C  
Boil

0
60
70
60
① 
② 15
0

## ABOUT THIS BREW

| | |
|---|---|
| Volume | 23 litres |
| Boil volume | 27 litres |
| Alcohol | 5% (4% – 5.5%) |
| Bitterness / IBU | 26 IBU (15 – 30 IBU) |
| Colour | 6 EBC (6 – 12 EBC) |
| Original Gravity | 1.052 (1.040 – 1.055) |
| Final Gravity | 1.013 (1.008 – 1.013) |

### EXTRACT RECIPE:

Add 3.75kg of liquid wheat malt extract and bring to the boil and add hops as normal to the boil.

# AMERICAN WHEAT

Like their German cousins, American wheat beers feature large proportions of malted wheat and are naturally a bit cloudy in appearance. American wheat beers have a bit more hop character and a clean, neutral finish. With a spicy noble hop aroma and tart finish, it's a spritzy, refreshing crowd-pleaser.

| CORE RECIPE | | | | MAKE IT YOUR OWN | | | | | |
|---|---|---|---|---|---|---|---|---|---|
| MALT | Ideal qty | % | Overall qty kg | Qty min | Variance score | Qty max | max % | Impacts | |
| White wheat malt | 2.5kg | 50 | 5 | 2kg | | 2.5kg | 60 | ABV + flavour | |
| Pale malt | 2.5kg | 50 | | 2kg | | 2.5kg | 60 | ABV + flavour | |

**Mash in** at 64°C for 60min **Mash out** at 76°C for 10min

| HOP | Qty g | AA | Time | g min | Variance score | g max | Impacts | Alternatives |
|---|---|---|---|---|---|---|---|---|
| ❶ Willamette | 30 | 5 | 60 | 15 | | 55 | Aroma + bitterness | Hallertauer |
| | | | | | | | | Liberty |
| ❷ Cascade | 30 | 5.8 | 15 | 20 | | 43 | Aroma + bitterness | Amarillo |
| | | | | | | | | Centennial |
| | | | | | | | | Summit |

| YEAST | Temp °C | | Condition / Wks | | | Alternative yeasts | Temp °C | |
|---|---|---|---|---|---|---|---|---|
| | Min | Max | 1st | 2nd | Bot | | MIN | MAX |
| MJ's M20 Bavarian Wheat | 18 | 30 | 1-2 | 1-2 | 2 | Wyeast #1010 American Wheat | 14 | 23 |

## ABOUT THIS BREW

| | |
|---|---|
| Volume | 23 litres |
| Boil volume | 27 litres |
| Alcohol | 4.9% |
| Bitterness / IBU | 23 IBU |
| Colour | 20 EBC |
| Original Gravity | 1.051 |
| Final Gravity | 1.013 |

# PUMPKIN ALE

Autumn and a homebrewer's thoughts turn to capturing the experience of the season: crisp nights, colourful leaves, and ripe gourds being turned into pie. Clean and sweetly malty with just enough hop bitterness as balance and no hop aroma to mask the spices. A dose at the shutdown of the boil imbues the beer with a complex, lingering spice profile full of nutmeg, cinnamon, and ginger.

**ADJUNCTS:** Add 1tsp of pumpkin pie spice (ground ginger, cloves, cinnamon and nutmeg) at turn off. If you want to incorporate actual vegetables in this recipe, you'll need to use an 3-4kg provide pumpkin. Cut up the gourd, discard the innards, and roast or microwave the pieces until soft and cooked through, then peel. Mash the peeled, cooked pumpkin flesh with the included grains at 64°C for an hour.

## CORE RECIPE / MAKE IT YOUR OWN

| MALT | Ideal qty | % | Overall qty kg | Qty min | Variance score | Qty max | max % | Impacts |
|---|---|---|---|---|---|---|---|---|
| Pale malt | 3.5kg | 69 | | 3kg | | 4kg | 80 | ABV + colour |
| Munich malt | 1.2kg | 24 | 5.06 | 1kg | | 2kg | 10 | Malt flavour |
| Caramel 80 | 250g | 5 | | 200g | | 400g | 10 | Colour + aroma |
| Caramel 60 | 110g | 2 | | 100g | | 200g | 20 | Colour + aroma |

**Mash in** at 64°C for 60min ▬ **Mash out** at 76°C for 10min

| HOP | Qty g | AA | Time | g min | Variance score | g max | Impacts | Alternatives |
|---|---|---|---|---|---|---|---|---|
| ① Cluster | 30 | 7 | 60 | 20 | | 40 | Aroma + bitterness | Galena<br>Eroica |

| YEAST | Temp °C Min | Temp °C Max | Condition / Wks 1st | Condition / Wks 2nd | Condition / Wks Bot | Alternative yeasts | Temp °C MIN | Temp °C MAX |
|---|---|---|---|---|---|---|---|---|
| MJ's M15 Empire Ale | 18 | 22 | 1-2 | 1-2 | 2 | Wyeast #1056 American Ale | 15 | 22 |

Mash 67°C
Mash out 74°C
Boil

0
60
70
60
①
0

## ABOUT THIS BREW

| | |
|---|---|
| Volume | 23 litres |
| Boil volume | 27 litres |
| Alcohol | 4.5% (4.8% – 10%) |
| Bitterness / IBU | 20 IBU (10 – 30 IBU) |
| Colour | 11 EBC (10 – 60 EBC) |
| Original Gravity | 1.047 (1.044 – 1.090) |
| Final Gravity | 1.012 (1.007 – 1.015) |

# ITALIAN GRAPE ALE

A fascinating hybrid of wine and beer, the Italian grape ale is expanding beyond the speciality menus of Italian craft breweries and moving into international markets, with the result being a refreshing beer with noticeable grape aromatics and a fine, delicate acidity.

//////////////////////////////////////////

**NOTES:** Grape or grape must can be used up to 40% of the grist and added into the boil, during secondary fermentation or in ageing. This is one for experimentation!

## CORE RECIPE     MAKE IT YOUR OWN

| MALT | Ideal qty | % | Overall qty kg | Qty min | Variance score | | | | Qty-max | max % | Impacts |
|---|---|---|---|---|---|---|---|---|---|---|---|
| Pale malt | 4.8kg | 86 | | 4kg | | | | | 7kg | 90 | ABV + colour |
| CaraAroma | 400g | 7 | 5.6 | 100g | | | | | 800g | 10 | Colour + aroma |
| White wheat malt | 400g | 7 | | 100g | | | | | 1kg | 30 | Aroma + flavour |

🡒 **Mash in** at 64°C for 60min 🡒 **Mash out** at 76°C for 10min

| HOP | Qty g | AA | Time | g min | Variance score | | | | g max | Impacts | Alternatives |
|---|---|---|---|---|---|---|---|---|---|---|---|
| ① Nelson Sauvin | 20 | 11.3 | 60 | 15 | | | | | 50 | Aroma + bitterness | Pacific Jade |
| | | | | | | | | | | | Pacifica |
| ② Nelson Sauvin | 30 | 11.3 | 0 | 20 | | | | | 90 | Aroma | Pacific Jade |
| | | | | | | | | | | | Pacifica |

| YEAST | Temp °C Min | Temp °C Max | Condition / Wks 1st | 2nd | Bot | Alternative yeasts | Temp °C MIN | Temp °C MAX |
|---|---|---|---|---|---|---|---|---|
| MJ's M15 Empire Ale | 18 | 22 | 2 | 1-2 | 2 | Wyeast #1056 American Ale | 15 | 22 |

## ABOUT THIS BREW

| Volume | 23 litres |
|---|---|
| Boil volume | 27 litres |
| Alcohol | 5.8% |
| Bitterness / IBU | 15 IBU |
| Colour | 10 EBC |
| Original Gravity | 1.060 |
| Final Gravity | 1.015 |

# KOYT

Koyt is a historical Dutch beer which first appeared in the 14th century. This indigenous ale was made with oats and herbs similar to a gruit. At some point hops were used, and while there is some controversy, today the style is recognised for its creamy body (mainly thanks to the large amount of oats, bready aromas and low hop profile. There are very few recipes around, but this is our take on it.

## CORE RECIPE / MAKE IT YOUR OWN

| MALT | Ideal qty | % | Overall qty kg | Qty min | Variance score | | | | Qty max | max % | Impacts |
|---|---|---|---|---|---|---|---|---|---|---|---|
| Malted oats | 3kg | 50 | | 2kg | | | | | 4kg | 60 | ABV + colour |
| Pale wheat | 2kg | 33 | 6 | 1kg | | | | | 3kg | 40 | Body + flavour |
| Dark wheat | 1kg | 17 | | 1kg | | | | | 3kg | 20 | Colour + flavour |

▭ **Mash in** at 64°C for 90min ▬ **Mash out** at 76°C for 10min

| HOP | Qty g | AA | Time | g min | Variance score | | | | g max | Impacts | Alternatives |
|---|---|---|---|---|---|---|---|---|---|---|---|
| ⓘ Fuggles | 15 | 15 | 60 | 10 | | | | | 30 | Bitterness | Willamette |
| | | | | | | | | | | | Styrian Golding |
| | | | | | | | | | | | Tettnang |

| YEAST | Temp °C | | Condition / Wks | | | Alternative yeasts | Temp °C | |
|---|---|---|---|---|---|---|---|---|
| | Min | Max | 1st | 2nd | Bot | | MIN | MAX |
| MJ's M41 Belgian Ale | 18 | 28 | 1-2 | 2-4 | 2 | Wyeast #3522 Belgian Ardennes | 18 | 24 |

## ABOUT THIS BREW

| | |
|---|---|
| Volume | 23 litres |
| Boil volume | 27 litres |
| Alcohol | 8% (7% – 11%) |
| Bitterness / IBU | 9 IBU (7 – 15 IBU) |
| Colour | 7 EBC (8 – 44 EBC) |
| Original Gravity | 1.082 (1.076 – 1.120) |
| Final Gravity | 1.021 (1.016 – 1.020) |

### EXTRACT RECIPE:

Steep 300g of smoked malt in 27 litres of water for half an hour. Remove and then add 4.8kg of dried Pilsner extract or 6kg of liquid Pilsner extract, bring to the boil and add hops as normal to the boil.

# SAHTI

A traditional Finnish beer which dates back almost 500 years, the sahti is most noted for its use of juniper boughs in the brewing process. Coupled with the use of a warm-fermenting yeast and rye, the result is a sweet and heavy ale with distinct notes of juniper berry, juniper, banana and clove.

//////////////////////////////////////

**ADJUNCTS:** The addition of juniper berries (and juniper branches if you can get them!) is the easiest way to achieve a sahti. We recommend popping in 10g with 30 minutes of the boil to go.

## CORE RECIPE / MAKE IT YOUR OWN

| MALT | Ideal qty | % | Overall qty kg | Qty min | Variance score | | | Qty-max | max % | Impacts |
|---|---|---|---|---|---|---|---|---|---|---|
| Pilsner malt | 7kg | 88 | | 4kg | | | | 8kg | 80 | ABV + colour |
| Rye malt | 700g | 8 | 8 | 500g | | | | 1kg | 20 | Flavour + body |
| Smoked malt | 300g | 4 | | 100g | | | | 350g | 10 | Flavour |

**Mash in** at 64°C for 60min **Mash out** at 76°C for 10min

| HOP | Qty g | AA | Time | g min | Variance score | | g max | Impacts | Alternatives |
|---|---|---|---|---|---|---|---|---|---|
| ❶ Saaz | 20 | 3.8 | 60 | 15 | | | 40 | Aroma + bitterness | Sladek |
| | | | | | | | | | Lublin |
| | | | | | | | | | Sterling |

| Juniper | 10g | | 30 | |
|---|---|---|---|---|

| YEAST | Temp °C Min | Max | Condition / Wks 1st | 2nd | Bot | Alternative yeasts | Temp °C MIN | MAX |
|---|---|---|---|---|---|---|---|---|
| MJ's M42 Strong Ale | 16 | 22 | 2 | 3m | 2 | Wyeast #1187 Ringwood Ale | 17 | 24 |

## ABOUT THIS BREW

| Volume | 23 litres |
|---|---|
| Boil volume | 27 litres |
| Alcohol | 3.6% (2.5% – 3.6%) |
| Bitterness / IBU | 9 IBU (20 – 35 IBU) |
| Colour | 7 EBC (6 – 12 EBC) |
| Original Gravity | 1.037 (1.028 – 1.032) |
| Final Gravity | 1.009 (1.006 – 1.012) |

# GRODZISKIE

This historical style from the Polish city of Grodzisk is currently undergoing a bit of a renaissance. Made with oak-smoked wheat malt and a clean ale yeast strain, the highly sessionable Grodziskie is noted for its light body, lively carbonation, oak-smokiness and a clean hop bitterness.

////////////////////////////////////

**NOTES:** Because of the amount of wheat, you may struggle with mashing out. Rice hulls may help with it.

## CORE RECIPE / MAKE IT YOUR OWN

| MALT | Ideal qty | % | Overall qty kg | Qty min | Variance score | Qty max | max % | Impacts |
|---|---|---|---|---|---|---|---|---|
| Oak-smoked wheat malt | 2.8kg | 76 | 3.7 | 2.5kg | | 3kg | 80 | ABV + colour |
| Pilsner malt | 900g | 24 | | 500g | | 900g | 30 | ABV + colour |

**Mash in** at 64°C for 90min  **Mash out** at 76°C for 10min

| HOP | Qty g | AA | Time | g min | Variance score | g max | Impacts | Alternatives |
|---|---|---|---|---|---|---|---|---|
| ① Saaz | 40 | 3.8 | 60 | 20 | | 45 | Bitterness | Sladek |
| | | | | | | | | Lublin |
| | | | | | | | | Sterling |
| ② Saaz | 30 | 3.8 | 15 | 10 | | 40 | Aroma + bitterness | Sladek |
| | | | | | | | | Lublin |
| | | | | | | | | Sterling |

| YEAST | Temp °C Min | Temp °C Max | Condition / Wks 1st | Condition / Wks 2nd | Condition / Wks Bot | Alternative yeasts | Temp °C MIN | Temp °C MAX |
|---|---|---|---|---|---|---|---|---|
| MJ's M54 California Lager | 18 | 20 | 1-2 | 2-4 | 2 | Wyeast #2565 Kolsch | 13 | 17 |

Mash 67°C
Mash out 74°C
0
60
70
60
Boil
15
0

## ABOUT THIS BREW

| | |
|---|---|
| Volume | 23 litres |
| Boil volume | 27 litres |
| Alcohol | 4.3% |
| Bitterness / IBU | 20 IBU |
| Colour | 18 EBC |
| Original Gravity | 1.045 |
| Final Gravity | 1.011 |

### EXTRACT RECIPE:

Steep 500g of medium crystal in 27 litres of water for half an hour. Remove and then 2.4kg of dried malt extract or 3kg of liquid malt extract, bring to the boil and add hops and spices as normal to the boil.

# SPICED WINTER ALE

Before hops became the conventional flavouring for beer, medieval European brewers used proprietary spice mixtures, and many modern breweries still use a blend of spices along with hops for seasonally-brewed holiday beers. We started with a Scottish-style ale and added a blend of spices to create a medium-bodied, malty, clean base beer with a sweet, exotic spice character reminiscent of mulled wine.

**ADJUNCTS:** The addition of a 10g mulled spice mix bag, just like you get at Christmas for wine, is added at 0 minutes of the boil.

## CORE RECIPE | MAKE IT YOUR OWN

| MALT | Ideal qty | % | Overall qty kg | Qty min | Variance score | Qty-max | max % | Impacts |
|---|---|---|---|---|---|---|---|---|
| Pale malt (Golden Promise) | 4kg | 89 | 4.5 | 3kg | | 4.5kg | 90 | ABV + colour |
| Medium crystal | 500g | 11 | | 500g | | 700g | 200 | Colour + flavour |

▭ **Mash in** at 64°C for 60min ▬ **Mash out** at 76°C for 10min

| HOP | Qty g | AA | Time | g min | Variance score | g max | Impacts | Alternatives |
|---|---|---|---|---|---|---|---|---|
| ❶ East Kent Goldings | 20 | 4 | 60 | 15 | | 35 | Aroma + bitterness | Hallertau |
| | | | | | | | | Tettnanger |
| | | | | | | | | Mt. Hood |

| Spices | 10g | 0 |
|---|---|---|

| YEAST | Temp °C Min | Temp °C Max | Condition / Wks 1st | 2nd | Bot | Alternative yeasts | Temp °C MIN | Temp °C MAX |
|---|---|---|---|---|---|---|---|---|
| MJ's M15 Empire Ale | 18 | 22 | 1-2 | 1-2 | 2 | Wyeast #1728 Scottish Ale | 13 | 21 |

## ABOUT THIS BREW

| Volume | 23 litres |
|---|---|
| Boil volume | 27 litres |
| Alcohol | 4.9% (4.5% – 6%) |
| Bitterness / IBU | 34 IBU (20 – 35 IBU) |
| Colour | 8 EBC (8 – 14 EBC) |
| Original Gravity | 1.050 (1.038 – 1.050) |
| Final Gravity | 1.013 (1.004 – 1.006) |

### EXTRACT RECIPE:

Steep 250g Cara Malt and 340 of wheat malt in 27 litres of water for half an hour. Remove and then add 2.7kg of Pilsner malt extract or 3.375kg of liquid Pilsner malt extract, bring to the boil and add hops as normal to the boil.

# AUSTRALIAN ALE

Patterned after a descendant of a descendant of Burton ale, this Australian ale shows its influences on the sleeve. There's no consensus whether 'sparkling' refers to effervescent carbonation or brilliant clarity - that's for you to figure out. Hopped entirely with Pride of Ringwood, a bold, earthy, powerfully expressive hop descended from the best of the UK hops.

| CORE RECIPE | | | | MAKE IT YOUR OWN | | | | |
|---|---|---|---|---|---|---|---|---|
| MALT | Ideal qty | % | Overall qty kg | Qty min | Variance score | Qty max | max % | Impacts |
| Pilsner malt | 4.3kg | 88 | | 3.8kg | | 4.5kg | 80 | ABV + colour |
| White wheat malt | 340g | 7 | 4.89 | 200g | | 400g | 10 | Mouthfeel |
| Cara Malt | 250g | 5 | | 200g | | 400g | 10 | Colour |

**Mash in** at 64°C for 90min **Mash out** at 76°C for 10min

| HOP | Qty g | AA | Time | g min | Variance score | g max | Impacts | Alternatives |
|---|---|---|---|---|---|---|---|---|
| ① Pride of Ringwood | 30 | 8.5 | 60 | 20 | | 40 | Aroma + bitterness | Cluster |
| | | | | | | | | Galena |
| ② Pride of Ringwood | 15 | 8.5 | 15 | 10 | | 30 | Aroma | Cluster |
| | | | | | | | | Galena |

| YEAST | Temp °C | | Condition / Wks | | | Alternative yeasts | Temp °C | |
|---|---|---|---|---|---|---|---|---|
| | Min | Max | 1st | 2nd | Bot | | MIN | MAX |
| MJ's M36 Liberty Bell | 18 | 22 | 1-2 | - | 2 | Wyeast #1275 Thames Valley | 15 | 22 |

Mash 67°C

Mash out 74°C

0

60
70
60

①

Boil

②  15

0

# GET STARTED

When Beer Hawk wanted to start stocking homebrew equipment, we knew exactly where to go: Northern Brewer in the US, a respected outfit that concentrates on quality beer making apparatus. We now stock a huge range of top quality beer gear and ingredients whether you're complete beginner or an expert.

**beerhawk.co.uk**

# Equipment

Beer Hawk stocks a huge amount of homebrew equipment from propane burners to muslin hop bags, from stir plates to bungs and airlocks, much of it exclusively from the hugely respected US homebrew stockists Northern Brewer. We've designed the range to fit in with what you already own. If you're just starting out, we have starter kits for the stove top.

# Ingredients

Beer Hawk's huge range of ingredients includes malts, dried and liquid malt extracts, yeasts, hops and sugars. They can be bought in a variety of quantities. We also stock an extensive selection of all-grain and extract recipe kits for stove top brewing or full 23-litre brews. All the ingredients are weighed out and include all you need to brew the beer.

# Resources

At www.beerhawk.co.uk we have an ever-expanding range of information and tutorials, frequently asked questions, recipes and videos. Our friends in the US, Northern Brewer (www.northernbrewer.com) also have loads of calculators and resources. Another online tool we like includes brewgr.com that calculates the outcome of your recipe.

# Index

| RECIPES | |
|---|---|
| Altbier | 138 |
| Amber ale | 90 |
| Amber ale | 164 |
| American IPA | 169 |
| American lager | 160 |
| American pale | 162 |
| American porter | 167 |
| American red | 181 |
| American rye | 180 |
| American stout | 168 |
| American wheat | 182 |
| Australian sparkling lager | 189 |
| Baltic poter | 98 |
| Barley wine | 96 |
| Belgian blond | 144 |
| Berliner Weisse | 140 |
| Bière de garde | 157 |
| Black IPA | 173 |
| Bock | 122 |
| Bohemian Pilsner | 116 |
| Breakfast | 105 |
| Brown ale | 165 |
| California common | 166 |
| Coffee stout | 104 |
| Cream ale | 163 |
| Doppelbock | 120 |
| Dortmunder Export | 123 |
| Double IPA | 177 |
| Dry Irish stout | 100 |
| Dubbel | 145 |
| Dunkel | 135 |
| Dunkels Bock | 121 |
| Dunkelweizen | 134 |
| Eisbock | 126 |
| English IPA | 88 |
| Flanders red | 153 |

| | |
|---|---|
| Foreign extra stout | 101 |
| Fruit lambic | 152 |
| German Pilsner | 117 |
| Golden ale | 89 |
| Golden strong | 147 |
| Gose | 141 |
| Grapefruit IPA | 178 |
| Grodziskie | 187 |
| Gueuze | 151 |
| Heather ale | 113 |
| Hefewiezen | 131 |
| Helles Weizen | 132 |
| Imperial Black IPA | 174 |
| Imperial mild | 94 |
| Imperial stout | 106 |
| Irish draft | 108 |
| Irish red | 107 |
| Italian grape ale | 184 |
| Kellerbier | 124 |
| Kolsch | 137 |
| Koyt | 185 |
| Kvass | 188 |
| Lambic | 150 |
| Maibock | 119 |
| Marzen | 128 |
| Mild | 93 |
| Milk stout | 102 |
| Mosaic IPA | 179 |
| Munich Helles | 118 |
| Northern brown | 91 |
| Oatmeal stout | 103 |
| Old ale | 95 |
| Old bruin | 154 |
| Patersbier | 156 |
| Petite saison | 148 |
| Porter | 25, 97 |
| Pre-prohibition lager | 161 |

| | |
|---|---|
| Pumpkin ale | 183 |
| Raspberry wheat | 130 |
| Rauchbier | 136 |
| Red IPA | 175 |
| Roggenbier | 129 |
| Rye IPA | 172 |
| Sahti | 186 |
| Saison | 149 |
| Schwarzbier | 125 |
| Scottish 60/ | 109 |
| Scottish 70/ | 110 |
| Scottish 80/ | 111 |
| Session IPA | 170 |
| Smoked porter | 99 |
| Southern brown | 92 |
| Sticke | 139 |
| Tripel | 146 |
| Vienna lager | 127 |
| Wee heavy | 112 |
| Weizenbock | 133 |
| West Coast IPA | 171 |
| White IPA | 176 |
| Witbier | 155 |

| INGREDIENTS | |
|---|---|
| **MALTS AND ADJUNCTS** | |
| Acidulated malt | 24, 30, 43 |
| Amber malt | 30, 27 |
| Aromatic malt | 30 |
| Barley hulls | 31 |
| Base malts | 25, 27, 30 |
| Belgian pale ale | 30 |
| Belgian pilsner | 30 |
| Belgian Special B | 30 |
| Biscuit malt | 30 |
| Black malt | 30 |
| Brown malt | 30 |

| | | | | | | | |
|---|---|---|---|---|---|---|---|
| Candi sugar | 28, 31 | Munich | 24, 30 | First Gold | 34 |
| CaraAmber | 30 | Pale malt | 24 | Fuggles | 34 |
| CaraAroma | 30 | Pale chocolate | 31 | Galaxy | 34 |
| Carafa I | 30 | Peated malt | 31 | Galena | 34 |
| Carafa II | 30 | Pilsner | 24, 25, 31 | Glacier | 34 |
| Carafa III | 30, 24 | Rice hulls | 31 | Hallertau Mittelfrüh | 34 |
| Carahell | 30 | Rice syrup solids | 31 | Heather | 32 |
| Caramel malts | 27, 30 | Rye | 25, 27 | Hersbrucker | 34 |
| Caramunich | 30 | Roasted barley | 24, 27, 31 | IBU (International Bitterness Unit) | 32 |
| Carapils | 27, 30 | Six-row | 30 | Liberty | 34 |
| CaraRed | 30 | Smoked malt | 31 | Magnum | 35 |
| Chocolate | 30 | Spelt malt | 31 | Mosaic | 35 |
| Chocolate rye malt | 31 | Speciality malts | 25, 30, 31 | Motueka | 35 |
| Corn sugar | 28, 31 | Torrified wheat | 28, 31 | Mt Hood | 35 |
| Crystal malt | 24, 27, 31 | Two-row | 30 | Neson Sauvin | 35 |
| Dark crystal | 31 | Victory | 24, 30 | Northdown | 35 |
| Dark Munich | 31 | Vienna | 30 | Northern Brewer | 35 |
| Dark wheat | 31 | Wheat | 27, 30 | Nugget | 35 |
| Dextrin malt | 31 | White wheat malt | 30 | Pellet | 32 |
| Flaked barley | 31 | HOPS | 32 | Perle | 35 |
| Flaked maize | 27, 31 | Admiral | 34 | Pride of Ringwood | 35 |
| Flaked oats | 27, 28, 31 | Ahtanum | 34 | Progress | 35 |
| Flaked rice | 27 | Alpha acid | 32 | Saaz | 35 |
| Flaked rye | 31 | Amarillo | 34 | Simcoe | 35 |
| Flaked wheat | 31 | Apollo | 34 | Sorachi Ace | 35 |
| Golden Promise | 25 | Aroma hops | 67 | Strisselspalt | 35 |
| Golden naked oats | 31 | Bittering hops | 67 | Styrian Goldings | 35 |
| Honey | 28, 31 | Bramling Cross | 34 | Summit | 35 |
| Honey malt | 31 | Brewer's Gold | 34 | Target | 35 |
| Lactose | 28, 31 | Cascade | 34 | Tettnang | 35 |
| Malts - general | 25, 30, 31, 57 | Centennial | 34 | Tradition | 35 |
| Malted oats | 27 | Challenger | 34 | Vanguard | 35 |
| Maple syrup | 28, 31 | Chinook | 34 | Warrior | 35 |
| Maris Otter | 25, 30 | Citra | 34 | Whole cone | 32 |
| Medium crystal | 31 | Cluster | 34 | Willamette | 35 |
| Melanoidin | 31 | Columbus | 34 | | |
| Mild ale | 30 | East Kent Golding | 34 | | |

# Index

| YEAST | 36 |
|---|---|
| Ale yeast | 37 |
| Attenuation | 38 |
| Bottom-fermenting | 37 |
| Brettanomyces | 37, 38 |
| Carbon dioxide | 37 |
| Cell count | 39 |
| Dry yeast | 36, 62 |
| Esters | 37 |
| Flocculation | 38 |
| Lactobacillus | 76 |
| Lager yeast | 37 |
| Liquid yeast | 36, 62 |
| Oxygen | 37 |
| Pediococcus | 76 |
| Pitching yeast | 69 |
| Saccharomyces cerevisiae | 37 |
| Saccharomyces pastorianus | 37 |
| Top fermenting | 37 |
| FRUIT AND SPICES | 40 |
| Cardamom | 40 |
| Coriander | 40 |
| Cherries | 40 |
| Chilli | 40 |
| Ginger | 40 |
| Lime | 40 |
| Orange | 40 |
| Pumpkin | 40 |
| Raspberries | 40 |
| WATER | 42 |
| Alkalinity | 42 |
| Bicarbonate | 42 |
| Carbon | 42 |
| Campden tabel | 42 |
| Chloramine | 42 |
| Chlorophenols | 42 |
| Filtering | 42 |

| Magnesium | 42 |
|---|---|
| pH | 42 |
| Sodium | 42 |
| Sulphate | 42 |

| BREWING | |
|---|---|
| Adjunct | 56, 27 |
| Airlock | 47, 56 |
| Ale | 56 |
| Alkali | 56 |
| Alkalinity | 42, 56 |
| Alpha acid | 32, 56 |
| Amino acids | 56 |
| Amylases | 56 |
| Bacteria | 56 |
| Barrel-ageing | 75 |
| Base malt | 56 |
| Batch | 56 |
| BJCP | 56 |
| Blow-off | 56 |
| Boil | 67 |
| Bottling | 72 |
| Carbon dioxide | 56, 74 |
| Carbonation | 72, 74 |
| Coldbreak | 56 |
| Cone | 56 |
| Conditioning | 71 |
| Converting recipes | 60 |
| Cooling | 68 |
| Copper | 56 |
| Chiller | 68 |
| Cleaning | 47, 49, 58, 63 |
| Crown caps | 56 |
| Decoction | 56 |
| Dry hopping | 56 |
| Diacetyl | 36 |

| Enzymes | 65 |
|---|---|
| Ester | 36, 56 |
| Extract brewing | 27, 60 |
| Fermentaion | 69, 70 |
| Force carbonation | 72 |
| Flame out | 67 |
| Grain bed | 47, 66 |
| Grain bill | 27, 56, |
| Grist | 25, 27, 57, 65 |
| Gypsum | 57 |
| Hardness | 57 |
| Heat wrap | 70 |
| Hop schedule | 67 |
| Hydrometer | 57 |
| IBU | 57 |
| Infusion | 57 |
| Infusion mash | 57 |
| Initial mashing | 57 |
| Isinglass | 57 |
| Kegging | 72, 74 |
| Krausen | 57, 70, 71 |
| Lactic acid | 57 |
| Lager | 71 |
| Lauter tub | 57 |
| Lovibond | 27 |
| Lupulin | 57 |
| Malt extract | 27, 57, 60 |
| Malt | 25, 27, 57 |
| Malting | 25, 27 |
| Maltose | 27, 57 |
| Mashing | 25, 42, 47 64, 65 |
| Must | 57 |
| Original gravity | 57, 69 |
| pH | 42, 57 |
| Phenols | 42, 57 |
| Pitch | 57, 69 |
| Priming | 57, 72 |

| | |
|---|---|
| Protein rest | 65 |
| Rack | 57, 71, 72 |
| Reinheitsgebot | 37 |
| Recirculate | 66 |
| Run off | 66 |
| Sanitising | 49, 58, 62 |
| Secondary fermentation | 71 |
| Sediment | 72 |
| Souring | 76 |
| Sparging | 50, 57, 65, 66 |
| Specific gravity | 69, 70 |
| Spontaneous fermentation | 76 |
| Star San | 58 |
| Starter | 57 |
| Steeping grains | 57, 60 |
| Step infusion mash | 65 |
| Strike temperature | 64 |
| Stuck fermentation | 69, 70 |
| Stuck mash | 66 |
| Torrified | 57 |
| Transfer | 68 |
| Trub | 57, 71, 72 |
| Vorlauf | 66 |
| Wort | 25, 57, 66, 68, 69 |
| Yeast | 57 |
| Yeast energiser | 70 |
| Yeast starter | 39 |
| Water volume | 64 |
| Wild yeast | 57, 76 |

## EQUIPMENT

| | |
|---|---|
| Airlock | 47, 48 56 |
| Bottles | 48, 72 |
| Bottling bucket | 72 |
| Bottle caps | 48 |
| Bottle capper | 53 |

| | |
|---|---|
| Bottle drying tree | 48 |
| Bottle filler | 48, 53 |
| Bucket | 48 |
| Burner | 48, 50 |
| Colander | 47, 49 |
| Counterflow chiller | 68 |
| Cleaning | 47, 49 |
| Demi-john | 48 |
| Digital scales | 46, 47 |
| False bottom | 47, 62 |
| Fermenting vessel | 46, 47, 51, 68 |
| Fizz Drops | 72 |
| Hot liquor tank | 47, 50, 62, 64 |
| Hydrometer | 48, 52 |
| Keg (Corny/Cornelius) | 46, 48, 53, 74 |
| Kettle | 48, 49, 64 |
| Oxygenation kit | 52 |
| pH meter | 48 |
| Propane burner | 46, 47 |
| Malt mill | 48 |
| Mash tun | 48, 50, 62, 64, 65 |
| Muslin grain and hop bags | 48 |
| Refractometer | 52 |
| Regulator | 53, 74 |
| Stir plate | 39, 51 |
| Stock pot | 46, 47 |
| Stove top | 47, 48 |
| Syphon | 47, 48, 71 |
| Thermometer | 47, 49, 65, 70 |
| Water pumps | 48 |
| Wort chiller | 47, 48, 51, 68 |

# THANK YOU

Putting a book together is a group effort, either directly or indirectly.
It is an all-consuming experience and one that affects many people.
I'd like to express my gratitude and to the people listed here...

Photo by Anders Brogaard

# Cheers guys...

Firstly I'd like to thank Mark Roberts, co-founder of Beer Hawk, who had the idea to do a homebrew book in the first place. We got there! Also to fellow co-founder Chris France for stocking all this fantastic homebrew equipment in the first place.

I'd like to express my gratitude to the Northern Brewer guys who did much of the hard work creating many of these recipes and whose expertise we have used throughout the book.

The entire Beer Hawk team have been hugely supportive, and a special thanks go to Beer Hawk's Beer Sommelier Maggie Cubbler who wrote parts of the book and supported wherever she could. Big thanks to Homebrew Buyer Mark James as well for dealing endless questions. Thanks too, to finance dude Andy Hill who can seemingly sort anything out, and everyone in the Filling Factory (you know who you are). Everyone in the entire marketing have also been amazing. You're all amazing!

Thanks to the supremely talented Rob Vanderplank who took many of the photographs in this book (all the nice ones!). Also to Adrian Tierney-Jones for casting his knowledgeable brain over the words, and to Pete Brown for writing the foreword.

A special mention needs to go to Adam McNaught-Davis who not only designed this lovely book but spent many many hours figuring out how to always make it better. And also for putting up with me, anytime, all the time.

It's been an incredible journey. Did anyone say volume 2?